Johnny Temple

ALSO BY WILLIAM A. COOK
AND FROM McFARLAND

Bibb Falk: The Man Who Replaced Shoeless Joe (2015)

Big Klu: The Baseball Life of Ted Kluszewski (2012)

Jim Thorpe: A Biography (2011)

King of the Bootleggers: A Biography of George Remus (2008)

August "Garry" Herrmann: A Baseball Biography (2008)

The Louisville Grays Scandal of 1877: The Taint of Gambling at the Dawn of the National League (2005)

Waite Hoyt: A Biography of the Yankees' Schoolboy Wonder (2004)

Pete Rose: Baseball's All-Time Hit King (2004)

The Summer of '64: A Pennant Lost (2002)

The 1919 World Series: What Really Happened? (2001)

Johnny Temple

All-Star Second Baseman

WILLIAM A. COOK

McFarland & Company, Inc., Publishers
Jefferson, North Carolina

LIBRARY OF CONGRESS CATALOGUING-IN-PUBLICATION DATA

Names: Cook, William A., 1944– author.
Title: Johnny Temple : all-star second baseman / William A. Cook.
Description: Jefferson, North Carolina : McFarland & Company, 2016. | Includes bibliographical references and index.
Identifiers: LCCN 2016036226 | ISBN 9781476663913 (softcover : acid free paper) ∞
Subjects: LCSH: Temple, Johnny, 1927–1994 | Baseball players—United States—Biography.
Classification: LCC GV865.T37 C66 2016 | DDC 796.357092 [B]—dc23
LC record available at https://lccn.loc.gov/2016036226

BRITISH LIBRARY CATALOGUING DATA ARE AVAILABLE

**ISBN (print) 978-1-4766-6391-3
ISBN (ebook) 978-1-4766-2353-5**

© 2016 William A. Cook. All rights reserved

No part of this book may be reproduced or transmitted in any form or by any means, electronic or mechanical, including photocopying or recording, or by any information storage and retrieval system, without permission in writing from the publisher.

Front cover: Houston Colt .45s infielder Johnny Temple (courtesy Houston Astros)

Printed in the United States of America

*McFarland & Company, Inc., Publishers
   Box 611, Jefferson, North Carolina 28640
   www.mcfarlandpub.com*

To
Joseph Thullen
One of the Cincinnati Reds' Greatest Fans

Table of Contents

Introduction   1

One. A Stormy Road to the Big Leagues   5

Two. Breaking In with the Reds   14

Three. Taking Over at Second Base   23

Four. An All-Star Performer   39

Five. Earl Lawson Gets Punched   58

Six. Shake-Up in Cincy   75

Seven. A Deal That Sinks the Reds   86

Eight. Traded to Cleveland   105

Nine. A Fading Star   129

Ten. A Complicated Return to Cincinnati   149

Eleven. The Tragic Fall of Johnny Temple   164

Afterword   172

Appendix A. Temple Among His Peers   173
Appendix B. All-Star Game Statistics   174
Appendix C. Major League Career Highlights   175

Chapter Notes   177

Bibliography   183

Index   185

Introduction

Johnny Ellis Temple is one of those forgotten ballplayers in major league history. His lifetime statistics do not warrant his election to the Hall of Fame, but his story needs to be told. Temple's career was marked by bold determination and a great deal of success, but after baseball he slipped into an absurd freefall, living in near poverty and engaging in petty crime. The shocking reality, however, is that Johnny Temple's story is not unlike those of other major leaguers who retired before the dawn of the free agency era.

Before free agency, players did not receive a fair share of the enormous profits made by major league teams. In 1959, Los Angeles Dodgers owner Walter O'Malley had estimated gross revenues of $5,177,612.50 from Dodger ticket sales and wound up using the Los Angeles Coliseum for free. O'Malley paid the Coliseum Commission $319,383 in rent, but the Commission then turned around and paid him $337,882 for concessions sales. So O'Malley made a profit of $18,499 on renting the Coliseum. The Los Angeles Dodgers payroll in 1959 was $406,000, and Duke Snider was the team's highest paid player at $43,500 for the season. Future Dodgers star pitcher Sandy Koufax was paid $14,000 for the season, well below the major league average of $16,997.

In the 1950s, 1960s and early 1970s, when a major league player hung up his spikes, he was on his own. There were no millions of dollars in deferred payments waiting for him from previous contracts to tide him over and provide a comfortable transition. Consequently, many ex-major league players of the pre-free agency era struggled economically to support themselves and their families. Some ex-players such as Ernie Lombardi and Chico Cardenas suffered silently as they pumped gas for a living. Some, such as Lou Johnson, became drug addicts; some, such as Denny McLain, wound up in prison for racketeering. Johnny Temple's post-career struggle, notwithstanding the fact the he entered into a dark alliance with thieves, has a common theme running through it among so many pre–free agency era ex-major leaguers.

Johnny Temple was a classy ballplayer, a four-time All-Star selection at second baseman with the Cincinnati Reds in the National League (1956, 1957 and 1959) and in the American League with the Cleveland Indians (1961). While he never played on a pennant-winning team and never had the opportunity to showcase his brilliant skills with the bat and glove in a World Series, statistically Johnny Temple is capable of standing shoulder to shoulder with his contemporaries during the era of 1950s.

In almost every game that Johnny Temple ever played he did something to help his team: a dazzling play in the field, a timely base hit, or a stolen base. There simply has never been any other player in the modern era who played with more intensity than Johnny Temple. He was in the game up to his ears.

All of Johnny Temple's lifetime batting and fielding statistics are near equal to or better than those of Billy Martin. But Martin played in five glorious World Series with the fabled New York Yankees of the 1950s and had his number retired, then was memorialized with a plaque in Monument Park at Yankee Stadium. Nonetheless, Billy Marin's one-time selection as an All-Star in 1956 pales in comparison to the four-time All-Star selection of Johnny Temple.

When the term clutch-hitter comes up, most baseball fans, sportswriters and historians mention players such as Tony Perez, Johnny Mize, Derek Jeter, Eddie Murray and others. But then there was Johnny Temple too. There have been few players who could hit like Temple with two out and the tying run on third.

Johnny Temple was also an expert glove man and in baseball's golden era of the 1950s, he and shortstop Roy McMillan formed one of the premier double play combinations in the major leagues, if not major league history.

A tobacco-chewing, hustling, hard-talking player, Johnny Temple had a fiery disposition on the playing field, which led many sportswriters, teammates and opposing players to refer to him as a throwback player to the old days, an Eddie Stanky–type player, who would challenge anyone. But in retrospect it may be that Eddie Stanky was a Johnny Temple–type player. Temple had higher lifetime statistics than Stanky in almost every category and had more fights on the field too.

Pete Rose stated that when he was teenager growing up in Cincinnati and attending games at Crosley Field in the 1950s, Johnny Temple was his favorite Reds player.

Introduction

Birdie Tebbetts, manager of the Reds from 1954 to 1958, stated, "Temple is a manager's player. He does everything he's capable of doing. He's the best second baseman in the National League."[1]

Despite such accolades, Johnny Temple felt that he never got the credit as a ballplayer that he deserved. More than a decade after he left the game, Temple was to state, "One of the things that really hurts me—I was probably the best second baseman the Reds ever had until Joe Morgan, but I'll be remembered for taking a punch at Earl Lawson, who was my best friend in sportswriting and still is."[2]

It's true that Temple's pugnacity probably has historically overshadowed his better-than-average playing statistics and All-Star performance in major league baseball. Among the forty or so players who manned second base for the Cincinnati Reds during the seventy-five years before Temple became the club's starting second baseman in 1954, only a few compare with him statistically.

The list would include Bid McPhee, who played eighteen years with Cincinnati between 1882 and 1899 in the American Association and National League and had 2291 career hits. There was also Hughie Critz, the Reds' second baseman during most of the "roaring twenties" between 1924 and 1930. In 1924 as a rookie, Critz hit .322 playing in 102 games. Also there is Lonnie Frey, the sentimental favorite among the most knowledgeable Reds fans. Frey, a three-time All-Star, came to Cincinnati from the Chicago Cubs in exchange for cash in 1938 and held down second base for the Reds through the 1943 season, when he then entered military service. Frey played second on the Cincinnati Reds pennant-winning team of 1939 and World Series champions of 1940. Later Frey would play on the 1947 World Champion New York Yankees and room briefly with Yogi Berra.

Tony Cuccinello played second base for the Reds in 1930 and 1931, hitting above .300 both years, but he was traded before the 1932 season to the Brooklyn Dodgers in a trade that brought the Reds future Hall of Fame catcher Ernie Lombardi. So a big "what if" exists in regard to Cuccinello, who would ultimately play fifteen years in the major leagues for the Cincinnati Reds, Brooklyn Dodgers, Boston Braves, New York Giants and Chicago White Sox, finishing his career with 1729 hits. Also Cuccinello was a three-time All-Star. He was selected to play in the very first All-Star game in 1933 and had the distinction of being the last batter in the first All-Star game when he struck out against Lefty Grove of the Philadelphia Athletics as the American League downed the National 4–2.

Despite Cuccinello's solid achievements, Johnny Temple had a higher lifetime batting average and played in more All-Star Games.

Another "what if" that exists in Temple's assertion that he was the best second baseman the Cincinnati Reds ever had before Joe Morgan is Pete Rose. Between 1963 and 1966, Rose played second base for the Reds and was selected as the National League Rookie of the Year in 1963. The reason that Rose vacated second base in the 1967 season and moved to the outfield was to make room for his buddy Tom Helms, whom he had known since both were teammates with the Macon Peaches in the minor leagues, playing alongside each other at shortstop and second base.

Whatever the statistics may reveal, they cannot capture the essence of Johnny Temple on the diamond. There just isn't a Sabermetrics model that measures hustle and determination. Temple was the kind of ballplayer who had tremendous confidence in himself, and when he played he truly believed he was the best at what he did. While Temple was cautious to demonstrate the utmost respect for veteran second basemen such as Red Schoendienst, talented young players coming into the National League faced the scourge of his personal scrutiny. In the late 1950s Johnny Temple asserted to the press that the Pittsburgh Pirates' young second baseman, future Hall of Fame member Bill Mazeroski, couldn't carry his glove.

The high-flying major league career of Johnny Temple would eventually crash and burn in late 1964 when he left Cincinnati in disgrace after a fight with a fellow coach.

After a five-year stint of sportscasting on a Houston TV station, slowly the task of just making daily ends meet became a monumental struggle for Temple. The life of Johnny Temple had become a Greek tragedy and would eventually end in profound disappointment and disgrace.

In completing this work it is my intention to present a remembrance of both the life and brilliant major league career of Johnny Temple and offer a more positive legacy for an athlete and a person who so richly deserves it. At the very least, to take his imperfect life and make it appear better.

In gathering information for this work I am most grateful for the contributions of the Library of Cincinnati and Hamilton County, Cincinnati, Ohio; the Cincinnati Museum Center at Union Terminal–Cincinnati Historical Society, Cincinnati, Ohio; and the National Baseball Hall of Fame Library, Cooperstown, New York.

ONE

A Stormy Road to the Big Leagues

The early life of Johnny Ellis Temple is filled with mystery and contradictions. It begins with his birth date. The *Baseball Encyclopedia* list Temple's birth date as August 8, 1928. The Web site Baseball Reference.com lists it as August 8, 1927, and Temple's 1957 Topps baseball card lists his birth date as August 8, 1929. An arrest record involving Temple in 1977 in the files of the Buncombe County Clerk of Superior Court, Asheville, North Carolina, lists his age as 47. That would indicate that Johnny Temple was born in 1930.

Temple's actual birthplace is also in question. Whatever the date of his birth actually was, it is pretty much agreed that Temple was born in Reeds, North Carolina, although the record books, including the *Baseball Encyclopedia,* list his birthplace as Lexington, North Carolina. Temple maintained that he was responsible for that. "I just got tired of having to explain where Reeds is every time somebody asked me where I'm from. At least Lexington is on the map."[1]

It can be said for certain that his parents were Leslie and Alma Temple. He grew up in the village of Reeds, North Carolina, where his parents farmed, growing corn and tobacco crops. He had three brothers, Aubrey J. Temple, Shelbourne L. Temple and Coy E. Temple.

Tragedy entered the life of Johnny Temple as a teenager when the family house caught fire. As Temple was helping family members escape the inferno, part of the house fell on him, breaking his leg. Then he was badly burned from the knee to the ankle when his left trouser leg caught fire. The leg eventually became covered with scar tissue. The doctors told Temple he would be fortunate just to walk again, much less play any sports. But that didn't stop him. All during his major league career he wore a protective device on his left leg. By the late 1950s he had a shinguard made out of fiberglass that was very light.

Johnny Temple had no dreams of ever becoming a big league ballplayer, although from his early teens on he demonstrated signs of being a gifted athlete. He was captain of both his high school basketball and baseball teams at Reeds High School (now West Davidson). Temple was also a good student and graduated in 1945 as the class valedictorian.

Following high school, Temple enrolled at Catawba College, a liberal arts college founded in 1851 in Newton, North Carolina, nestled in the Piedmont district in Salisbury. Today the college is thriving as a coeducational institution with a student population of about 1300.

Another mystery that exists in Johnny Temple's background is that there has been some historical disagreement as to whether or not he won letters in both football and basketball while enrolled at Catawba College. Most evidence suggests that he did not win a letter in either, and a myth seems to have been created in part by the modern day Web and partly by Johnny Temple.

Currently there are numerous Web sites on the Internet that state Johnny Temple was a letterman at Catawba College, including the usually reliable Baseball Reference.com. Furthermore, a few other Web sites state that Temple played baseball at Catawba, but there is no record of his ever participating on the diamond during his brief college experience.

Johnny Temple told Furman Bisher during an interview for an article, "Rough Neck at Second Base," published in *Sport Magazine*, January 1960, that he lettered in football and basketball at Catawba before leaving school prior to the baseball season.

When Temple enrolled at Catawba College in the fall of 1945, he tried out for the Indians football team as a 140-pound back with no previous playing experience on the gridiron. That much can be substantiated by an article in the *Salisbury Post* on August 30, 1945.

In the middle 1940s the Catawba Indians were a "crackerjack" football team taking on all comers, which included teams from Appalachian State, William and Mary, Virginia Military Institute, Western Carolina, Eastern Kentucky and the 82nd Airborne (NC). In the 1945 season, Catawba finished with an outstanding record of 10–1.

The following season the 1946 Catawba Indians finished with a record of 10–2 and proceeded to defeat Maryville College 31–0 in the Tangerine Bowl. Then in 1947 the Indians finished with a record of 11–1 and defeated Marshall 7–0 in a return appearance to the bowl game at Orlando, Florida.

In the article written by Mike London in the *Salisbury Post* in 2011,

"The Curious Case of Johnny Temple," he points out that in 1945, when Johnny Temple supposedly tried out for the football team, Catawba had a backfield squad consisting of several skilled veterans, including Carroll Bowen, Bill Greene, Bill Speacht, Jack Ward and Charlie "The Slinging Kid" Gabriel. According to London, he could not find Johnny Temple listed in archive copies of the *Salisbury Post* as being on the first, second or even third teams.

With all those experienced players it is doubtful that there would have been any room for Johnny Temple on the Catawba Indians football squad that year. One of those veteran backs, Bill Speacht, ran back two kickoffs in 1946 for touchdowns; that set a school record which stood until 2010, when it was tied by L.J. McCray. Another of the veteran backs on the 1945 squad, Bill Greene, set a season record of 13 touchdowns in 1945 that still ranks fifth in school history.

It seems that Johnny Temple's athletic career at Catawba College is a grossly exaggerated tale manufactured by Temple. Throughout his later major league career, while a gifted and accomplished All-Star player, Johnny Temple would exhibit a strong penchant for "the blarney."

Having Catawba athletic letters or no letters at all, Johnny Temple left the school before the 1946 baseball season began. According to Temple, he had a limited scholarship and there wasn't enough money for clothes and other essentials.

So Temple dropped out of college and joined the U.S. Navy and served aboard the aircraft carrier USS *Randolph*. For a while it looked as if he might make a career out of the Navy and spent two weeks at the U.S. Naval Academy. "I spent two weeks running to class, running to my room, running to chow," said Temple. "I decided that I'd rather play baseball, so I got my discharge and went home."[2]

Later Temple stated that he fully intended to return to Catawba College after his tour of duty in the Navy, but was sidetracked by a baseball tryout camp that he attended.

While several Internet sources wrongfully credit Johnny Temple as having played baseball at Catawba, when he in fact did not, this does not diminish the fact that Catawba College has produced a modest list of players from its baseball program who did go on to play major league baseball. This list includes Sam Gibson (Detroit Tigers 1926–1928, New York Yankees 1930, New York Giants 1932), Buz Phillips (Philadelphia Phillies 1930), Vern Benson (Philadelphia Athletics 1943, St. Louis Cardinals 1946, 1951–1953), Clyde Klutz (Boston Braves 1942–1945, New York Giants 1945–1946, St. Louis Cardinals 1946, Pittsburgh Pirates 1947–1948, St.

Louis Browns 1951, Washington Nationals 1951–1952), Bobby Wilkins (Philadelphia Athletics 1944–1945) and Ben Callahan (Oakland Athletics 1983).

The most recent former Catawba College player to reach the major leagues is outfielder Jerry Sands. In the 2008 draft, Sands was the 25th-round selection of the Los Angeles Dodgers. At the start of the 2015 season, Jerry Sands was playing for the Cleveland Indians.

When Jerry Sands made his major league debut on April 19, 2011, with the Dodgers, immediately the fact that he had graduated from Catawba College was cause for another gusher of misinformation to be released by sportswriters, announcers and bloggers in regard to the college athletic experience of Johnny Ellis Temple.

Regardless of the aforementioned documented list of current and former major league players who attended Catawba College, it seems that Johnny Temple, without ever having one documented at-bat with the Catawba College baseball team, or ever having donned the Indians uniform, during his brief affiliation to the school, along with his guarded comments about his experience, combined with the lack of in-depth research by baseball fans and sportswriters, has elevated Temple to the status of being the person who is most historically associated with the Catawba baseball program. While it may be a classic case of sports history vs. sports mythology, it seems Johnny Ellis Temple has put Catawba College on the baseball map by simply having enrolled at the school for a few months in the fall of 1945 and early 1946. Although it's fabrication, it's still a pretty damn good PR job for Temple and the school.

Johnny Temple's rise to the big leagues is even more mysterious. Temple maintained that he got in touch with nearly every Class D club in North Carolina. He tried out for six or seven of them, but they all said he was too small. The rejections hardly stopped Temple from proving himself to the baseball establishment, and brazenly he tried out for big league teams too. He attended tryouts with both the Brooklyn Dodgers and Philadelphia Athletics. Both clubs turned him down as being too small.

Then Temple, along with brother Chub (a pitcher) and a friend by the name of George Snyder (an outfielder), read in a newspaper about a one-day tryout camp that a couple of scouts from the Cincinnati Reds were holding in Mooresville, North Carolina, about fifty miles from Reeds. At the time all three were working as house painters.

When the three arrived at the Mooresville tryout camp site they were surprised to learn that they were the only ones who were attending. The scouts were decidedly disappointed with the low turnout. But when they asked where this shabby trio had come from, the scouts decided that if they had traveled that far, they deserved a look. So the three put on their old town ball uniforms and worked out. The scouts liked what they saw in Chub Temple and offered him $700 to sign with the Reds. But they felt Johnny was too small to have much of chance at making the major leagues. But when Chub held firm that he wouldn't sign unless they signed his brother, the scouts relented. While the scouts signed both of the Temples and Snyder too, the only one who got a signing bonus was Chub. Johnny and George Snyder had to settle for $150 each. They all were told to report to the Morganton club of the Class D Western Carolina League. By the end of that summer Chub would be out of baseball.

Prior to being signed to a professional contract, in early summer of 1948 Johnny Temple was playing American Legion baseball. Alton Myers was a teammate who said of Temple, "The summer he signed with the Reds we played in Elkin. Cincinnati scout Tex Miller signed Johnny and his brother Chub. He was not a highly gifted player, but he was a battler. He was super competitive person. I thought maybe he'd go as high as Triple-A ball. He didn't have much speed, but he had a knack for getting on base, or getting a key hit, at the right time."[3]

After signing his $150-a-month contract with the Reds, Temple felt that he was on his way to the big leagues. He was, of course, naïve in those days and didn't know anything about meal money or first class travel. He went to see the scout who had signed him and asked if the club paid for his travel expenses.

The scout was thunderstruck and threw up his hands, stating, "Temple, you only been under contract three days and you're already trying to run things."[4] Temple said that the scout put three dollars' worth of gasoline in his gas tank and sent him along his way.

While it was a less than ostentatious beginning, Johnny Temple was on his way to working his way through the backwater towns of organized ball to the big leagues.

At the age of twenty, Johnny Temple made his entry into organized baseball, playing at the Class D level with Morganton in the Western Carolina League. Temple arrived in Morganton on June 25, 1948, the night of the second bout between Jersey Joe Walcott and Joe Louis for the heavyweight championship that saw Walcott KO Louis in the 11th round.

Upon his arrival the Morganton, manager pulled Temple aside for a private conversation. He told him to be darned sure not to tell anyone on this club how much money he was making. Some of the veterans on the ball club would be real unhappy if they knew he was making that much money. While later Temple came to the realization that the manager was pulling his leg, at the time he took his $150 every month and remained silent about it.

It was storybook beginning for Temple in organized ball as in his very first game he drove in the winning run. For the year he would hit .316.

The following season in 1949 Temple moved up to Class C ball playing shortstop for Ogden in the Pioneer League and hit .400 in 116 games to lead the league. In fact, Temple had 200 hits for 500 at bats. At the time, both future big league catchers Gus Triandos and Hal Smith were playing in the league.

Playing in the Pioneer League in the late 1940s required fortitude. Eight-hundred-mile bus trips were frequent between games. Sometimes to break up the boredom the team bus driver would stop at Yellowstone Park, where the players could view Old Faithful. Meal money was fixed at $1.25 a day.

It was just as much a Spartan existence for managers in the Pioneer League too. Charlie Metro, who later managed in the major leagues for the Chicago Cubs and Kansas City Royals, was the manager at Twin Forks in 1948. Not only was Metro the team manager, he was also the bus driver and clubhouse attendant.

During the off-season that year, once again, fate dealt a severe blow to the possible baseball career of Johnny Temple. He was working as a house painter and fell off a ladder, breaking his back. Miraculously he recovered in time for spring training and continued to move up the ladder of organized ball, and in 1950 was playing at the Class A level with the Columbia Reds of the South Atlantic League (a.k.a. Sally League).

At Columbia, Temple was playing between two Cincinnati Reds legends, one currently in the making and the other in the near future. Ted Kluszewski, who had preceded him at Columbia in 1946, had hit for a league-leading average of .352, and eighteen-year-old Frank Robinson would follow him in 1954 hitting .336 for the Columbia Reds.

Temple's salary was $375 month with Columbia. Because of the slow recovery with his back, he made quite a few errors that year; nonetheless he hit for an average of .322, which was fourth best in the league behind future nine-year major league veteran outfielder Rip Repluski .323, Pete Kraus .324 and league leader John Fiscalini .333.

On September 5, 1950, the second-to-last day of the Sally League season, Johnny Temple married Rebekah (Becky) Sheely. The ceremony, performed by the Reverend Paul McCullough, took place at home plate at Capital City Park in Columbia, and Temple, all decked out in a white tuxedo jacket and black pants, made one more error for the year, when he dropped the wedding ring at home plate. Following the game the Temples received a broad array of gifts from various Columbia merchants, the Columbia team and various well-wishers.

Throughout his career Temple would speak of his wife with overwhelming, sincere affection. In a 1952 interview Temple stated that Becky "has been a great inspiration to me on and off the field."[5]

Johnny Temple's ballpark nuptials were hardly uncommon; such ceremonies in minor league parks were common in the years before World War II and shortly after. Another notable infielder who got married at home plate was Don Zimmer, who had his marriage ceremony performed with his wife Soot on August 16, 1951, prior to a minor league game at Elmira, New York.

In the game the night of Temple's wedding the Columbia Reds defeated the Savannah Indians 4–1 to move into a tie for second place. Temple went 0 for 4.

One of Johnny Temple's teammates that year on the Columbia Reds was nineteen-year-old Bob Hazel, who played left field and hit .313. Hazel would eventually play for three years in the major leagues with the Cincinnati Reds and Milwaukee Braves, where he played in the 1957 World Series. Despite the steady hitting of Temple and Hazel, the Columbia Reds finished in second place in the Sally League in 1950 with a record of 83–70, 7 games behind the Macon Peaches.

On the day that Johnny Temple was married, the first major league ballplayer was called to duty for the Korean War. It was the Philadelphia Phillies' left hander Curt Simmons, who was a member of the Pennsylvania National Guard. At the time Simmons had won 17 games for the Phillies who were locked in a heated battle for the 1950 National League pennant with the Brooklyn Dodgers.

Temple had already served a post–World War II hitch in the U.S. Navy and was not eligible for the draft or call-up. However, the Korean War would interrupt the major league careers of a couple of hundred players. Some players called up or drafted would see combat, such as Lloyd Merriman, Ted Williams, Jerry Coleman and Bobby Brown. But most of the major league players drafted or called up during the Korean War, such as Whitey Ford, Don Newcombe, Carl Sawatski, Billy Martin, Willie Mays, Harvey Haddix, Johnny Antonelli, Jim Brosnan and others, would serve stateside throughout the war and play on service baseball teams.

By 1951 Johnny Temple was property of the Cincinnati Reds AA affiliate Tulsa Oilers of the Texas League. Although Temple had been an All-Star shortstop in every league he had played in up to that point in time, at the suggestion of Tulsa manager Al Vincent, he was moved from shortstop to second base. It was around that time Temple began to believe that he had a genuine shot at becoming a big leaguer.

Eventually the move to second base would become a very significant and strategic event in Temple's rise to the major leagues. Later he was to state, "Can you imagine me walking into Crosley Field and challenging Roy McMillan for his job?"[6]

Temple was surprised that after his promotion to Tulsa his salary was only increased by $25 a month more than he had been making at Columbia. It was typical minor league nonsense of the time. Tulsa management informed him that he had to prove himself to make more. Dismayed by the level of his salary, Temple sent a letter to the Cincinnati front office informing the Reds brass that he wanted to make a deal with them. "If I make the Tulsa club, you pay me $550 a month. If I don't you pay me $350, $25 less than I was making last year."[7]

Johnny Temple was now determined more than ever to reach the major leagues and began to reason that no matter how hard he played, how well he fielded or ran the bases, or how high his batting average was, something had to be added to his game to reach "the show." To that end, Temple determined that in order to get the attention of the Cincinnati Reds front office he had to become an ultra-aggressive player. So Johnny Temple became resolved to fight his way into the big leagues. In the 1951 season Temple exhibited his new sense of hyper-machoism by having almost as many fights in Texas League games as he did hits.

One of the more memorable diamond bouts that Temple had that summer occurred in Beaumont, Texas, when a pitcher by the name of Harry Schaeffer slid hard into Temple at second base, taking him out of a sure double play. Immediately Temple was on top of Schaeffer, pounding him with his fists. Both teams poured out of their dugouts and joined in the melee. The police had to come onto the field to untangle the brawling players and it took about fifteen minutes to restore order. At the bottom of the pile, there lay Johnny Temple in a state of bloody pulp with spike wounds all over his head. It took sixteen stiches to sew Temple's cranium back together. The spike wounds to his head tore into his scalp so badly that his hair never grew right in the spot again. Some observers have suggested that was why Temple so often wore a hat and later a toupee.

Nonetheless, with his head shaved and heavily bandaged, Temple was back in the lineup at second base for the following evening's game. Tulsa teammate pitcher Joe Nuxhall later said that Temple looked like an Indian playing at second base. "You should have seen him after he was spiked," said Nuxhall, "with his head swathed in bandages, he looked like a Comanche Indian running around on the ball diamond."[8]

Harry Schaeffer, the Beaumont pitcher who started the melee, would have a brief major league career with the New York Yankees, pitching in five games in the 1952 season. If Schaeffer hadn't sparked the brawl with Temple, he would not have even been a footnote in professional baseball history.

A week after the brawl in Beaumont, Temple was hit in the head by a pitch and was out of action for two weeks. The ball had struck his head just above the temple and actually bounced up in the air.

Johnny Temple's next on-field-bout came a few weeks later playing against Fort Worth. He had laid down a bunt and took off for first base. Immediately after crossing the bag, he heard a roar from the crowd. As he turned to determine what was going on, he was hit in the mouth by 220-pound Fort Worth first baseman Ben Taylor. Temple attempted to retaliate but got roughed up pretty good, with one of Taylor's punches hitting him in the teeth so hard that it split his lip. When the Tulsa catcher Walt Wrona arrived at the scene of the battle, he took hold of Taylor, and Temple immediately got a few good retaliatory licks in on him.

Very quickly Johnny Temple had gained the reputation he wanted as a feisty player, one who would admonish his teammates for not hustling. Later in the major leagues this personality trait would serve to create a psychological wall between him and some of his teammates.

During the 1951 season Temple was fined a least a dozen times. Despite his frequent on-field fisticuffs and the fact that his batting average dipped below .300 for the first time in his professional career (.291), Temple led the Texas League in hits (180), singles (151) and stolen bases (30). Also he solidified his growing reputation as a contact hitter, striking out only 18 times in 675 trips to the plate.

In the end all the hustle and blood and guts style of play paid off for Temple—it got him what he wanted, to be noticed in the Cincinnati Reds front office. On October 13, 1951, Temple's contract was purchased from Tulsa by Cincinnati and he was invited to spring training with the Reds in 1952.

Two

Breaking In with the Reds

As spring training began in 1952, the Cincinnati Reds had not finished in the first division in the National League since 1944. In the 1951 season Cincinnati finished in sixth place and only 588,768 fans had gone through the turnstiles at Crosley Field. It was the second worst season attendance record in the National League.

The pre–World War II glory days of the Cincinnati Reds winning back-to-back National League championships in 1939 and 1940, the thrill of Johnny Vander Meer's back-to-back no hitters in 1938, Ernie Lombardi's National League batting championship and the club's exciting victory over the Detroit Tigers in the 1940 World Series, had become distant memories in the hearts and minds of the loyal Queen City fans. One fan used to listen to the Reds on radio with twin plaster of Paris bulldogs situated on each side of his easy chair. He called the dogs Bucky (Walters) and Paul (Derringer) and rubbed their heads for good luck when their namesakes were on the mound. But by now in 1952 both Walters and Derringer were long gone from Crosley Field; the fan had long given up on the Reds and confined his gypsum canines to the closet.

Reds radio broadcaster and former New York Yankees pitcher Waite Hoyt later recalled that on one occasion in the middle 1940s, Reds general manager Warren Giles had called him into his office and asked why he wasn't more enthusiastic about the ball club in his broadcasts like other broadcasters, citing the Chicago Cubs' Bert Wilson as an example. Hoyt said that he told Giles, "Your top hitter's a lousy .267 or whatever the hell it is. Your top pitcher's won eight games. What is there to cheer about? Christ, if I cheered like Bert Wilson with the bums we got, people would think I was blind or the village idiot. Or maybe both."[1]

The 1952 edition of the Cincinnati Reds didn't promise to be much better than the dismal 1951 club. Despite the fact that the first baseman, big Ted Kluszewski, would hit .320 in the coming campaign, it wouldn't be enough to help the Reds climb out of the second division. Overall the 1952 Reds would prove to be a weak hitting club and finish with a team batting average of .249, the sixth worst average in the league.

The Reds' pitching staff was also pathetic and had only one reliable starter, left-hander Ken Raffensberger, who would finish with a record of 17–13 with an ERA of 2.81. Collectively the 1952 Reds pitching staff would achieve an ERA of 4.01, seventh worst in the league.

It would be this lackluster, rag-tag Cincinnati Reds club, with a heavily ingrained culture of losing, on which Johnny Temple would reach the major leagues.

Manager Luke Sewell, who had been at the Reds' helm since the last three games of the 1949 season, knowing that he had a weak pitching staff, was determined to put a team on the field in 1952 that could score runs. Over the winter the Reds had acquired Andy Seminick, a power-hitting veteran catcher from the Philadelphia Phillies, in a trade for second baseman Connie Ryan and catcher Smoky Burgess, who had been acquired by the Reds from the Chicago Cubs over the winter.

With Ted Kluszewski, the team's best hitter, holding down first base, Sewell inserted Joe Adcock, another power-hitting first baseman, in left field. But there were concerns with Adcock; despite his power he had hit into twenty-five double plays in the 1951 campaign.

The team leader was third baseman Grady Hatton, an All-Star and the matinee idol of the Ladies Day crowd at Crosley Field. But with Ryan traded to the Phillies, Sewell decided to move Hatton from third base to second base to make room for Bobby Adams at the hot corner, a player who could swing the bat with authority. Also Sewell had given up on Virgil Stallcup, who had been the Reds' starting shortstop since 1948 but who hit just .241 in the 1951 season. To replace Stallcup at shortstop, Sewell inserted young Roy McMillan, who had come up from the minors in 1951 and played in 85 games. While McMillan was also a weak hitter and would only hit .244 in the 1952 season, he would prove to be by far the best fielding shortstop in the National League and was capable of winning games with his glove. In early May, Stallcup was packaged with Dick Sisler, acquired in the deal for Seminick, and traded to the St. Louis Cardinals.

While Grady Hatton had some doubts at his ability to play second base, he knew if he learned to handle the pivot at second that he could do the job. So with Hatton slated to play second, McMillan at shortstop and yet another second baseman acquired in the trade with Philadelphia– Eddie Pellagrini—there really wasn't any room for rookie Johnny Temple.

It was, however, surprising to Temple that when he arrived at the Reds' spring training camp in Tampa, Florida, in early March 1952, his reputation as a fiery young, battling, tobacco-chewing, hustling player had preceded him. The press began to question Temple about his donnybrooks while playing at Tulsa. Standing by the batting cage waiting his turn, Temple told the assembled press corps, "I don't look for trouble, but I'm not going to let anyone push me around."[2] The die for Temple's style of play in the majors had been cast.

Controversial Ben Chapman was a coach with the Reds in 1952. When Chapman had been manager of the Philadelphia Phillies in 1947, he had been one of Jackie Robinson's most notable adversaries during his quest to break into traditionally all-white major league baseball. Recently Chapman had been complaining that ballplayers of the current day lacked the spirit, aggressiveness and hustle of those of who had previously played the game. But Chapman was all smiles in regard to Johnny Temple and was sure that he had the right stuff to be a major leaguer and maybe even be a throwback to players of an earlier day.

About halfway through spring training, Grady Hatton twisted his ankle in a game with the Philadelphia Phillies. Those around the Reds' camp in Tampa wondered if this might be a window of opportunity for Johnny Temple. When sportswriter Earl Lawson of the *Cincinnati Times-Star* asked Temple if he thought that Hatton's injury might give him a shot at the second base job, he surprised not only Lawson, but everyone else within hearing distance with his bold retort. "That's OK with me," said Temple. "It's a tough break for Hatton, but in this game it's everyone for himself."[3]

There was some ambiguity in Temple's statement that left some wondering just what he had meant. Was it a tough break for Grady Hatton that he had injured his ankle, or was it tough break for Hatton that Temple might now be playing in his position?

As it turned out, Johnny Temple didn't get an immediate chance to seize the opportunity provided by Hatton's disability; Luke Sewell inserted Eddie Pellagrini at second base for the first two games. But in the third game of Hatton's absence from the lineup, Temple got to play against the Boston Red Sox and made the most of it. Left-hander Mickey McDermott, the Boston pitcher, had set down seven Reds in order, striking out five, when Temple came up to the plate. Temple immediately hit a single. In the game Temple had three singles in five at bats and handled twelve chances in the field flawlessly. His performance raised more than a few eyebrows among the press corps.

Two. Breaking In with the Reds

A couple of days later Luke Sewell decided to see what Temple could do as the Reds' leadoff hitter in a game against the Philadelphia Athletics. In the Reds' half of the first inning, with a sparse crowd of only 563 snowbird fans on hand, Temple stepped up to the plate facing Philadelphia pitcher Edward "Moe" Burtschy, a native of Cincinnati who had attended Roger Bacon High School. Temple quickly lined a hit into right center, and as he rounded first he noticed Athletics right fielder Elmer Valo taking his time fielding the ball, so he sprinted toward second base and slid in with a double just ahead of the throw. The Reds won the game 6–5; Temple got three of the Reds' nine hits and for the third time he played errorless ball in the field. For three games Temple had got eight hits in thirteen at bats for an average of .615.

While Luke Sewell was pleased with Temple's performance, he still had some doubts about the rookie. "The kid's a ballplayer," said Sewell. "He wants to play. He's no 'fancy Dan' in practice, but he's the kind that's at his best in a game. Still, I'll have to wait for a couple of weeks to see what he can do at the plate when the pitchers, the good ones, begin bearing down."[4]

When sportswriters asked Luke Sewell how Grady Hatton's ankle was healing, Sewell remarked that the kid (Temple) will cure his ankle. The Cincinnati press now began to mention Johnny Temple as a dark horse for the Reds' second base position.

On opening day, April 15, 1952, Johnny Temple made his major league debut with the Cincinnati Reds. A large crowd of 28,517 fans packed Crosley Field for the game with the Chicago Cubs. Johnny Temple got his first major league at bat when he pinch-hit for pitcher Herman Wehmeier in the bottom of the third inning and flew out to center field. The Cubs won the game in ten innings 6–5. But it was official–Johnny Temple was in the record book.

Luke Sewell decided to go with Grady Hatton at second base in the lineup rather than Johnny Temple. With twenty-one-year-old Roy McMillan at shortstop, Sewell believed that he would benefit from the steady influence of a veteran playing next to him. Sewell also felt that Hatton had a little more power in his bat than Temple had, despite the fact that he had only hit 65 home runs in the six years he had played for the Reds.

Temple would not get in another game for two weeks, when manager Luke Sewell sent him up to pinch-hit against the New York Giants in the eighth inning. This time Temple lofted a soft fly ball to shortstop Alvin Dark as the Reds went down to defeat 4–1.

Two days later Temple was inserted as a pinch runner for catcher

Andy Seminick in the ninth inning in a 2–1 loss to the Boston Braves. Some fans and sportswriters were beginning to ask why a player with Temple's potential was wasting his time on the bench. Why not send him back down to the minors for more seasoning? The facts were that Luke Sewell was reluctant to farm Temple out, and furthermore, Temple didn't want to leave, as he felt he was ready to play in the big leagues.

The Reds had a substantial investment in Grady Hatton, who up until this point in his career had never hit for an average higher than .281. When the former University of Texas star was discharged from the service, the Reds paid him a $25,000 signing bonus. Former Reds president Warren Giles, who by then in 1952 was president of the National League, took a personal liking to Hatton and never cut his contract after he had a couple of consecutive sub-par seasonal performances. This circumstance made Hatton somewhat unattractive on the trade market. Also Hatton was well liked by his teammates, who had selected him as their player representative. So all this made it look unlikely that Johnny Temple would play much in the 1952 season.

On May 7, Johnny Temple got his first major league hit. In the ninth inning of a game played at Ebbets Field in Brooklyn, Temple pinch-hit for pitcher Frank Hiller and stroked a line drive single off Johnny Rutherford as the Dodgers beat the Reds 5–4.

The fact that Temple got his first major league hit against the Dodgers was a harbinger of things to come, as he would tend to feast on Dodger pitching throughout his career in the National League, doing just about all things possible with the bat other than hitting home runs. In 1957, the Dodgers' last year playing in Brooklyn, Temple would hit .354 against them. In a late season series he would assault the Brooklyn staff for a .643 average, going 9 for 14. Temple was particularly fond of Dodgers lefty Johnny Podres' pitches, as he hit .412 against him that year.

The Reds' front office and manager Luke Sewell just could not determine where Johnny Temple fit in on the team. So on June 4 they decided to send him down to Tulsa. On his way out of the door to AA ball, Temple penned a note and pinned it on the clubhouse bulletin board. The note read, "So long fellows, I'll be back though. Only I'll stay."[5]

Meddling owners and micro-managing general managers aside, it is fully recognized by alert major league managers that fans and their strong protests, usually orchestrated by the press, could shorten their terms of service with a ball club. Perhaps a little of this type of negativity hastened the departure of Luke Sewell from Cincinnati.

By July 26 the Reds were floundering in familiar ground, holding

Johnny Temple, Cincinnati Reds, circa 1953 (Rhodes/Klumpe Reds Hall of Fame Collection).

down seventh place with a record of 38–57. At that point Luke Sewell resigned as manager. As he packed his bags for parts unknown, Sewell expressed dissatisfaction with both the Cincinnati fans and press, stating that he had been harassed by both. In particular Sewell stated that Cincinnati was "the worst fan clientele in the country."[6]

On July 28 the legendary Rogers Hornsby was hired by general manager Gabe Paul as the new Reds manager. Hornsby had recently been fired that season by Bill Veeck, Jr., as manager of the St. Louis Browns after posting a record of 22–29. At that point in time Hornsby had eleven years' experience as a big league manager for four teams. By the end of his brief tenure as manager of the Reds, Hornsby would hold much the same opinion of the Cincinnati fans and press as Luke Sewell, but would remain less vocal about it.

As a player Rogers Hornsby was one of the greatest hitters in the history of the game. In twenty-three years in the big leagues, playing with the St. Louis Cardinals, New York Giants, Boston Braves, Chicago Cubs and St. Louis Browns, Hornsby had 2930 hits, 301 home runs and 1584 RBIs. He led the National League in hitting seven years and batted over .400 three times (.401, 1922; .424, 1924; and .403, 1925). His lifetime batting average of .358 is second all-time to Ty Cobb's .367. Most baseball historians acknowledge Rogers Hornsby as the greatest right-handed hitter of all time.

Earle Bruckner acted as interim manager and guided the Reds to a 3–2 record; then on August 5 Hornsby took over. In his first game as manager, Ken Raffensberger pitched a shut-out and Ted Kluszewski hit a key two-run triple as the Reds defeated the Chicago Cubs 4–0. There was a lot of hype in regard to the game and even Reds owner Powell Crosley, Jr., who had been vacationing in Canada, flew in for the game. But a disappointing crowd of only 12,651 showed up at Crosley Field to witness Hornsby's debut as Reds manager.

Immediately and methodically Rogers Hornsby started to remake the Cincinnati Reds into a team in his own image. He began recommending player changes and acquisitions. During the week before he started his managerial duties with the Reds, Hornsby went on a scouting mission, watching the Reds' affiliate American Association minor league teams in Milwaukee and Kansas City. Hornsby had been impressed by outfielder Jim Greengrass on the Tulsa club. Hornsby liked the power he demonstrated at the plate and the all-round hustle displayed by Greengrass. So he urged Gabe Paul to acquire him. But Greengrass was under contract to the New York Yankees.

However there was no honeymoon for Hornsby with the Reds' players. Almost from the time he walked into the Reds' clubhouse, various players began having trouble with him. One of those players was pitcher Ewell "The Whip" Blackwell, who held the opinion that Hornsby was too temperamental. After experiencing Hornsby's managerial style for about three weeks, Blackwell requested to be traded.

In 1947 when the Reds finished in fifth place, Blackwell had been the franchise with a record of 22–8, leading the league in complete games with 23 and strikeouts with 193. Also Blackwell had thrown a no-hitter that year on June 18, beating the Boston Braves 6–0.

By 1952 Blackwell had been coming up with periodic arm problems and the front office decided that his best days on the mound were behind him. So on August 28 the Reds traded him to the New York Yankees for

Jim Greengrass, Johnny Schmitz, Ernie Nevel, Bob Marquis and $35,000 cash.

Rogers Hornsby also saw the acquisition of Jim Greengrass as the solution to replacing the good-hitting but moody Joe Adcock, who was not happy playing in the outfield. Although Adcock was a budding power hitter, he was not going to dislodge Ted Kluszewski from first base. As soon as Greengrass arrived in Cincinnati in early September, he replaced Adcock in the lineup.

Another player who quickly became unhappy with Hornsby's managerial style was Grady Hatton, who was struggling at the plate since being moved by Luke Sewell to second base at the beginning of the season.

Rogers Hornsby could not comprehend that only a few players were gifted with the natural ability to hit like he had in the major leagues. His preference was for infielders who could hit over those who were great fielders. In regard to Roy McMillian, the Reds' extraordinary slick-fielding, weak-hitting shortstop, Hornsby remarked, "You can shake good fielders out of any tree."[7]

The 1952 Cincinnati Reds keystone combination of Roy McMillian at shortstop and Grady Hatton at second base was simply appalling to Rogers Hornsby in regard to their ability at the plate. At the end of August, Roy McMillan was hitting around .235 and Grady Hatton .212. Hornsby had hit .424 in 1924, almost as much as the combined averages of McMillan and Hatton. Hornsby had only a few options in beefing up the lineup in that area, especially at second base to take over from Grady Hatton, where he could call on veteran utility infielder Eddie Pellagrini or rookie Johnny Temple, who had been recalled from Tulsa on August 30.

In early September, with the Reds out of the pennant race and fighting hard for sixth place, Hornsby chose to insert Eddie Pellagrini at second base. But he was hitting only .172 and didn't improve.

Johnny Temple had hit .306 after being sent down to AA ball and had only been struck out 14 times in 435 at bats. There were a lot of observers who felt that Temple should have been playing second base for Rogers Hornsby. Temple fit the model of a player that Hornsby preferred— he was blunt and feisty. Speculation was that there was a clash of personalities between Temple and Hornsby.

On September 9, the Reds and Braves were scheduled to play a double-header in Boston—one of the last National League twin bills ever to be played in the city. With the Braves committed to leave Boston for Milwaukee in the 1953 season, only 3,175 fans were on hand.

Rogers Hornsby decided that it was time to let Johnny Temple prove that he belonged in the big leagues and demonstrate he could improve on the performance of both Grady Hatton and Eddie Pellagrini at the plate.

In the first game of the double-header the Reds were shut out 1–0 by Warren Spahn, who threw a three-hitter. Temple went 0 for 4 in the game and his batting average dipped to .105.

In the second game the Reds turned the tables behind a four-hitter by Harry Perkowski, defeating the Braves 2–0. Facing the pitching of Max Surkont and Bob Chipman, Johnny Temple again went hitless, going 0 for 5 as his batting average dropped to a paltry .083.

Although Temple was struggling, Hornsby was cognizant of his own struggles when he came up. The fact that he had only hit .246 in his first 18 games in the major leagues in 1915 prompted Hornsby to stay with the rookie.

On September 12 the Reds played a double-header with the New York Giants at the Polo Grounds. In the first game Temple went 0 for 3 as the Reds were defeated 4–2.

Then in the second game the Reds defeated the Giants 8–7, led by Johnny Temple. In the second inning, Temple, who was hitting just .103 at the time, hit a grand slam home run off Jim Hearn. It was the rookie's first major league home run.

Two days later at Ebbets Field in Brooklyn, the Reds beat the Dodgers 4–0 with outfielder Jim Greengrass hitting his first major league home run. It was also a grand slam, accounting for all the Reds runs and making Greengrass the second Reds rookie to hit a grand slam in three days. Johnny Temple had two hits in the game to raise his batting average to .146.

The 1952 Cincinnati Reds finished in sixth place in the National League with a record of 69–85, 27½ games behind the pennant-winning Brooklyn Dodgers, but the club showed promise under Rogers Hornsby, going 27–24.

Grady Hatton played 120 games at second base in the 1952 season hitting for an average of .212. Eddie Pellagrini played second base in 22 games, hitting .170. Johnny Temple also played in 22 games at second base and hit .196. At that moment Johnny Temple's future with the Reds didn't seem very secure. Rogers Hornsby was disgusted with all three, Hatton, Pellagrini and Temple, and unless the Reds made a move over the winter, the second base position would be up for grabs in the 1953 season.

Three

Taking Over at Second Base

As soon as the 1952 season ended, Rogers Hornsby and Gabe Paul got down to the business of improving the Cincinnati Reds for the coming 1953 campaign. On October 14, Gabe Paul made one the best trades in his career.

By that time Branch Rickey had sold his interest in the Brooklyn Dodgers for a million dollars and moved on to become the general manager of the Pittsburgh Pirates. Pittsburgh had been floundering in the standings for a couple of decades and Rickey was in a hurry to rebuild the team. But Rickey was hampered in his efforts by one of his personality traits—his frugality. While Branch Rickey's legacy is highlighted by his historic action of signing Jackie Robinson to a major league contract and breaking the game's color barrier, lying just below the surface of all that human justice inherent in Rickey's psychological makeup were the blatant characteristics of a major league front office miser.

The stories of Branch Rickey's obsessive penny-pinching are endless. Dizzy Dean referred to Rickey as a cheap bastard. Enos Slaughter remarked that Branch Rickey "would go to the vault to get change for a nickel." Ralph Kiner remarked that following a season in which he had hit 47 home runs and asked for a raise, Branch Rickey replied, "We finished last with you and we can finish last without you."[1]

Effa Manley, who along with her husband Abe had owned the Newark Eagles, had a very negative opinion about Branch Rickey. She was to state that Branch Rickey took a million dollars' worth of ballplayers from the Negro Leagues and never bothered to say thanks.

In the 1950 season the Pirates had brought a young power-hitting outfielder by the name of Gus Bell up to their major league roster and he had quickly established himself as a potential All-Star. But problems between Bell and Rickey started immediately. In 1952 Bell wanted Rickey to pay for a train ticket to spring training in Florida for his wife and their infant son, but Rickey refused.

According to Gabe Paul, Branch Rickey didn't like Gus Bell's wife. "He thought she was extravagant."[2] After coming to Cincinnati, Bell told Paul that Rickey saw his wife throwing diapers away. He didn't know they were a new product—disposable diapers.

Those disposable diapers that Bell's wife was using were being put on the couples' first born son, Buddy Bell, who would later become one of the best third baseman of his generation, playing eighteen years in the major leagues with Cleveland, Texas, Cincinnati and Houston while becoming a five time All-Star and winning six Gold Gloves.

As might be expected, Branch Rickey's personality clouded his judgment on Gus Bell, and with the recommendation of Rogers Hornsby, on October 14, 1952, Gabe Paul acquired the slugging outfielder from the Pirates for three marginal players, Cal Abrams, Joe Rossi and Gail Henley.

As for second base, in the 1953 season it looked like Johnny Temple would be the heir apparent. Then, just prior to the start of spring training on February 16, the Reds were involved in a multi-team trade. Brooklyn sent outfielder Jim Pendleton and infielder Rocky Bridges to Milwaukee for pitcher Russ Meyer. Milwaukee in turn sent Rocky Bridges and $50,000 cash to Cincinnati for disgruntled outfielder/first baseman Joe Adcock.

Previously, the Boston Braves (about to become the Milwaukee Braves) had offered Reds general manager Gabe Paul $175,000 cash for Adcock, and now he would become the key player in the multi-team deal. The trade would ultimately turn out to be one of the worst that Gabe Paul would make in his distinguished career, balancing out his theft of Gus Bell from Branch Rickey and the Pirates. But Paul had little or no alternatives in the matter; there was no way that Joe Adcock was going to play first base in Cincinnati while Ted Kluszewski was there.

Joe Adcock would go on to play in two World Series for the Milwaukee Braves, hit .308 in the 1958 World Series, and finish a 17-year major league career with 336 home runs and 1122 RBIs.

During spring training the previous season it had been rumored that the Reds were interested in acquiring Rocky Bridges. But at that time former manager Luke Sewell stated he wouldn't trade Johnny Temple for Bridges one for one, so talk of a deal for Bridges died.

But now with Sewell gone and as a result of the trade, Rocky Bridges would become the Reds' regular second baseman in the 1953 season and Johnny Temple would continue to sit on the bench. Still, current Reds

Three. Taking Over at Second Base

manager Rogers Hornsby was far from being enamored with Bridges and was open-minded about giving Johnny Temple a shot at second base.

Rocky Bridges was a tobacco-chewing, weak-hitting infielder who could play second base, third base and shortstop. He had come up to the majors with Brooklyn in the 1951 season. According to Chuck Harmon, who would become the first Afro-American player to play for the Cincinnati Reds: "One day Hornsby was watching Bridges taking batting practice. He turned away from the batting cage and remarked, 'I can piss farther than he can hit.'"[3]

Gabe Paul justified the snub of Temple and the acquisition of Bridges, stating, "We didn't want to put all of our eggs in one basket [Temple]."[4] In other words the Reds' general manager felt strong competition would produce a better second baseman.

Comparing the two's past performance didn't really provide a definitive answer to who might be the better candidate for the second base job. In terms of major league experience Rocky Bridges had been in the big leagues for two years with Brooklyn but mostly sat on the bench. While neither Bridges nor Temple had much power at the plate, Temple had the better minor league statistics. Just once in five years in the minors had Temple's batting average dipped below .300. That was in 1951 when he hit .296 at Tulsa. Rocky Bridges's best minor league batting average was .280 in 1950 at Montreal. As for the field, Temple had the edge in speed. Bridges had a stronger arm, but Temple's arm was strong enough to pivot for the double play. Both players were known to be aggressive players.

When opening day 1953 came to Crosley Field, Rogers Hornsby inserted Johnny Temple in the lineup at second base. The job was his to keep or lose. The Reds opened the 1953 campaign against the Braves, now of Milwaukee rather than Boston. The usual opening day packed house of 30,000 plus fans was on hand in Cincinnati to witness Max Surkont shut out the Reds 4–0.

Johnny Temple went 0 for 4 in the opening game, but after the fourth game of the season he was hitting .333. Then Temple's average started to decline. By the ninth game of the season his average had dipped to .231 and the Reds had a record of 2–7. From that point on Rocky Bridges took over at second base.

In the 1953 season Johnny Temple played in 63 games, 44 games at second base, and hit .264 with 1 home run and 14 RBIs. Rocky Bridges played in 122 games, 115 at second base, while .hitting 227 with 1 home runs and 21 RBIs. Also Grady Hatton was still with the Reds and played 35 games at second base while hitting .233.

The 1953 Reds turned out to be not much better than the 1952 edition—a ball club with fairly good hitting, good fielding and weak pitching. On September 17, with eight games to go in the season, Rogers Hornsby was fired. While everyone knew that there had been tension between Hornsby and the front office, as well as between Hornsby and the Reds players, no one was talking and the official statement released by Gabe Paul was that everyone, Reds owner Powell Crosley, Jr., himself and Hornsby, were all parting on the best of terms.

While the Reds had failed to improve overall as a team under Rogers Hornsby, he had made one significant contribution to the ball club during his brief tenure as manager: he had converted first baseman Ted Kluszewski from a line drive hitter into a pull hitter. As a result Big Klu had a banner year in 1953, hitting for an average of .308 with 40 home runs and 108 RBIs.

Coach Buster Mills took over as manager for the balance of the schedule and the Reds finished in sixth place with a record of 68–86. It was the ninth consecutive year that the Reds had finished in the second division. The Reds were never over .500 the entire season and finished 37 games behind the pennant-winning Brooklyn Dodgers while having the lowest season attendance in the National League, 548,086 paid admissions.

Immediately following Roger Hornsby's departure, speculation as to who would be the new Reds skipper was rampant. Names being mentioned included Lefty O'Doul, Bobby Bragan, Al Lopez, Harry "The Hat" Walker, Del Baker and Ernie White. The favorite among the hot stove league set seemed to be Al Lopez.

After sitting on the bench for most of his first full season in the major leagues, Johnny Temple was extremely dissatisfied and he expressed himself. He remarked, "If this happens again next year, I'm going to quit. I ought to quit if I can't play second base for this club."[5] He felt that if he couldn't beat out a guy hitting .215 (Rocky Bridges) that there was absolutely no use in his trying to play in the major leagues.

To that end, Temple went to Venezuela to play winter ball and let his bat do the talking. As the league was about to conclude its schedule in February 1954, Johnny Temple was hitting a robust .330. Buster Mills had resigned his coaching post with the Reds after the 1953 season and accepted a similar job with the Boston Red Sox for the coming season. He was Temple's manager in the Venezuelan Winter League. Mills contacted Gabe Paul and told him, "Temple has played great ball all season and is hitting around .330. He is your second baseman for 1954, strictly a major leaguer."[6]

Another Reds player who distinguished himself that winter in Venezuela was rookie catcher Ed Bailey, who demonstrated that he was the team's future receiver. Andy Seminick would still be the Reds' starting catcher in 1954, but he also tutored Bailey and it paid off. Bailey would catch in 61 games for the Reds. While he would only hit for an average of .197, he would hit 9 home runs in just 183 at bats.

Ed Bailey was from Strawberry Plains, Tennessee (population 680), a small village outside of Knoxville. His teammates referred to him as "Gar" (Edgar Bailey). When the Reds were on the road coming north from spring training, they passed through Johnny Temple's one-traffic-light hometown of Reeds, North Carolina, prompting Bailey to quickly remark, "Don't ever let me hear anyone kidding me about Strawberry Plains."[7]

As the 1954 major league season approached, the Cincinnati Reds had a new manager and Cold War politics entered into major league baseball.

The new skipper of the team was Birdie Tebbetts, a former big league catcher. Between 1936 and 1952, Tebbetts had played in 1162 games in the American League with Detroit, Boston and Cleveland, and played for the Detroit Tigers in the 1940 World Series against the Cincinnati Reds. In the 1953 season Tebbetts had managed the Cleveland Indians' AAA team in Indianapolis. Tebbetts also had additional managerial experience as he had managed big league ballplayers on service teams for three years during World War II.

Cleveland general manager Hank Greenberg had been grooming Tebbetts to take over as Indians manager in a year or two, but he was not going to step in the way of his former teammate and friend's advancing himself to a major league job more quickly. During the winter meetings in Chicago, opportunity knocked for Tebbetts when he was approached by Cincinnati general manager Gabe Paul about becoming the Reds' manager. When Tebbetts asked Paul if he had any money, he replied that he didn't. So Paul offered Tebbetts the big league job with Cincinnati for the same amount he had made in the minors with Indianapolis. However, Paul sweetened the pot when he offered Tebbetts incentive pay based on season attendance. He offered Tebbetts an extra $1000 for every 100,000 fans the Reds drew over 600,000 for the season. The deal was done.

Andy Seminick said of Tebbetts, "He was a younger guy, having been catching just a couple of years before, so he could relate to the players much better than Rogers Hornsby."[8]

As for Cold War politics having an effect on Cincinnati baseball in the 1954 season, in the nation's capital Senator McCarthy's hearings had been in full swing since the fall of 1953 and were engulfing the nation's headlines. Consequently there was considerable anti-communist hysteria prevailing across America and the Cincinnati Reds were concerned about the team's name. The term "Reds" was a popular euphemism used to designate communists. Therefore in order to protect their brand, the Cincinnati Baseball Club, Inc. made an executive decision to change the name of the ball club from Reds to Redlegs.

Such a corporate anxiety attack would get a chuckle today, but in the Cold War environment of 1954, with the winds of communism blowing hard across Europe and Asia, there was genuine paranoia about even the suggestion of being a "commie." The Cincinnati Reds were owned by Powell Crosley, Jr., an American industrialist of some considerable stature, and he personally felt it was in the ballclub's best interest to ensure that they were not to be allegorically misconnected to the Soviets, who were commonly referred to as "Reds." So the team's name was officially changed to Redlegs. It would remain in effect until 1959, when the team name was returned to Reds. The team moniker Redlegs was really nothing new. In fact many Cincinnati fans referred to the team as the Redlegs, and *Cincinnati Times-Star* sportswriter Earl Lawson had been referring to the team as the Redlegs in his columns for several years.

Regardless of the fact that Johnny Temple had a terrific winter playing ball in Venezuela, when he got to the Reds' spring training camp in Tampa, Florida, in March, he found it crowded around second base. Those candidates looking to fill the job in the 1954 season included Grady Hatton, Rocky Bridges and Connie Ryan, whom the Redlegs had reacquired in a trade with the Philadelphia Phillies in December along with sore-armed pitcher Saul Rogovin in exchange for outfielder Willard Marshall. It was apparent that someone had to go.

Manager Birdie Tebbetts asked Temple if he wanted to take it easy for a while after playing ball in Venezuela over the winter. Temple replied that he didn't have time to take it easy. From that point on Johnny Temple went out and had a terrific spring. By March 19, Temple had got 12 hits in 32 official at bats, three of them coming on bunts. In the field he vacillated between being spectacular and erratic.

Temple was also determined to show both Birdie Tebbetts and his Redlegs teammates that the reputation he had acquired in the Texas League as a fiery, hustling throwback player was indeed accurate. In a spring training game against Milwaukee, Temple came barreling into home plate full-throttle into Braves catcher Dell Crandall. The collision caused the ball to pop out of Crandall's glove and he remained on the ground as

Temple got up and limped toward the Redlegs bench. Immediately someone shouted to Temple that Crandall was still down. Temple quickly replied, "That's nothing—I'm afraid to look and see if I've still got a kneecap."[9] Then before he sat down, Temple staggered over in the direction of the Redlegs' 240-pound behemoth first baseman Ted Kluszewski and shouted, "Let that be a lesson to you, you big slob."[10] Big Klu, stunned by the brash remark, was speechless.

When the press asked Birdie Tebbetts about Temple during spring training, he remarked, "He's the toughest little monkey I've come across in a long time. Up to now he's called every man on the team a dirty name, except me, and I expect to be next. He's a real throwback to the old days."[11]

Birdie Tebbetts brought a more disciplined managerial style to the Redlegs than had been practiced by Rogers Hornsby. The Cincinnati front office had high hopes that their new manager would finally lead the ball club out of their second-division funk, where they had been mired down since 1944.

On Birdie Tebbetts's first day in the Redlegs clubhouse in Tampa, he called a team meeting to introduce himself. In the 1953 season first baseman Big Ted Kluszewski had set a club record hitting 40 home runs and was the idol of every kid in the Queen City. Tebbetts looked across the room and saw Kluszewski reading a newspaper. Tebbetts later remarked that all the other players were watching him intensely to see what he would do with the benevolent slugger. Tebbetts looked towards Kluszewski and said, "Mr. Kluszewski, the remarks I am making are for the whole team."[12] Kluszewski looked up, put the paper down and nodded politely. According to Tebbetts, Kluszewski got the message and after that they got along just fine.

There were several things that Tebbetts couldn't tolerate from his players. One was complaining about the weather. "I'd fine anybody $25 for bitching that it was too hot or too cold or raining. I wanted my ball players to come on the field wanting to play,"[13] said Tebbetts.

By the end of spring training in 1954, Johnny Temple would take over the Cincinnati second base job and continue to hold it until he was traded following the 1959 season.

With Johnny Temple playing second base and batting sixth in the lineup, the Cincinnati Redlegs opened the 1954 campaign at Crosley Field before 33,185 fans by defeating the Milwaukee Braves 9–8. In the second inning Temple drove in the Redlegs' first run with a single off Bob Buhl that sent Jim Greengrass scampering across the plate.

The Cincinnati front office and Birdie Tebbetts quickly reached the conclusion that Johnny Temple was their man at second base and began moving players. On April 18, Grady Hatton, who had been with Cincinnati since 1946, was traded to the Chicago Cubs for veteran shortstop Johnny Lipon. Lipon would play in one game for Cincinnati and be released. Connie Ryan would play in one game for the Redlegs before being released on April 26.

Rocky Bridges became a utility infielder for the Redlegs, playing second, third and shortstop, a job he did remarkably well. In the 1955 season Bridges would play in 95 games for the Redlegs (59 at third base, 26 at shortstop and 9 at second base) while hitting .286. Bridges would continue to play that role with the Redlegs until early in the 1957 season, when he was sold to Washington on waivers.

On May 5 at Crosley Field, the Redlegs defeated Sal Maglie and the New York Giants 7–1 with Fred Baczewski pitching a complete game. Due to the power hitting of Ted Kluszewski and steady contributions of Johnny Temple, who had entered the game with a .364 batting average—highest on the team—the Redlegs found themselves in second place, one game behind in the standings. While Kluszewski kept hitting home runs, Temple kept flirting with a batting average above .300 and was running the bases like Ty Cobb, stealing home three times since opening day. But the Redlegs began to run out of gas and just couldn't keep pace with the Braves, Dodgers and Giants. By mid–May they were fighting for fifth place and just hoping to finish in the first division.

At the All-Star Game break, although the Redlegs were scoring some runs led by Ted Kluszewski (22 home runs and a .313 average), Gus Bell (12 home runs and a .344 average) and Johnny Temple (0 home runs, but hitting .308), the Redlegs had a record of 41–42 and were holding down fifth place 13½ games behind the New York Giants.

In a weekend series with the St. Louis Cardinals played on August 13–15, the Redlegs lost two out of three games. But in the series Johnny Temple got on base nine straight times. The streak started in the Friday night game when Temple was hit by a pitch from Brooks Lawrence in his last at bat. Then in the Saturday night game, in five trips to the plate, Temple hit two singles (one a bunt single), a triple and walked twice. In the Sunday game he singled, doubled with the bases full, and walked before ending the streak with a fly ball to left field. In his last at bat he walked.

It was on Friday evening, September 3, 1954, that a feud between Milwaukee Braves shortstop Johnny Logan and Redlegs second baseman Johnny Temple began. Hard feelings between the two would continue for several seasons and become one of the longest player feuds in major league history.

Three. Taking Over at Second Base

As the 1954 pennant stretch drive began, the Milwaukee Braves were on the road in Cincinnati. The Braves were in third place, 6½ games behind the league-leading New York Giants and 2½ games behind second-place Brooklyn. The Redlegs, although in fourth place, were 19 games behind the Giants and in a battle for the first division with a one-game lead over the fifth-place Philadelphia Phillies.

With a typical Friday night crowd of 13,901 on hand at Crosley Field, the Redlegs' Corky Valentine took the mound opposed by the Braves' Lew Burdette. The Braves took a 1–0 lead into the bottom of the eighth inning when Burdette walked Redlegs centerfielder Gus Bell. This brought Ted Kluszewski to the plate, who hit a line drive home run into the right field bleachers to give the Reds a 2–1 lead. It was Big Klu's 42nd home run of the season.

The next Redlegs batter was left fielder Jim Greengrass, who singled. Johnny Temple then stepped up to the plate and hit a sharp ground ball to Braves shortstop Johnny Logan, who stepped on second to force Greengrass. But as Greengrass slid into the bag, he wrapped his legs around Logan. When the players got up, Greengrass threw a punch at Logan, who as an ex-prize fighter artfully dodged the blow and swung back. Then Greengrass, a 200-pounder, picked up the 175-pound Logan and body slammed him to the ground.

Players from both benches swarmed onto the field, and three separate fights began and a couple of wrestling matches. Johnny Temple joined the fracas by jumping into one of the piles at second base and wound up fighting Logan. It took fifteen minutes before order could be restored.

Both Logan and Greengrass were ejected from the game. Logan was replaced at shortstop by Roy Smalley and Greengrass in left field by Bob Borkowski. Jim Greengrass said, "I thought he tried to swing at me with the ball. I didn't spike him. I had my feet tucked under me."[14]

Then, as Logan was passing first base on his way to the Braves' clubhouse, he snarled at Johnny Temple, "I'll get you."[15] Temple responded that there was no time like the present, and the two began to trade punches, fighting their way down to second base and out to right field.

Later, in an attempt to rationalize the brawl, Johnny Logan was to say that he was just tired of being pushed around in the game. Logan said that earlier Wally Post had hit him in the thigh. Then in the seventh inning Corky Valentine had rolled over him in a football-like block. Then there was Johnny Temple jumping into the pile at second base. "I'm fighting this 210-pounder and I see this 155-pounder wants to take me on. You think I'm crazy? I switch to the little man,"[16] said Logan.

The game continued into the ninth inning and the Braves' Del Crandell hit a home run to tie the score 2–2. The Braves eventually won the game 3–2 in the 12th when Jack Dittmer hit a home run off Reds reliever Frank Smith.

Johnny Temple had gone 1 for 5 in the game and was now hitting .301. He had yet to hit a home run in the season, but was the club leader in triples with 8 and stolen bases with 17. The only Redlegs with more hits than Temple were Ted Kluszewski, Gus Bell and Jim Greengrass.

Temple had only missed eight games because of injuries. As for the brawl with Johnny Logan, he sustained a couple of minor cuts around the eye. Bad blood had been created by the incident, and going forward the two players and their teams would continue to feud like a baseball version of the Hatfields and McCoys for several seasons.

According to Temple, after the 1954 brawl, "every time he [Logan] came into second base he would attempt to hurt me, and I in turn would come in and try to hurt him."[17] He added, "We must have had a dozen fights. We had two in one day. When either of us got on second base, the umpire automatically moved between us to try to stop a fight before it started."[18]

For several seasons following the brawl there was tension in the air when the Redlegs and Braves met. Any hard slide into second was suspect and scrutinized, while pitchers on both clubs threw dangerously close inside. Redlegs manager Birdie Tebbetts even started a campaign against alleged spitballs thrown by Lew Burdette.

Adding fuel to the bonfire that became the Braves vs. Redlegs rivalry was the private agenda of Braves first baseman Joe Adcock, who disliked the Cincinnati Redlegs because they had given up on him. But the bottom line in the rivalry was that the Redlegs just had a very difficult time beating the Braves. It even seemed that all left-hander Warren Spahn had to do to beat the Redlegs was throw his glove on the mound. Spahn would eventually hold a career record of 61–26 vs. Cincinnati.

The Redlegs were at a disadvantage when battling the Braves because notwithstanding Johnny Logan, they had such terrific street fighters as Eddie Mathews and Carl Sawatski. Mathews was a prodigious brawler, as exemplified by his punching out the Reds' Frank Robinson in a battle at third base in the 1960 season at Crosley Field. According to Hank Aaron, "Whenever a melee broke out, you could count on Mathews to take on everybody. Logan was a battler too, but his role was starting the fights, Mathews would finish them."[19]

Eventually Johnny Temple and Johnny Logan did make peace. One day Logan hit a double and while standing at second base, Temple came over and told Logan, "John, I know you're not afraid of me. You know I am not afraid of you. Before one of us gets hurt, why don't we call this thing off?" Logan replied, "That's just the way I feel about it."[20] So they stopped attempting to kill each other.

By Labor Day the Redlegs were battling for fourth place with the Cardinals and Phillies and a share of the World Series revenues. While they were still scoring runs with Ted Kluszewski leading the way, having hit 44 home runs and hitting .329, Gus Bell was hitting .297, also driving in runs, while Johnny Temple was hitting .304. But the pitching wasn't there for the Redlegs and they were allowing their opponents to score more runs than they produced.

Joe Nuxhall was the ace of the Cincinnati staff and would finish the 1954 season with a record of 12–5 and an ERA of 3.89; also Frank Smith was a reliable reliever. But once opposing teams got past "Hamilton Joe" Nuxhall, Birdie Tebbetts was dependent on a thin cast of starting pitchers to carry the water, including Art Fowler, Corky Valentine and Bud Podbielan, all of whom were just not capable of rising to the task.

On Labor Day the Redlegs could only attract 6,570 customers through the turnstiles at Crosley Field for a game with the St. Louis Cardinals and Stan Musial. While Johnny Temple had three hits in the holiday game, the Cardinals won 8–1 behind the pitching of Harvey Haddix.

Still, in late September it appeared that the Cincinnati Redlegs had a shot at finishing in the first division and getting a share of the World Series revenues. After defeating the Braves on September 20 and September 21, in the first two games of a three-game series in Milwaukee, the Redlegs were in fourth place with a record of 74–77 with three games left on the schedule. The fifth-place Philadelphia Phillies, with a record of 70–77, were four games behind the Redlegs with seven games remaining on their schedule, including two double-headers, one with the Pittsburgh Pirates and the other with the New York Giants, who had just clinched the pennant.

Then on September 22, in the third game of the series with the Braves, the Redlegs became involved in one of the most controversial umpiring decisions in major league baseball history since the "Merkle Boner" decision that occurred near the end of the 1908 season.

In the top of the ninth inning with the Braves leading 3–1, left-hander Warren Spahn replaced Charlie White on the mound. Spahn then proceeded to walk Gus Bell.

This brought Ted Kluszewski to the plate. Big Klu had hit forty-nine home runs so far during the season and was looking to become the seventh man in the history of the game to hit fifty in a season. In fact, if he had not gone 0 for 8 in his last eight at bats, he may have had an outside chance at winning a triple crown. However, the slump continued and Spahn got Klu to fly out to centerfield, and he was now 0 for 9 in his last nine trips to the plate.

Next up was Wally Post and Spahn walked him.

With Redlegs runners on first and second, manager Birdie Tebbetts sent Bob Borkowski, a right-handed batter, up to pinch-hit for left-handed-swinging Lloyd Merriman. Then circumstances in the game became controversial and even a bit bizarre.

Warren Spahn quickly got two strikes on Borkowski, who then swung at a wild pitch for strike three. But the pitch got away from Braves catcher Del Crandall. Immediately Borkowski started to run to first base. Meanwhile Gus Bell was heading from second to third base, and when Crandall recovered the ball, he threw it to third baseman Eddie Mathews, who cut the throw off and threw the ball across infield, where it hit Bob Borkowski in the back before rolling into right field. At that point Gus Bell crossed the plate with Wally Post close on his heels, scoring all the way from first base.

It appeared that the game was now tied at 3–3. Then umpire Hal Dixon ruled that both Redlegs runners were out on an unassisted double play. Dixon ruled that Borkowski had struck out, and by running to first base had illegally interfered with the play. Subsequently, the lead base runner Gus Bell was declared out, retiring the side, because the batter Bob Borkowski had illegally drawn the throw to first.

Birdie Tebbetts came charging out of the dugout to protest Dixon's call and a heated exchange continued for twenty minutes as the happy Braves fans departed County Stadium.

Meanwhile the umpiring crew of Dixon, Al Barlick, Bill Jackowski and Lee Ballanfant discussed the ruling for an additional eighteen minutes before affirming Dixon's decision based on Section 709, subsection E of the rule book which stated, "When any batter or base runner who has been retired interferes with any following play being made on a base runner, such base runner shall be declared out for the interference of his teammate or teammates."[21]

The fact was that Bob Borkowski was automatically out, missing the third strike with a runner on first base and resulting in two outs, but the case of Gus Bell's being out was questionable.

Birdie Tebbetts finally gave up, went into the Redlegs' clubhouse, picked up the telephone and called National League President Warren Giles. Tebbetts told Giles he was playing the game under protest and proceeded to plead his case on the obscure rule. In making his argument, Tebbetts told Giles that the game had ended by a runner's being called out because of something done by another runner on a different part of the field. According to Tebbetts, "Borkowski erred in running to first base when automatically out but he was no more in error than Mathews in throwing the ball in an attempt to retire Borkowski. Both should have known no play was required to retire Borkowski."[22]

Tebbetts stated that if the rule was valid, any time it was one out and a catcher had two strikes on a batter with men on base, all that the catcher had to do in order to make a double play was call for a pitchout, drop the ball, then when the batter made a move toward first base, he could throw the ball into the outfield and get a double play. Apparently the rule had been in the book for ages.

After listening to Tebbetts rant for several minutes, Giles told him that he had heard what he said and now needed to think about what he might do about it. For the moment Tebbetts was satisfied.

In the meantime, as Giles ruminated on the matter, on Thursday the Cincinnati Redlegs moved on to Chicago to wait playing the final two games on the 1954 schedule with the Cubs.

It didn't take Warren Giles long to reach a decision. Later the following day Giles ruled that the game of September 22 between the Redlegs and Braves would be played off from the point of the protest on September 24. He acknowledged that the outcome of the game could possibly affect the final standings and the World Series shares of five clubs. This circumstance created an extraordinary situation that had to be dealt with in an extraordinary manner.

Under the existing regulations of the time, the second-, third- and fourth-place teams in the National and American Leagues received a share of the World Series revenues from the first four games, of which the players of each of those teams decided how it was appropriated.

While the Redlegs were waiting in the Conrad Hilton Hotel in Chicago for Giles's decision, the Philadelphia Phillies had won both ends of a double-header over the Pittsburgh Pirates and were now tied with Cincinnati for fourth place. Also the St. Louis Cardinals still had a slim chance to finish in fourth place, the Milwaukee Braves were battling the Brooklyn Dodgers for second-place money.

In his official statement on his ruling Warren Giles stated in part, "It is understandable that the umpires under pressure of making the decisions on the field, applied the only rule which specifically deals with the action of a player who has been retired. Elements of interference and confusion both existed, but in the opinion of our office, not to the extent or manner sufficient to declare Bell out. It is therefore directed that the Reds return to Milwaukee and resume play at that point immediately after Crandall's throw to Mathews."[23]

Therefore the game scenario was that the Redlegs would be at bat in the top half of the ninth inning with two outs, Gus Bell on third base, Wally Post on second and Johnny Temple coming up to the plate. However, Braves manager Charlie "Jolly Cholly" Grimm did not have to use the same lineup. Therefore Grimm was free to replace Warren Spahn on the mound. Likewise Birdie Tebbetts could pinch-hit for Johnny Temple if he chose to.

Charlie Grimm had no problem with Giles's decision to restart the game. Grimm stated, "We are happy to go along with his decision. We know that he spent so much time in rendering the decision it is the right one as the play involved has never happened in baseball before."[24]

Returning to Milwaukee to play the ninth inning with the Braves on September 24 would not be a problem for the Redlegs as they had an open date. They would just have to rent a bus to make the 180-mile round-trip jaunt from Chicago to Milwaukee and then rent rooms in a hotel to change into their uniforms before going to County Stadium. To that end, Warren Giles waived the existing rule that prohibited players from dressing in their uniforms in hotels for a game.

Warren Giles also ruled that the Redlegs would be allowed fifteen minutes of batting practice and ten minutes of fielding practice prior to the game.

The Braves had a game scheduled that day with the St. Louis Cardinals scheduled to start 1:30 p.m. Therefore the actual starting time would depend on whether or not the disputed game was completed in a reasonable amount of time or went into extra innings. To complicate matters further, it was announced that the Braves vs. Cardinals game would begin with just enough time for the pitchers to warm up, no batting practice or fielding practice.

The Redlegs were in a tough battle for the first division with the Phillies and the game meant a lot. Johnny Temple suddenly found himself in a crucial role as he would be the first batter in the disputed game. So he had all night to lie awake and think about it.

As the disputed game resumed on Friday, September 24, there were about 16,000 fans in County Stadium, about 5,000 more than had been on hand for the original game. Charlie Grimm decided to replace Warren Spahn on the mound with Dave Jolly. Birdie Tebbetts sent Nino Escalera in to run for Wally Post, who had been on second base.

So with Gus Bell on third, Escalera on second, two outs in the top half of the ninth and the Braves leading 3–1, Johnny Temple came up to bat and hit the first pitch from Jolly into center field for a single, scoring Bell. But Bill Bruton fumbled the ball in center, allowing the speedy Escalera to also score, tying the game at 3–3. The rally was short-lived, however, as Andy Seminick struck out looking at the pitch. It was the third time in the game that Seminick had fanned.

Going into the bottom of the ninth, Birdie Tebbetts replaced the Redlegs' starting pitcher Corky Valentine with Frank Smith. The first batter for the Braves was Jim Pendleton, who singled off the glove of Roy McMillan. Johnny Logan followed with a sacrifice, sending Pendleton to second. Danny O'Connell was then intentionally walked. George Metkovich was the next batter and drove the third pitch from Smith over Bob Borkowski's head in left to bring Pendleton home with the winning run.

A few years later Johnny Temple was asked by a reporter if being the first batter in the protest game in Milwaukee was the toughest spot he had been in during his major league career. He said that the pressure was far less than what he had experienced when he went to bat the first time in the 1956 All-Star Game. "That's a game," declared Temple, "when everyone is in a tight spot because individual performance stands out much more than team performance."[25]

The Cincinnati Redlegs went back to Chicago, lost the final two games of the season to the Cubs, and finished in fifth place with a record of 74–80. The Philadelphia Phillies overcame the Redlegs' four-game lead in the final week of the season to finish with a record of 75–79, one game ahead of Cincinnati.

Nonetheless the 1954 season was one of personal triumph for Johnny Temple. He had demonstrated to all of his doubters that he belonged in the big leagues. Temple had become the first Cincinnati regular second baseman to hit over .300 since Tony Cuccinello hit .315 in 1931. In his first full season as a regular, Temple hit .307, second highest average on the team behind Ted Kluszewski, who hit .326. Overall during the 1954 season Johnny Temple reached base 219 times via 155 hits, 62 walks and being hit by the pitcher twice. He also reached base a few times on errors. In addition he stole 21 bases, including three thefts of home.

In the field during 1954, Johnny Temple had teamed up with shortstop

Roy McMillan to give the Cincinnati Redlegs one of the premier keystone combinations in major league baseball. Along with Ted Kluszewski, who led National League first basemen in fielding with an average of .996, Johnny Temple led all National League second basemen in putouts with 428, while Roy McMillan led all National League shortstops in putouts with 341, and the Cincinnati Redlegs led the National League in double plays with 194.

At the winter meetings in Houston following the 1954 season, Gabe Paul decided to pursue a trade that made absolutely no sense. Paul arranged a pending trade with the Brooklyn Dodgers that would send Redlegs outfielder Wally Post to the Dodgers for second baseman Jim Gilliam.

On the way home to Cincinnati, Paul stopped in Dallas to see the Notre Dame vs. SMU football game. In the stadium he bought a newspaper, turned to the sports pages and discovered that Dodgers general manager Buzzie Bavasi had decided to put the kibosh on the trade.

In the 1955 season Wally Post would hit 40 home runs for the Redlegs. If he had gone to Brooklyn that total may have increased significantly.

Jim Gilliam was a good ballplayer, a switch hitter who could play second base, third base and the outfield, and ultimately would play 14 years for the Brooklyn/Los Angeles Dodgers. Most baseball insiders saw Gilliam as the successor to the aging Jackie Robinson. But the 1955 season would be one the least productive seasons in his career, as he hit only .249 with 7 home runs while playing 99 games at second base and 46 in the outfield.

Of course, if the Post for Gilliam trade had been completed, it is certain that Johnny Temple would have been wearing another major league uniform than that of the Cincinnati Redlegs before the 1955 campaign began and his career would have either been shortened or enhanced depending on where he wound up playing.

Four

An All-Star Performer

The 1955 National League season from opening day to the last day belonged to the Brooklyn Dodgers. They began the season by winning ten games in a row and proceeded to win twenty-two out of the first twenty-four games. By July 4, the Dodgers were 12½ games in front of the pack. They won the National League pennant with a record of 98–55, finishing 13½ games ahead of the second-place Milwaukee Braves. Along the way the Dodgers hit a major league best 201 home runs.

Cincinnati pitcher Art Fowler was to later remark that no one could beat the Dodgers until they were so far in front that it didn't matter anymore.

While the Cincinnati Redlegs finished in fifth place with a record of 75–79, 23½ games behind the Dodgers, they were just a couple of pitchers away from becoming a serious contender. At the plate the Redlegs were starting to show some remarkable power as they hit 181 home runs in 1955, third best in the National League, just one home run behind Milwaukee. The Redlegs' power surge was led by Ted Kluszewski with 47 home runs; Wally Post hit 40, Gus Bell 27 and Smoky Burgess 20.

During the 1954 season, manager Birdie Tebbetts had batted Johnny Temple in the sixth spot, reasoning that he would bring speed to the bottom half of the order. For the 1955 season Tebbetts moved Temple up from the sixth spot to leadoff hitter. Cincinnati had not had a capable leadoff hitter since the franchise's back-to-back pennant-winning years of 1939 and 1940 when Billy Werber was at the top of the order.

Tebbetts's moving Temple into the leadoff spot was a huge vote of confidence in him. But Temple got off to a slow start and by the end of April he was hitting just .143. Immediately a whispering campaign began around the league that, although Temple had hit .308 in 1954, it had been a fluke and now most teams had become wise to him—that with no power to drive outfielders back, he was an easy out. The fact was that opposing outfielders were playing Temple shallow.

Nonetheless, during the early weeks of the 1955 season, it just wasn't Johnny Temple who was in a slump; it was the entire Redlegs team. By the end of April, Ted Kluszewski had hit only four home runs and the Redlegs were holding down seventh place with a record of 4–12.

It was apparent that general manager Gabe Paul had to act. On April 30 the Redlegs made a six-player swap with the Phillies, sending Andy Seminick, Glen Gorbus and Jim Greengrass to Philadelphia in exchange for Smoky Burgess, Steve Ridzik and Stan Palys.

Then, as the month of May unfolded, suddenly Johnny Temple found his stroke and began driving the ball in holes, and the Redlegs began to make a moderate rise in the standings. In a fifteen-game span Temple got 21 hits in 57 at bats, a .368 clip. By mid–May he had raised his batting average to .262.

On May 26 the Redlegs moved into fourth place with a record of 17–19. Then Cincinnati lost both ends of a Memorial Day double-header to Milwaukee, fell back into sixth place, and would continue to fight hard to get out of the second division the rest of the season.

At the season's end Johnny Temple finished with a batting average of .281, highest in the league for a second baseman, with more than 300 at bats. He also had 50 RBIs, a remarkable number considering the fact that he did not hit a home run in the 1955 campaign.

In the field Johnny Temple and Roy McMillan continued their remarkable play as they led all second basemen and shortstops in double plays in the National League for the 1955 season (Temple 119 and McMillan 111). There was not a better double play combination in the major leagues.

Although he did an outstanding job at second base, Johnny Temple was highly cognizant of the fact that no matter how feisty he was or how much he hustled or played with a square jaw, he was no Roy McMillan when it came to fielding the ball. It was simply impossible to match the magic that McMillan displayed at shortstop time after time going deep into the hole, fielding a ground ball backhanded, then sharply turning and firing a perfect peg to Ted Kluszewski at first base, usually beating the runner by more than a foot. The fact was that no other shortstop in the National League, not Pee Wee Reese, Dick Groat, Johnny Logan or Ernie Banks, did it better than Roy McMillan when it came to covering ground at shortstop.

Among the memorable highlights of the 1955 season for Johnny Temple was the on-base streak he had between June 28 and July 2, when he

Four. An All-Star Performer

Reds double play combination Johnny Temple (2B) (left) and Roy McMillan (SS) circa 1957 (Rhodes/Klumpe Reds Hall of Fame Collection).

got on base safely twelve straight times before lining out to Danny O'Connell of the Braves for a double play in the fifth inning.

Temple's on-base streak began on the night of June 28 in St. Louis as the Redlegs defeated the Cardinals 9–1. After grounding out his first time up, Temple proceeded to drive in a run with a single. The next time up he drove in three runs with a triple, and then in the fifth inning he squeeze bunted Roy McMillan home from third for his fifth RBI of the game. Temple also had a stolen base in the game.

Another season highlight for Johnny Temple occurred on July 21. The Redlegs swept a double-header from the Pittsburgh Pirates 6–5 and 7–4, and Temple had seven hits in the twin bill.

The 1955 season was the third consecutive season that Big Ted Kluszewski hit forty or more (47) home runs. While he was productive, knocking in runs almost every game, and everyone loved Big Klu—his teammates, the fans, the press—he just wasn't much of a leader; he never said much, he just played.

Pitcher Art Fowler said that he liked to hang around Kluszewski because "my salary was just $6,000 and $9,000 in my first two years and he was making $40,000 or $50,000, so I knew he'd buy me two or three beers. That would make my day."[1] The fact was that by 1955 Ted Kluszewski had become the highest-paid player in the Cincinnati Redlegs/Reds franchise history.

Johnny Temple, on the other hand, was attempting to become the Redlegs' team leader. He played hard, wasn't averse to getting into fights, wanted to win at all cost, and expressed himself to that end. Unfortunately it mattered little how hard Temple played and how many home runs Big Klu and Wally Post hit, or how many double plays Roy McMillan and Johnny Temple made—without better pitching, the Cincinnati Redlegs were destined to be a perpetual second-division club.

The subject of pitching came up one evening when general manager Gabe Paul and Birdie Tebbetts were invited by Redlegs owner Powell Crosley, Jr., to dine with him at his mansion in College Hill. At one point during the dinner, Crosley turned towards Tebbetts and said, "Birdie, I want you to fire the pitching coach." Tebbetts was stunned! He asked Crosley why and he replied, "Because our pitching is terrible." Tebbetts thought over his reply carefully, then said, "That's because our pitching is terrible. And as long as I'm manager of the Cincinnati Reds you can fire me any time you want to, but you cannot fire my pitching coach."[2]

The Redlegs' pitching coach at that time was Tom Ferrick, and Birdie Tebbetts truly believed that he was the best in the business and was determined to stand behind him. As Crosley kept pressing the issue, Tebbetts walked out of the dinner. Crosley had previously stated that hiring Tebbetts as manager was the smartest move he had made in baseball. Now, confused by Tebbetts's abrupt departure, Crosley dropped the subject and told Gabe Paul to let Birdie know that he never intended to make him mad.

Over the winter of 1955–1956, Gabe Paul made an attempt to address the Redlegs' pitching deficit by making a couple of trades. He sent pint-sized southpaw Jackie Collum to the St. Louis Cardinals in exchange for right-hander Brooks Lawrence. In 1954, his rookie year, Lawrence had won fifteen games for the Cardinals. However, he became expendable when he struggled on the mound in the 1955 season, unable to follow with another brilliant performance.

In another deal, Gabe Paul obtained right-handed starter/reliever Hal Jeffcoat from the Chicago Cubs in exchange for backup catcher Hobie Landrith. Jeffcoat had begun his professional career as an outfielder, but after six years with the Cubs switched to mound duty in 1954.

Every writer who has ever chronicled the National League's 1956 campaign has stated that, at the beginning of the season, every informed person in baseball predicted a two-team dogfight for the pennant between the Brooklyn Dodgers and Milwaukee Braves. No one saw the Cincinnati Redlegs as even remotely being a part of the equation in deciding the 1956 pennant—but as things turned out, they were.

Since the tenure of Rogers Hornsby as manager, the Cincinnati Redlegs had been assembling an offensive time bomb, a team filled with a lineup of power hitters: Ted Kluszewski, Gus Bell, Wally Post, Ed Bailey, Smoky Burgess—then, going into the 1956 season, rookie sensation and future Hall of Famer Frank Robinson joined the club. It was only a matter of time before that offensive time bomb would explode. In 1956 it did.

Between August 4 and August 24, 1956, the Cincinnati Redlegs would hit a home run in 21 consecutive games. Overall in the 1956 season the Redlegs topped the National League by scoring 775 runs, while socking a record-tying 221 home runs, and hammering out a league-leading slugging average of .441.

On the mound in 1956, Brooks Lawrence (19–10) and Hal Jeffcoat (8–2) would have a combined record of 27–12 and play a vital role in keeping the Redlegs in contention, while the National League's top relief pitcher Hershell Freeman would finish with a record of 14–5, along with 18 saves and an ERA of 3.40. Also three other Redlegs hurlers would have double-digit win seasons: Joe Nuxhall 13–11, Art Fowler 11–11 and Johnny Klippstein 12–11.

As a result of the Redlegs' power surge and improved pitching, they would be in the 1956 pennant race with the Dodgers and Braves until the final weekend of the 1956 season, winning 91 games—the most wins by a Cincinnati ball club since 1940.

Beginning with infielder Chuck Harmon in 1954, Afro-American players had been added to the Cincinnati roster. In 1955 pitcher Joe Black had come to the Redlegs in a trade with the Brooklyn Dodgers and outfielder Bob Thurman in a trade with the Chicago Cubs. From that point going forward there was a concentrated effort by Gabe Paul and the Redlegs' front office to completely ignore race when adding players to the

Cincinnati roster and attempt to find the best ones available. Frank Robinson had been signed by the Redlegs right out of McClymonds High School in Oakland and would join the team in 1956. If he hadn't become ill during the spring of 1955 he most probably would have joined the team as a 19-year-old rookie.

Another Afro-American player that the Cincinnati Redlegs had signed from Oakland was Curt Flood, who played most of his high school baseball at McClymonds with Frank Robinson. Flood was signed by scout Bobby Mattick for $4,000 and told to report to spring training in Tampa, Florida, where he would rejoin Robinson. At the end of spring training Flood was sent to the Redlegs' minor league facility in Douglas, Georgia. The Redlegs' front office considered Curt Flood a highly prized prospect with terrific defensive skills, and before the 1956 season had been concluded, he had advanced to the Class B ball with High Point-Thomasville in the Carolina League. Flood didn't disappoint the Redlegs brass: he led the Carolina League with a .340 batting average, scored 128 runs and hit 29 home runs in 1956.

Curt Flood's performance at the Carolina League would be rewarded with a late season call-up with the Redlegs. He joined the team in New York and eventually played in five games, primarily as a pinch-runner. But he did get his first major league at bat going 0 for 1.

Chick Harmon would be traded to the St. Louis Cardinals early in the 1956 season. Nonetheless with Frank Robinson, Brooks Lawrence, Joe Black, Bob Thurman and George Crowe (obtained from Milwaukee soon after the season began), all players of color on the roster, the 1956 Cincinnati Redlegs would be the franchise's first fully racially integrated team, and every one of the Afro-American players on the team would play a significant role in the Redlegs' nearly winning the pennant that year.

While the playing field was integrated and the black and white players on the Redlegs got along, off the field, they were reluctant to do things together. There was fraternization on the train, but only rarely did the black and white players on the Redlegs go out together for dinner.

It had nothing do with the cultural makeup of the Redlegs roster that included a lot of Southern-born players (Johnny Temple, North Carolina; Smoky Burgess, North Carolina; Ed Bailey, Tennessee; Hershell Freeman, Alabama; Alex Grammas, Alabama; Art Fowler, South Carolina; Hal Jeffcoat, South Carolina; Roy McMillan, Texas; and Johnny Klippstein, Washington, D.C.). The socialization process was pretty much the same between black and white players on all major league teams in the 1950s regardless of what region of the country they had come from—away from the ball park they kept their distance from one another.

Four. An All-Star Performer

The racial divide on major league teams in the 1950s is best described by Howard Bryant in his book *The Last Hero: A Life of Henry Aaron*. Bryant states, "There was no clear rules, no road maps to follow in 1957 about asking a black player to join his teammates for a drink, or inviting him over to the house for an off-day barbecue. An invisible line cut through American society—and a major league clubhouse was no different—one that nobody was quite sure how to cross."

In the 1950s, Cincinnati was the smallest city in the major leagues (population 525,000). Ten minor league cities in the International and Pacific Coast Leagues and the American Association had greater populations. Regardless of the fact that annual attendance at games had shrunk, the Cincinnati Reds had one of the most loyal fan bases in all of organized ball, and due to the city's geographical location, the team drew heavily from surrounding states such as Indiana, Kentucky and West Virginia.

Those Cincinnati fans were also keenly aware of their team's heritage and unique place in major league history. The 1869 Cincinnati Red Stockings were the first professional (paid) team in baseball. Opening day for more than half a century had a Mardi Gras atmosphere about it with a parade and city-wide celebrations. The city also embraced the Reds' players as being intimately connected to the city. To Cincinnati fans, if you played for the Reds you were family. Most Cincinnatians were far more capable of naming the nine players who made up the Cincinnati Reds' opening day lineup than they were of naming the nine members of Cincinnati City Council. The ball club reciprocated with its fans and annually honored them with a huge Fan Appreciation Night event, Ladies Days and Knothole Day Games and other promotions.

The 1956 Cincinnati Redlegs were a team with a lot of players who were fun to be around—Rocky Bridges, Ray Jablonski, Joe Nuxhall, Art Fowler, Gus Bell, Roy McMillan and others. The Redlegs were also a team that was family oriented.

According to pitcher Johnny Klippstein, who joined the Redlegs in the 1955 season via a trade with the Chicago Cubs, "Cincinnati was a good place for a ball player with a family. Almost everybody had small children and a mortgage. The wives were friendly with one and another and there were a lot of family-oriented picnics and parties."[3]

Center fielder Gus Bell had the largest family with six children. One of Bell's children, oldest son Buddy, would grow up to become an All-Star third baseman with the Cleveland Indians. Near the end of his career Buddy Bell would play for the Reds from 1985 to 1988.

For the 1956 season, Johnny Temple's wife Becky, along with their five-year-old son Mike, relocated from Columbia, South Carolina, to Cincinnati. The Temples made sure that Mike got to take advantage of the numerous recreational opportunities in the city, like the Cincinnati Zoo and the huge Coney Island amusement park. But as far as baseball went, Mike Temple was a little young to connect with the game and preferred watching Pinky Lee on TV to watching his father play at Crosley Field.

While on the road, Johnny Temple hung out with his roommate Ted Kluszewski. During home stands, Temple and his family often joined Wally Post and his family for a picnic or other outings. While at home in Cincinnati, Kluszewski hung out with Roy McMillan and his family for cookouts.

While the Temples rented an apartment during the season in the north Cincinnati neighborhood of College Hill where owner Powell Crosley lived, some players lived in Cincinnati or the surrounding area year round. Ted Kluszewski and his wife Eleanor owned a house in the Cincinnati neighborhood of Kennedy Heights, while Gus Bell and family lived in suburban Monfort Heights. Roy McMillan rented former Reds teammate and Cincinnati native Herm Wehmeier's home in the west-side neighborhood of Westwood.

Unfortunately, the Cincinnati of the 1950s was a city that had redlined real estate and segregated housing. Consequently, the Afro-American players on the team, Frank Robinson, George Crowe, et al., resided in predominantly black neighborhoods such as Avondale.

During the season a lot of the white Redlegs players with families resided in the northeast side of the city in a new apartment complex called Swifton Village.

Relief pitcher Hershell Freeman was one of the Redlegs legally domiciled in Swifton Village. Freeman stated that during home stands a bunch of the players who lived in the apartment complex would commute together for night games at Crosley Field. They might say, "Okay, Hersh, you're driving tonight, so we can have a few. You knew guys like Nuxhall and Fowler were going to bend their elbows, but they'd never let it control their baseball lives."[4] Some guys like Roy McMillan would have a couple and go home. Ray Jablonski, one of the best beer drinkers on the team, stayed until nearly closing time.

A couple of the Redlegs, Joe Black and Smoky Burgess, completely abstained from alcohol and didn't smoke either. Burgess preferred milkshakes. Gabe Paul, knowing that Burgess was a teetotaler, strategically had him room with Art Fowler on the road, hoping that Smoky might be a positive influence on the Redlegs' hurler, who had a penchant for hoisting more than a few brews. Smoky attempted to lecture Fowler, but it didn't help; he just preferred the sudsy camaraderie of Nuxhall, Post and Bell.

Other than being a seasonal residence for Cincinnati Redlegs ballplayers during the 1950s, Swifton Village is deserving of another historical footnote.

The apartment complex had been built in 1953 by New York developer Jonathan Wood for $10 million. By 1962 the complex was plagued with high vacancy rates and was losing considerable money. The New York State Employees Retirement System had invested a one-fifth share of the property.

At that time New York developer Fred Trump came to the rescue of the failing property by plunking down $5.7 million in a sheriff's sale, as the only bidder, to purchase Swifton Village lock, stock and barrel.

When Fred Trump bought Swifton Village, it had a 50 percent vacancy rate in its 800 units. Fred's son Donald Trump was attending business school. So in order to get his son's feet wet in the real estate market, Fred sent Donald out to Cincinnati to manage the struggling property.

Young Donald Trump would fly out to Cincinnati a couple of days a week, inspect the property and do some menial work. The Trumps propped up the failing complex with a cash infusion of $500,000 and in 1972 they sold it for $6.75 million. In his 1987 memoir *The Art of the Deal*, Donald Trump boasted that Swifton Village was his first multimilliondollar deal.

Nonetheless there has been some historical disagreement as to the level of influence "The Donald" had in making Swifton Village a profitable venture. Author Gwenda Blair alleges in her book *The Trumps: Three Generations That Built an Empire* that Donald Trump's account "was loaded with 'energetic exaggerations'—it was his father, not Donald, who was the force behind Swifton Village."[5]

The Cincinnati Redlegs actually got off to slow start in the 1956 campaign, losing five of their first six games. The only Redlegs getting hits were the keystone combination of Johnny Temple, who was hitting .300, and Roy McMillan, who was hitting .320. With the Redlegs in last place, manager Birdie Tebbetts benched Smoky Burgess, Frank Robinson and Ted Kluszewski for not hitting. The tactic worked, and between April 27 and May 2 the Redlegs won six in a row, and by May 6 had won ten out of the last eleven games and were in first place.

The Redlegs' power-packed batting order was changing the way Temple had to play. On 2 and 1, and 3 and 1 counts, he was getting the take sign from first base coach Jimmy Dykes. Temple was the only Redlegs regular who hadn't hit a home run since 1953. So with Smoky Burgess or Ed Bailey, Ted Kluszewski, Wally Post, Gus Bell, Frank Robinson and Ray Jablonski coming up behind Temple, Birdie Tebbetts wanted him on base. With Temple on base, one of those guys was likely to hit the ball out of the park, giving the Redlegs two runs instead of one. The opposing pitchers knew that, too, and now began bearing down on Temple.

Birdie Tebbetts was ordering Temple to take the first pitch. So Temple let a lot of balls that came in right down Broadway go unchallenged, pitches that he might have driven into the gap. Temple was a bit frustrated, knowing that more hits meant a higher salary. But he attempted to cope with the circumstances, knowing he fit Tebbetts's model for a leadoff hitter; he had speed, good eyesight and patience. "In a leadoff hitter, bases on balls reflects a man's value more than base hits," said Tebbetts. We want a man to get on base, so our batting order can start bringing runs home."[6]

The Redlegs skipper knew he was going to have to be a creative manager in order to win the pennant as an imbalance existed in the Redlegs' pitching as opposed to their hitting. At the beginning of the season Birdie Tebbetts called a pitchers' meeting and told his staff that the media had given them a bum rap; he knew that the Redlegs staff was a good one and that his pitchers would do anything to win for him.

Unknown to the Redlegs' pitchers, Tebbetts was attempting to use reverse psychology and had previously called a meeting with the Redlegs hitters and told them that they knew what kind of a pitching staff the team had, therefore they were going to have to score a lot of runs to win.

There was one day in the 1956 season when the Redlegs' pitching staff could have used some runs as they put forth a truly gallant effort against the powerful Milwaukee Braves and received no support from the hitters.

On Saturday, May 26, 1956, the Redlegs were in Milwaukee to play a day game against the Braves. With the third-place Redlegs nipping at the heels of the second-place Braves, 22,936 fans showed up at County Stadium to see Johnny Klippstein square off on the mound against Ray Crone. Klippstein began by shutting down the Braves in order in the first inning. Then in the bottom of the second, he hit Hank Aaron with a pitch and proceeded to walk Bobby Thomson and Bill Bruton to load the bases. Frank Torre followed with a sacrifice fly to center to score Aaron and give the Braves a 1–0 lead. But the Braves still didn't have a hit.

Klippstein continued to hold the Braves hitless through the seventh inning. Meanwhile Crone continued to dominate the Redlegs and they couldn't score a run. In the eighth inning Hershell Freeman took over from Klippstein and continued to hold the Braves hitless in the game. But the Braves still led the Redlegs 1–0.

Finally in the top of the ninth inning Ted Kluszewski singled and Birdie Tebbetts sent Jim Dyck in to run for him. Wally Post followed with a double, scoring Dyck to tie the score 1–1.

In the bottom of the ninth inning Joe Black relieved Freeman and held the Braves hitless. So three Redlegs pitchers, Johnny Klippstein, Hershell Freeman and Joe Black, had no-hit the Braves through nine innings.

Then in the bottom of the tenth inning, with two outs, the Braves got their first hit when Jack Dittmar doubled.

The game entered the eleventh inning with the score still knotted at 1–1, and the Redlegs failed to score in the top half of the inning. In the bottom half of the eleventh, Hank Aaron led off against Joe Black with a triple. Two batters later, Frank Torre singled to drive Aaron home with the winning run.

The Redlegs' catcher in the nine-inning no-hitter had been Smoky Burgess. It would be ironic that three years later on yet another May 26, (1959), Burgess, then playing for the Pittsburgh Pirates, would catch a twelve-inning perfect game thrown by Harvey Haddix, once again vs. the Braves at Milwaukee. The Braves' victory in 1959 made Smoky Burgess the only catcher in major league history to catch two no-hit games and lose both contests.

In that epic game Birdie Tebbetts used nineteen players but could only produce one run. The Redlegs' keystone combination of Johnny Temple and Roy McMillan entered the game hitting .284 and .311 respectively, but failed to get a hit off Ray Crone, who went the distance. The loss left the Cincinnati Redlegs in third place, one game behind the league-leading St. Louis Cardinals and a half game behind the second-place Milwaukee Braves.

At the All-Star Game break on July 10, 1956, the National League standings found the Cincinnati Redlegs hitting home runs at record pace and in first place, one and a half games ahead of the second-place Milwaukee Braves and two games ahead of the surging Brooklyn Dodgers. Suddenly the stage had been set for a dramatic second half of the season, with those three teams entering into hand-to-hand combat for the pennant.

Leading up to the 1956 All-Star game, a ballot box–stuffing campaign by the Cincinnati fans urged on by local newspapers and radio stations, including Redlegs radio broadcaster Waite Hoyt, resulted with a record five Cincinnati players being voted to the starting lineup: Ed Bailey (catcher), Frank Robinson (left field), Roy McMillan (shortstop), Gus Bell (center field) and Johnny Temple (second base). Then National League manager Walter Alston added Cincinnati first baseman Ted Kluszewski and pitchers Joe Nuxhall and Brooks Lawrence, making a total of eight Cincinnati Redlegs on the National League All-Star team.

In the inaugural All-Star game in 1933 through the 1934 game, players were chosen by the managers and fans. Then from 1935 to 1946, managers selected the entire team for each league. The fans became part of the selection process again from 1947 to 1957, voting for the starting lineups for each league other than the pitcher. During that period the managers picked the pitchers and the reserves. The selection of five Cincinnati players on the National League All-Star team in 1956 by the fans was highly controversial and would eventually lead to the fans' only selecting starters for one more game in 1957 before a change was implemented in the selection process.

The following season major league baseball changed the procedure after another Cincinnati ballot box–stuffing episode, and between 1958 and 1969, all player selections were made by the managers, players and coaches. Finally in 1970 the vote for the starting lineups was returned to the fans, and there it remains today. Nonetheless, fans will be fans, and ballot box stuffing still occasionally takes place, as demonstrated most recently by the overzealous Kansas City Royals fans in the 2015 All-Star balloting.

The stuffed All-Star ballot box in favor of the Redlegs for the 1956 game generated some harsh criticism from various influential individuals in the game, such as American League president William Harridge, Boston Red Sox outfielder Ted Williams, and New York Giants vice-president Chub Feeney. All began advocating that the All-Star voting process be turned over to the managers or the players.

On the other hand, Cincinnati manager Birdie Tebbetts was quick to respond and defend his players' selections by the fans, stating, "The only reason Cincinnati has so many players on the All-Star team is because they happen to be the best players in the league."[7]

One baseball executive who remained firm on letting the fans vote was National League president Warren Giles. "I would rather have 100,000 fans voting for a player than one vote by a manager," said Giles. "The fan angle, on which the game was founded in 1933 in Chicago by Arch Ward, must be adhered to."[8]

Four. An All-Star Performer

The fans' selections of players for the All-Star Game have always been an acknowledgment of their individual superior performance during the first half of the season, but the presence of five Cincinnati players on the starting National League team was controversial and unprecedented.

There was no question that catcher Ed Bailey, the league's leading hitter at the time with an average of .335, and rookie sensation left fielder Frank Robinson, who was hitting .312 with 18 home runs, deserved to be selected by the fans.

On the other hand, no one complained that Dale Long of the Pittsburgh Pirates had been selected as the starting first baseman over Ted Kluszewski. The facts were that without Kluszewski's contributions the Cincinnati Redlegs would not have been in first place at the All-Star Game break.

Dale Long, the Pittsburgh Pirates' first baseman, was chosen by the fans over Kluszewski because he had got off to a fast start in the 1956 season. By June 7, Long was hitting a hefty .382. Between May 19 and May 28, Long had set a major league record by hitting home runs in eight consecutive games. This feat would remain a major league record until tied by the New York Yankees' first baseman Don Mattingly in 1987 and later by Ken Griffey, Jr., playing for the Seattle Mariners in 1993.

In the four weeks preceding the 1956 All-Star Game, Dale Long had been in a slump and lost over 80 points in his batting average. At the All-Star Game break, while Dale Long was leading Ted Kluszewski in batting average .303 to .282, Kluszewski was leading Long in both home runs (22 to 17) and RBIs (55 to 50). Also in the week preceding the All-Star Game, Ted Kluszewski had hit eight home runs in eight games, but they were not in consecutive games as Long had done.

As for the fans' selection of Johnny Temple, he had certainly put forth an All-Star performance in the first half of the 1956 season. On July 10, Temple was hitting .281, third best for a second baseman in the National League behind his idol Red Schoendienst (.308) and Bill Mazeroski (.286). Furthermore, if fielding counts as much as hitting in winning games, then without a doubt Cincinnati's magnificent double play combination of Roy McMillan and Johnny Temple belonged on the 1956 All-Star team on that merit alone.

The 23rd All-Star Game was played on July 10, 1956, at Washington's Griffith Stadium. The game was won by the National League 7–3. The Nationals took a 1–0 lead in the third inning when the Redlegs' Johnny Temple singled home teammate Roy McMillan. In the fourth inning the Giants' Willie Mays pinch-hit for the Redlegs' Gus Bell and belted a home run off the Yankees' Whitey Ford with Ken Boyer on base to give the Nationals a 3–0 lead. For Mays it was his seventh straight hit off Ford. The Nationals scored again in the top of the fifth when Ken Boyer drove in Johnny Temple to increase the lead to 4–0.

The Redlegs' Ted Kluszewski entered the game in the sixth inning as pinch-hitter for Dale Long. Klu doubled and scored on a wild pitch to give the National League a 5–0 lead.

The American League fought back and in the bottom of the sixth they scored three runs, two of them on back-to-back home runs by the Red Sox' Ted Williams with Nellie Fox on base and a solo shot by the Yankees' Mickey Mantle to make the score 5–3 Nationals.

In the seventh inning, after Stan Musial homered to give the Nationals a 6–3 lead, Ted Kluszewski doubled home Willie Mays to increase the lead to 7–3, which was the final score.

It had been at the discretion of National League manager Walter Alston to make position player changes in the lineup after the third inning, but Alston elected to go all the way with McMillan and Temple. It was a wise decision; in the field McMillan and Temple gobbled up every ball that came their way, including making one double play. In fact all the Redlegs in the game played errorless ball.

At bat, collectively the controversial Cincinnati Redlegs delegation on the 1956 All-Star squad hit for an outstanding average of .400. Ted Kluszewski, who entered the game in the sixth inning, had two hits, while starters Johnny Temple was 2 for 4 and Roy McMillan was 2 for 4. Also Johnny Temple drove in a run and had the only stolen base in the game. Frank Robinson,

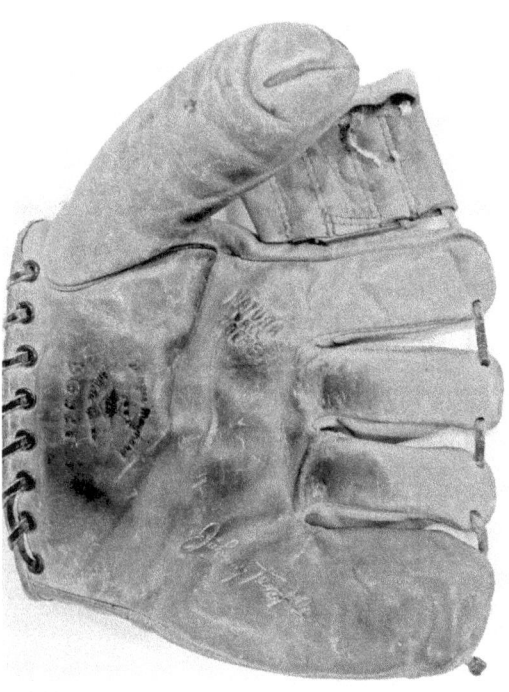

Johnny Temple's glove, circa 1956 (courtesy Joe Thullen, photograph by John Ruschulte).

Gus Bell and Ed Bailey collectively went 0 for 5. If any of these players had hit safely the Redlegs collective average would have approached .500. The two Redlegs hurlers on the squad, Brooks Lawrence and Joe Nuxhall, sat in the bullpen and did not pitch.

The strong competitive nature of Johnny Temple on the diamond was never more evident than that displayed in a game with the Pittsburgh Pirates at Forbes Field on July 30, 1956. The Redlegs were about to complete a series sweep of the Pirates with a 4–2 win. Then in the fifth inning, the Pirates, trailing 4–0, suddenly routed Redlegs pitcher Tom Acker with a triple by Frank Thomas, a walk and two singles off the glove of Johnny Temple to score two runs. Hershel Freeman, the Cincinnati relief ace, came in to put an end to the Pirates' rally.

As the inning ended, Temple, visibly upset over the two grounders that got away from him, went storming towards the Redlegs' third base side dugout and flung his glove into the stands. In the bottom of sixth, Temple took the field using pitcher Hal Jeffcoat's glove until another one could be obtained from his locker in the distant Redlegs clubhouse.

Now all shortstops and second basemen know that they have to protect themselves once in a while by low-bridging a runner. If they don't make a runner slide, then at some point they are going to find themselves knocked into the outfield. "It's up to the base runner to avoid getting hit by throws," said Temple. "The one sure way to do it is make him slide."[9]

The day before, Pirates outfielder Roberto Clemente had upended Temple by coming into second base high, crashing into him in a successful attempt to break up an inning-ending double play. When Clemente got up and started off the field it seemed like he was laughing about it. That upset Temple.

A few innings after the Pirates' rally, Clemente again came charging into second base, attempting to break up another double play when a ground ball was hit toward Ray Jablonski at third. The third baseman's throw was momentarily delayed, which caused Temple to not have enough time to pivot, and he was again tossed into the air by Clemente coming in high. But Temple had enough time to get off a hard underhand intentional throw that banged off Clemente's batting helmet and ricocheted into right field. The throw had actually been intended for Clemente's jaw. According to Temple, Clemente's helmet rang like a gong.

While Temple admitted his errant throw was bad judgment, because it permitted Clemente to take third, the message had been received, and going forward Roberto Clemente never again came into second high against Johnny Temple.

For a while following the All-Star Game it looked like the Milwaukee Braves might pull away from the Redlegs and Dodgers. After Charlie Grimm was replaced by Fred Haney as manager, the Braves went on a tear and won eleven games in a row. But the Redlegs and Dodgers just wouldn't go away. In fact by August 10 the Redlegs had pulled to within one half game of the first-place Braves.

Then bad things started to happen to Cincinnati. By July 17 Brooks Lawrence had won thirteen straight games without a defeat; then suddenly he seemed tired and overworked. By August 31 Lawrence's record had fallen to 17–7.

At the time Big Ted Kluszewski was well on his way to having his fourth consecutive season with 40 or more home runs. Then he reinjured his back, which had been bothering him since spring training, forcing Birdie Tebbetts to insert George Crowe at first base.

Coming down the stretch it all depended on pitching, and the Brooklyn Dodgers got the most. The Dodgers won the 1956 National League pennant on the final weekend of the season by sweeping a three-game series with the Pittsburgh Pirates behind the pitching of Sal Maglie, Clem Labine and eventual National League Cy Young and MVP winner Don Newcombe, while the Milwaukee Braves lost 2 out of 3 games to the St. Louis Cardinals.

The Cincinnati Redlegs, after losing a single game to Milwaukee 7–1 on September 25, had a three-day break before finishing with a two-game series at Chicago. At that time the Redlegs were on the verge of elimination, and on Friday, September 28, the *New York Times* reported that Birdie Tebbetts was considering playing a power lineup in Chicago for the final two games on the schedule to break the National League season record for home runs.

The *Times* stated that Tebbetts would remove Johnny Temple from the lineup and replace him at second base with Ray Jablonski, insert Frank Robinson at third, and leave Roy McMillian at shortstop. George Crowe was already playing first base, replacing the ailing Ted Kluzsewski, who had further reinjured his back running out a double play ball on a soggy field at Brooklyn on September 17. The outfield would consist of catcher Ed Bailey, Gus Bell and Wally Post. Bob Thurman, an outfielder/pinch hitter, would be on the mound and Smoky Burgess would catch.

Tebbetts never used any such lineup, and in fact on September 29 at Wrigley Field with the Redlegs in third place, 2½ games back and eliminated, they beat the Chicago Cubs 9–6 as the day-to-day regulars started the game and Joe Nuxhall pitched. Regardless it did seem as if Tebbetts was going for the record. He used twenty-one players with six pinch hitters, including Big Klu, in an attempt to play long ball. In the eighth inning pinch hitter Smoky Burgess came through, hitting a home run that tied the National League record of 221 for most team home runs in a season.

The following afternoon the Redlegs' regulars were in the lineup again as they beat the Cubs 4–2 in the season's finale, but they failed to hit the record-breaking home run.

In the end, the Cincinnati Redlegs, with overwhelming power at the plate and mediocre pitching, put up a good fight, finishing two games behind the pennant-winning Brooklyn Dodgers and one game behind the second-place Milwaukee Braves.

The 1956 National League pennant race between the Brooklyn Dodgers, Milwaukee Braves and Cincinnati Redlegs had been one of the most exciting seasons in recent National League history. Along the way, first place was occupied for 126 days by the Braves, 17 days by the Dodgers and 16 days by the Redlegs. The pennant race was not settled until the final weekend of the season.

In all three cities the fans rooted feverish for their team. All during the summer of 1956 the Redlegs were the main topic of conversation in Cincinnati, and the fans set an attendance record with 1,124,928 attending games at Crosley Field.

The Braves fans were even more zealous in their support of the Braves with 2,046,331 attending games at County Stadium. According to Hank Aaron, "The whole state [Wisconsin] became excited about the Braves. There were Braves hairdos and Braves cocktails and Braves banners stretched across the street."[10]

In Brooklyn 1,215,562 fans anticipating a back-to-back World Championship for the Dodgers jammed into Ebbets Field. It is almost unbelievable, with such strong fan support in a city that had three major league teams, that after just one more season the Dodgers would be playing in Los Angeles.

The 1956 Cincinnati Redlegs hit 221 home runs, tying the major league record that was set by the 1947 New York Giants. As a token of remembrance of the occasion every player on the Redlegs was presented with a ring engraved with the number 221 on it.

The 221 home runs would remain as the Cincinnati club record until 2005, when that Reds team would hit 222 home runs.

Five years later in the 1961 season, the New York Yankees would eclipse the Redlegs' 221 home runs by hitting 240. The current major league record of 264 home runs in a season was set by the 1997 Seattle

Mariners. The current National League record was set by the 2000 Houston Astros with 249 home runs.

Birdie Tebbetts was named manager of the year for 1956 by *The Sporting News*. Tebbetts and Bill McKechie (1940) remain the only Cincinnati Reds managers to have ever been named manager of the year by the paper. Not even Sparky Anderson, manager of the Big Red Machine teams of the 1970s, ever got the paper's honor.

Although the Redlegs lineup in 1956 was power-packed, the Cincinnati Baseball Writers Association named shortstop Roy McMillan as the team's most valuable player. McMillan deserved the recognition. In the 1956 season he had topped all other shortstops in the National League in every fielding category: most putouts, most assists, fewest errors, most double plays, total fielding chances per game and highest fielding average.

Frank Robinson led the 1956 Redlegs with 38 home runs and was voted the 1956 National League Rookie of the Year

Wally Post hit 36 home runs, Ted Kluszewski 35, Gus Bell 29, Ed Bailey 28 and Ray Jablonski had 15 home runs, while backup first baseman George Crowe hit 10. Pinch hitter extraordinaire and part-time catcher Smoky Burgess hit 12 home runs in 229 at bats, giving the Reds a combined total of 40 home runs from their two catchers. Also, part-time outfielder and pinch hitter Bob Thurman hit 8 home runs. Pitcher Joe Nuxhall hit 2. Reserve outfielder Stan Palys also contributed 2 home runs. Joe Frazier, an outfielder who played in 10 games after coming to the Reds in a trade for Chuck Harmon with St. Louis, hit 1 home run. Rounding out the record-tying total of 221 home runs were the contributions of the Redlegs' snappy double-play combination of Roy McMillan with 3 home runs and Johnny Temple with 2 home runs.

Prior to the 1956 season, Johnny Temple had not hit a home run since 1953. In fact, at that point in time Temple had hit just 15 home runs in his entire professional career, and 7 of those home runs came in his first year playing at Morganton.

Opposing teams in the National League, knowing that Johnny Temple was no threat to hit the long ball, began to play their outfielders so close to the infield that it made one wonder where Temple could drop the ball in for a hit. Pittsburgh Pirates outfielder Jerry Lynch played so close to the infield when Temple was at bat that on several occasions during the 1955 season he attempted to make plays on him at first base.

But Temple was philosophical about his lack of power and about being known as a singles hitter. "If I tried to hit home runs I wouldn't be in the major leagues today," said Temple. "I'm just too little. I go along with theory that you should do the things that you can do to the best of your ability."[11]

While Johnny Temple only contributed two home runs to the Redlegs' record-tying effort in 1956, nonetheless if getting on base via being hit by a pitch is eliminated from the equation, Johnny Temple got on base more than any other Cincinnati Redlegs player in the 1956 season, including Frank Robinson.

Johnny Temple was in fact little; he was not the 175-pound brute that press guides listed. The only way Temple was going to tip 175 on the scale is if someone had his foot on it. His actual playing weight was somewhere in the range of a little over 150 pounds.

Together with Roy McMillan at shortstop, who was listed at 170 pounds but really weighed in at about 160, they made up the smallest keystone combination in the major leagues behind the Chicago White Sox' Nellie Fox, 150 pounds, and Luis Aparicio, who tipped the scales at 155 pounds. McMillan and Temple also challenged Aparicio and Fox for acknowledgment as the best double play combination of the 1950s.

Johnny Temple's hitting statistics loom much larger, however, in a way that even the Sabermetrics enthusiasts have yet attempted to quantify when it is considered that he was forced to work extremely hard to get on base. As previously stated, the Redlegs were now a power-driven team, and opposing pitchers knew that if Temple got on base he was likely to be driven in, so they began to bear down on him hard.

Temple met the challenge head-on and in the 1956 season he led the National League in at bats with 632 and singles with 157. He hit for an average of .285 with 180 hits, sixth best in the league. Still there were many who felt perhaps Temple could have got 200 hits and had a higher batting average if he were not instructed by Tebbetts to take pitches when he was ahead on the count rather than swing the bat.

With a great season behind him, one in which he established himself as a legitimate All-Star, it was good to be Johnny Temple. Rational action dictated that over the winter of 1956–1957 Temple should use his newly acquired star status to add a few bucks to his bank account by hitting the speaker's circuit around the Cincinnati area on behalf of boosting Redlegs ticket sales. He also appeared on a few television programs over WLW-TV in the Queen City.

Five

Earl Lawson Gets Punched

As the Cincinnati Redlegs gathered for spring training at Tampa, Florida, in March 1957, there was little talk about the surprising campaign of the previous year. The Redlegs still had pitching problems and Gabe Paul and Birdie Tebbetts had done nothing to improve the situation.

Johnny Temple was telling sportswriters and fellow players that over the winter he had run into the Milwaukee Braves' first baseman Joe Adcock, and he said that all the fellows on his club believed that of all the Redlegs pitchers, Johnny Klippstein had the best stuff.

The record showed that in the 1956 season Klippstein had finished with a record of 12–11 with an ERA of 4.09, pitched 11 complete games (tied for first on the club), but didn't pitch any shutouts and struck out only 86 batters in 211 innings. So if Adcock's assertion was correct, Klippstein needed to prove it.

One pitcher that the Redlegs were hopeful about for the coming season was Tom Acker, a big right-hander from Paterson, New Jersey, who stood 6'4" and weighed 215 pounds. Acker had a good fast ball, but his curve ball needed improvement. While he had spent most of the 1956 season in the bullpen, late in the season Acker started against the Philadelphia Phillies and threw a three-hit shutout.

After a poor performance in winter ball in the Dominican Republic, Curt Flood was once again in Tampa for spring training. But the Redlegs outfield for the 1957 season seemed set with Frank Robinson, Gus Bell and Wally Post. So the Redlegs front office assigned Flood to Class A Savannah of the South Atlantic League (or SALLY League) with instructions that he should be converted to a third baseman.

Johnny Temple had a good season in 1956, when he hit .285 with 180 hits and was voted to the All-Star team by the fans. But he was far from satisfied. Temple believed that two circumstances were preventing him from being recognized as the premier second baseman in the National League.

The first was nothing more than sour grapes. Temple believed that he wasn't receiving due recognition as a second baseman because he didn't play for the one of the New York teams which were covered by an army of sportswriters.

Most sportswriters considered Red Schoendienst, who had hit .296 for the New York Giants, as the best second baseman in the league. However, those same sportswriters alleged that Gene Baker, who hit .258 for the Chicago Cubs, was the second best in 1956. But the record showed that Johnny Temple had better stats than Gene Baker in every category but home runs and RBIs in the 1956 season. Also Baker had made more errors at second than Temple.

The second issue raised by Temple had more substance. Temple was still insistent that his batting average would be higher if Birdie Tebbetts would remove the perpetual take sign he was under at the plate. He felt the mandate was preventing him from hitting .300.

Temple was concerned that opposing pitchers, knowing he was at the plate to take pitches, fed him a steady diet of slow pitches with impunity. "You should see some of these pitches I take for strikes," said Temple. "And the ones they throw up to me when they are behind, two and nothing and three and one. Why they're nothing but half-speed batting practice pitches most of the time. Those pitchers aren't worried about throwing fast pitches because they know I'm up there taking."[1] Temple was sure that if Tebbetts let him rip away at fifteen or twenty of those pitches the pitchers would soon change their tactics.

As spring training was about to conclude in 1957 it became apparent that a bad moon was rising over Tampa. Ted Kluszewski was ailing and the Redlegs were faced with the fact that they would have to make a run at the pennant without his big bat in the lineup.

In order to address the potential run deficit as a result of Big Klu's disability, on opening day April 16, Birdie Tebbetts created a discombobulated lineup in an attempt to shake things up offensively. He inserted Frank Robinson as the Cincinnati leadoff hitter and had Wally Post bat fourth. He moved Kluszewski, usually the cleanup hitter, to the sixth spot in the batting order behind Johnny Temple, who usually was the leadoff hitter. Although Temple went 2 for 4, the shakeup did nothing to change things as the Redlegs suffered a crushing opening day 13–4 defeat at the hands of the St. Louis Cardinals. It was the worst opening day defeat for Cincinnati since 1911.

In a game against the Braves on April 21 at County Stadium in Milwaukee, the Redlegs became involved in a highly controversial play that once again would lead to a rule change.

In the top of the first inning Frank Robinson led off for the Redlegs and was called out on strikes. Don Hoak followed by reaching first on a bunt single. The next batter was Gus Bell, who singled to left. Hoak took second. The Cincinnati cleanup hitter Wally Post followed by hitting a ground ball toward Braves shortstop Johnny Logan. However, Don Hoak fielded the ball and flipped it to Logan—thereby breaking up a potential inning ending double play. Wally Post was credited with a single because the ball hit the runner. So Hoak, who had made contact with the ball before it was fielded, was ruled out, and Gus Bell went to second on the play. The inning ended when the next batter, Johnny Temple, grounded out third to first.

While the Braves went on to win the game 3–1, the National League office quickly took notice that the Cincinnati Redlegs were making the tactic of having a base runner make contact with the ball part of their standard offensive modus operandi. Just the day before, Johnny Temple had let a ground ball hit by Gus Bell hit him with the same result—Temple was ruled out and Bell was awarded a single.

Although the strategy employed by the Redlegs had been legal, it prompted a review by both National League president Warren Giles and American League president Will Harridge. Subsequently a rule change was jointly announced that in any such play, both the runner and the batter would be declared out if the runner intentionally interfered with a batted ball and no runners would be allowed to advance.

After a couple of more games and losses, Birdie Tebbetts gave up on his lineup experiment and moved Johnny Temple back to the leadoff spot, and Frank Robinson became the Redlegs cleanup hitter.

By early May, Ted Kluszewski was on the thirty-day disabled list while undergoing a battery of medical diagnostic procedures on his ailing back and convalescing while sitting by the swimming pool in his Cincinnati residence listening to Waite Hoyt broadcast the games on the radio.

Suddenly the Cincinnati Redlegs got hot and by May 11 were in first place with a record of 14–7. Birdie Tebbetts, remarking on the Redlegs' surge, stated, "The way they're thinking now is that any one of them can make up for Klu. Even Frank Robinson is playing well, bad arm and all. McMillan and Temple—everyone is putting out. If the big man was in there but not hitting, it might be different, they'd be waiting for him to pick them up. Now they know they have got to pick themselves up."[2]

Five. Earl Lawson Gets Punched 61

Redlegs vs. Cardinals, Opening Day 1957, Crosley Field, Cincinnati (Rhodes/Klumpe Reds Hall of Fame Collection).

By mid–June, Ted Kluszewski was back with the team and attempting to play regularly, but it immediately became apparent that he was still suffering pain in his back and would have to be utilized as a pinch hitter. Still the Redlegs continued to hold on to first place.

In the Cincinnati Redlegs clubhouse it was an accepted fact that Johnny Temple could be moody and combative following lost games—especially after ones that had been the result of an error, bad play or perceived lack of hustle. After a loss to the Chicago Cubs, Temple confronted two teammates, telling them that they had performed in the outfield like mountain goats. His verbal attack nearly resulted in a donnybrook before several other teammates separated the players.

Temple knew no boundaries when it came to criticizing his teammates. On another occasion Temple nearly got the ire of 240-pound muscleman Ted Kluszewski, known throughout baseball to be a gentle giant. Following a game, Temple confronted Big Klu, accusing him of making a costly error. Temple's remarks just didn't sit right with Kluszewski, and as teammates assessed the mounting tension between the two, they quickly came to Temple's rescue, removing him to a safe distance from the behemoth slugger's reach. Club officials even went a step further and made sure they would no longer room together on the road.

On June 21, 1957, Johnny Temple's temper flared up, and when the dust had settled he was hit in the wallet over an incident with official scorer Earl Lawson. While the Temple-Lawson incident was far from anything unique to major league baseball, it would become a defining moment in Temple's career and have a tendency to historically categorize his personality as being a sort of "dry-drunk" version of Billy Martin.

Ballplayers have been questioning the judgment of official scorers since the days of Abner Doubleday. One of the more famous incidents of the modern era occurred on Friday evening, September 29, 1972, as Roberto Clemente was on the verge of collecting his 3000th career hit at Three Rivers Stadium in Pittsburgh with 24,193 fans on hand. The game turned out to be a pitcher's duel between the New York Mets' Tom Seaver and the Pirates' Nelson Briles. Seaver was victorious, shutting out the Pirates 1–0 while striking out thirteen and allowing only two hits to Al Oliver and Richie Hebner.

It appeared that Clemente had got his 3000th hit in the first inning when he reached first base on a play that confused everybody. Clemente hit a slow bouncer past the mound that Mets second baseman Ken Boswell bobbled. Everyone, the umpires, fans and Clemente, thought it was a hit. Clemente was even presented with the ball and shook hands with first baseman Don Leppert. Then the "Error" sign flashed on the scoreboard.

The official scorer Luke Quay of the *McKeesport Daily News* announced over the public address system that it was ruled an error on second baseman Ken Bosewell. Immediately the fans' cheers turned to boos and streams of toilet paper were thrown from the stands.

Later in the game, it looked like Clemente had his 3000th hit for sure when he sliced a drive deep down the right field line. However, Rusty Staub had been playing him close to the line and made the catch.

Following the game Clemente was livid. He was angry and saying that the press was out to get him. When Dick Young of the *New York Daily News* reached the Pirates clubhouse he found Clemente in water up to his neck in the whirlpool and grinning. He told Young that he was celebrating being robbed of his 3000th hit by "the assholes in the press box." Then he added, "I'm glad they didn't call it a hit. They've been fucking me all my life and this shows it."[3]

When Clemente was informed that Luke Quay was the official scorer, he calmed down. Quay was in fact Clemente's best friend among the Pittsburgh sportswriters. Clemente then stated that he would prefer to reach the milestone with a clean hit. With his sense of humor restored, Clemente signed the ball he had received and sent it to Quay with the inscription,

"It was a Hit. No it was an error. No, it was superman Luke Quay. To my friend Luke with best wishes—Roberto Clemente."[4]

The Johnny Temple—Earl Lawson incident began after the Pittsburgh Pirates had defeated the Redlegs 3–2 at Crosley Field in a Friday night game. In the ninth inning of the game with the Reds leading 2–1, Pirates catcher Hank Foiles hit a hard smash toward second base that got through Temple on a short hop. *Cincinnati Times-Star* sportswriter Earl Lawson was the official scorer for the game and charged Temple with an error.

On the play, John O'Brien, a pinch runner for Dick Groat, went to third just as he would have done if Temple had fielded the ball. Then O'Brien came home with the tying run on a wild pitch by Redlegs pitcher Joe Nuxhall. The Pirates then went on to win the game in extra innings as a Redlegs rally in the bottom of the eleventh inning was snuffed out when Johnny Temple, at bat with two out and the bases full, hit a bounder to third.

In the clubhouse following the game, Temple, badly agitated by his failure to deliver a hit in a critical situation in the eleventh inning, inquired who the official scorer had been for the game. Earl Lawson informed him that it had been he. Immediately, Temple went into a tirade, unleashing a torrent of verbal abuse upon Lawson. Temple wanted to know what he was supposed to do with the ball when he got it. Lawson replied he just called it the way he saw it. Then Lawson told Temple, "Why don't you grow up?"[5]

Temple had been sitting down and suddenly jumped up and punched Lawson in the left side of the face. It was a cheap shot, and Lawson, stunned by the blow, attempted to retaliate, but was separated from Temple by Ted Kluszewski. Lawson then returned to the *Times-Star* office where, with his eye watering, he dictated his story for the paper to Lee Allen, future historian for the National Baseball Hall of Fame, who was working the night sports desk. Then Lawson had a picture taken by one of the newspaper's photographers.

As was the case in the later Roberto Clemente–Luke Quay misunderstanding, Earl Lawson had been very supportive of Johnny Temple in his columns ever since he was rookie with the Redlegs in 1952, so it was very surprising that Temple would make the Lawson the target on which to act out his anger.

At a closed-door meeting the next day in the Cincinnati clubhouse, in front of his teammates, Johnny Temple apologized to Earl Lawson for attacking him. Going forward, Temple and Lawson would become the best of friends, and Lawson would be there for Temple and his family at the time of his greatest need.

The fact was that Earl Lawson had handled the attack on him by Johnny Temple with considerable poise, self-respect and a genuine concern for Temple's status in the game. Most players did not realize that under the baseball rules, official scorers had the right to turn in players for oral attacks and other insulting actions subject to fining or suspension by the league presidents.

It was stated under Section 10:00, (C) (1) of the Baseball Rule Book: "The scorer is an official representative of the league, and is entitled to the respect and dignity of his office, and shall be accorded full protection by the league president. The scorer shall report to the president any indignity expressed by any manager, player, club official or club officer in the course of, or as the result of the discharge of his duties."

It was obvious that Johnny Temple was ignorant of this section of the rule book. But the Lawson incident was hardly closed, and the fallout that began immediately after has tended to hang around historically and tarnish Johnny Temple's legacy in the game.

National League president Warren Giles didn't need to be notified. He was aware of the incident, as Dan Daniel, president of the Baseball Writers Association of America (BBWAA), immediately sent him a telegram pointing out that official scorers are officials of the game. Giles took immediate action. He sent a telegram to Temple that was read to him by general manager Gabe Paul. Giles stated that Earl Lawson had been acting in an official capacity for the National League as scorer for the game and consequently, he was fining Temple $100 for his action and that the ball club was not to reimburse him for the fine.

The BBWAA wanted a stiffer penalty for Temple. To that end, Dan Daniel wired both Warren Giles and American League president Will Harridge, asking them to warn players with a sign in the clubhouse that unwarranted attacks on an official scorer, who is recognized in the rule book as an official of the game, would mean a suspension as well as a fine.

It had also been reported in the press that a few weeks before his assault on Earl Lawson, Johnny Temple had questioned the judgment of Lou Smith, *Cincinnati Enquirer* sports editor, who was acting as the official scorer when he ruled that Temple had reached first base safely on an error rather than a hit. Temple was quoted as saying that Smith was taking bread and butter out of his mouth with his call. The facts were that Temple had four hits in the game, won by the Reds 22–2.

Johnny Temple was embarrassed by the story and aware that his altercation with Earl Lawson was not good for his image. He was starting to get endorsements around the Cincinnati area, including appearing in a

TV commercial for a Ford dealer with Redlegs TV telecaster George Bryson. If the public suddenly decided that he was running around half-cocked it could put those deals in jeopardy.

In an attempt to extricate himself from negative fan opinion, Johnny Temple came to the conclusion that perhaps he needed professional intervention to help him control his temper. So he went to see a psychiatrist. It was a rare act of self-introspection for a professional athlete—then and now. A decision that some might even say was dangerous in that the counseling could possibly compromise his competitive nature. The doctor told Temple that his penchant for fighting was a result of his needing to prove something about himself. Temple said at the time he became a nervous wreck, and attempting to follow the doctor's advice, he bit his lip until it bled. Seeking professional help was a good idea, but ill-timed; it would have been more beneficial for Temple in the long run if he had entered counseling when he had hung up his spikes and retired.

The controversy created by the Earl Lawson incident just wouldn't go away, and almost a month after Temple had punched the sportswriter the incident was still being replayed. Other sports scribes were needling Lawson each time he was required to make a scoring decision.

During a night game in late June, George Bryson was in the press box when Lawson made an official ruling. Bryson began to rib him, then followed up his ribbing with some remarks expressing his belief that anytime Temple complained he was justified. Lou Smith of the *Cincinnati Enquirer* and the chairman of the Cincinnati Chapter the BBWAA took offense to Bryson's remarks, told him his opinions were not wanted, and told him to leave the press box. Bryson became peeved about being booted out the press box and challenged Smith to a fight. Both he and Smith squared off, but fisticuffs were prevented when other writers in the bandbox press area quickly separated the two.

The fallout from the Temple-Lawson incident continued for weeks, with a considerable number of critics holding the opinion that National League president Warren Giles had been too lenient with Johnny Temple by letting him off with just a $100 fine. Finally, at the time of the All-Star game, both Giles and American League president Will Harridge, feeling the heat, announced that any further assaults on an official scorer would be met with a suspension.

Johnny Temple would not be the last Cincinnati player to punch Earl Lawson. On June 21, 1962, almost five years to the day after Temple had socked Lawson in 1957, prior to a game with the Pirates in Pittsburgh, Lawson was punched again. This time the assailant was Reds centerfielder

Vada Pinson, who became angered by a story written by Lawson on June 18 criticizing his fielding as well as the play of first baseman Gordy Coleman. So Pinson decided to express his displeasure with the article and landed a left hook to Lawson's chin in the locker room. Once again, as Lawson had done in the Johnny Temple incident, he attempted to retaliate, but the two were separated by various Reds players. A copy of Lawson's article had been circulating on the Reds' team bus as well as in the locker room. Apparently, Pinson was taking a lot of hazing from his teammates. Later around the batting cage both Pinson and Lawson apologized to each other. While Lawson said that he was tired of getting hit by ballplayers, he added, "Temple hit harder."[6]

As the 1957 All-Star Game approached, despite the fact that Ted Kluszewski had only contributed one home run and five RBIs to the cause, the Redlegs were in fourth place, 3½ games behind the league-leading St. Louis Cardinals. The Cincinnati fans, feeling great about their team, did it again—they stuffed the ballot box voting for their local heroes. This time seven of the starting eight players with the top vote counts (the pitcher was selected by the manager) were Redlegs. They included second base, Johnny Temple; shortstop, Roy McMillan; third base, Don Hoak; catcher, Ed Bailey; right field, Wally Post; center field, Gus Bell; and left field, Frank Robinson. The only player to avoid the avalanche of votes for Redlegs players was first baseman Stan Musial. However, for a time it looked like Redlegs first baseman George Crowe was going to edge out Musial in the vote totals, which would have made the entire starting eight all Cincinnati players.

In regard to the overzealous voting of Cincinnati fans, *Time Magazine* stated, "Cincinnati fans have already decided that the pennant is in the bag. They are so proud of their team that they have stuffed the All-Star game ballot boxes so full that All-Star game voting has been reduced to patriotic absurdity."[7]

Although the final ballots for the 1957 All-Star game had not yet been counted, Commissioner Ford Frick intervened and issued a ruling that only five of the selected Redlegs could have starting positions. So two of the selected Redlegs, Wally Post and Gus Bell, were replaced by Willie Mays in center field and Hank Aaron in right field. Both were in second place in the balloting and Frick felt they were more deserving. At the All-Star game break, Hank Aaron, who had been outvoted by Wally Post, was leading the National League in hitting with a .347 average and home runs with 27. Wally Post was hitting .231 with 11 home runs.

Of course a strong case could be made for a few of the Redlegs players

Left to right: Redlegs infielders Johnny Temple (2B), Roy McMillan (SS) and Don Hoak (3B), circa 1957 (Rhodes/Klumpe Reds Hall of Fame Collection).

voted to the starting eight by the fans. Johnny Temple was hitting .292, Frank Robinson was the fourth leading hitter in the National League with an average of .312, and catcher Ed Bailey was hitting .297 with 13 home runs. Furthermore, Redlegs third baseman Don Hoak's stats were competitive with those of the Braves' Eddie Mathews. Hoak was hitting .292 with 14 home runs and 55 RBIs, as opposed to Mathews, who was hitting .302 with 17 home runs and 47 RBIs.

Regardless, Ford Frick had enough of the Cincinnati fans shenanigans and further ruled that starting with the 1958 All-Star game, voting for the starting players would be transferred from the fans to the players and managers.

The 1957 All-Star game was played on July 9 at Sportsman Park in St. Louis with 30,643 fans in attendance. The managers for the game were the New York Yankees' Casey Stengel and the Brooklyn Dodgers' Walter Alston.

The starting pitchers were Jim Bunning of the Detroit Tigers for the American League and Curt Simmons of the Philadelphia Phillies for the

National League. Bunning would throw three perfect innings, then be replaced by Billy Loes of the Baltimore Orioles in the fourth inning.

Johnny Temple was the National League leadoff hitter and went 0 for 2 before being replaced by pinch hitter Red Schoendienst in the sixth inning.

In the seventh inning, with the Giants' Willie Mays and the Redlegs' Ed Bailey on board after each had singled, the Redlegs' Gus Bell pinch-hit for Frank Robinson, and hit a double, driving home two runs.

The game was won by the American League 6–5. The National League entered the bottom of the ninth inning down 6–2 and started to rally, scoring three runs. However, the rally was snuffed out when Minnie Minoso made a running catch of a line drive off the bat of Gil Hodges to end the game.

As the Redlegs continued to be in the thick of the pennant race throughout the month of June, Birdie Tebbetts appeared on the cover of *Time Magazine*'s July 8 issue. But circumstances for Cincinnati were about to worsen. On July 7, just prior to the 1957 All-Star game, the Redlegs lost a double-header to the St. Louis Cardinals. Then, following the All-Star game, they began to fade in the pennant race, eventually finishing in fourth place with a record of 80–74.

Offensive production was down in the 1957 season with the Redlegs scoring 747 runs as opposed to 775 in 1956. Also the Redlegs hit 187 home runs in 1957 which was 34 fewer than in the previous campaign. Still the Redlegs had drawn 1,070,250 paying customers into little dowdy Crosley Field, which amounted to a dizzying total for a team with one of the smallest fan markets in the major leagues.

Ted Kluszewski, the Redlegs' highest-paid player, had only played in only 69 games and hit just six home runs. But overall the loss of the sleeveless slugger in regard to the outcome of the Redlegs' performance in the 1957 season was negligible. George Crowe had taken over at first base and did a fine job, finishing with a batting average of .271 with a team-leading 31 home runs and 92 RBIs.

The Big Klu era in Cincinnati Reds baseball officially came to an end on December 28, 1957, when Gabe Paul traded Kluszewski to the Pittsburgh Pirates. Ted Kluszewski departed the Cincinnati Reds holding ten club records and as one of the most popular players ever in the long history of the franchise.

There had been great concern for Johnny Temple's welfare after he was beaned in a Friday evening game August 9 at Crosley Field by Chicago Cubs pitcher Don Elston and had been sent to Cincinnati's Christ Hospital for X-rays and treatment. When Temple arrived at the ballpark the following day, he was still suffering from recurring headaches and was sent back to the hospital for additional tests. Fortunately all the tests came back negative and Temple finished the season without further complications.

Regardless of the storm of controversy that had surrounded Johnny Temple in the 1957 season over the Lawson incident, there was no denying that he was now a legitimate All-Star. In the 1957 season among all second basemen in the National League, Temple led in games played (154), hits (180), singles (157), sacrifice hits (17) and stolen bases (14). Temple's 157 singles led the National League and his 94 walks tied Richie Ashburn for the best total by a leadoff hitter.

In 1957 sporting goods manufacturer Rawlings began the Gold Glove awards. The first year the award was given to only one position player in both leagues. The following year Rawlings began extending the award to position players in both the National and American Leagues.

In the 1950s Roy McMillan was regarded as the best defensive shortstop in major league baseball. When Rawlings began the Gold Glove awards in 1957, Roy McMillian was named the very first shortstop to receive the award. McMillan then proceeded to be named the National League Gold Glove award winner at shortstop for 1958 and 1959.

Roy McMillan, like Johnny Temple, was a tobacco chewer during games. Away from the ballpark the two players didn't socialize much together and didn't room with each other on the road. By 1957, after being removed as Ted Kluszewski's roommate by the ball club, Temple was rooming with third baseman Don Hoak, while McMillan roomed with relief pitcher Herschel Freeman. Nonetheless the two would get together occasionally on a husband-and-wife basis.

By that point in time the acrobatic double plays of McMillan and Temple had captured the attention of the media and the fans in every National League city who came out to see McMillan and Temple play as much as the Redlegs musclemen at the plate.

In the August 3, 1957, edition of *The Saturday Evening Post* there appeared a four-page article on McMillan and Temple titled "The Redlegs' Miraculous Twins." The article stated in part, "Roy McMillan and Johnny Temple, who are widely considered the best keystone pair in the business, have these qualities in abundant measure. No middlemen have ever worked harder at mastering the fine points of their jobs or come closer to figuring out all the angles."

It was accepted throughout most of the history of the game until the

1980s that pitchers were in fact infielders and were expected to field balls hit back through the box and to back up plays.

Jim Kaat pitched for twenty-five years in the major leagues and won a record sixteen Gold Gloves on the mound. St. Louis Cardinals pitcher Harry "The Cat" Brecheen was a legendary fielder, and Bob Gibson and Fernando Valenzuela rarely let a ball get through the mound. Tom Seaver often took thirty minutes of fielding practice on days he didn't pitch, and Whitey Ford was so skilled at fielding ground balls that the Yankees' second baseman and shortstop could play wide of the bag.

Jim Kaat's philosophy about the pitcher as a fielder was simple: "A pitcher's got to be aware that almost every time the ball is hit, there's someplace he's got to be other than the mound."[8]

But in today's game most pitchers have developed a style of delivery that leaves them off balance and useless as a fielder or for backing up plays. A lot of this unorthodox delivery style is a result of pitchers' attempting to throw as hard as possible. As a result, among noted pitchers today, Johnny Cueto nearly has his back to the ball when he finishes his delivery, and Tim Lincecum nearly falls off the mound on every pitch. The mechanics of these pitchers today are more the norm than an oddity and do little to improve their team's defense.

It's amazing that various persons hired to be baseball analysts today by ESPN and the MLB Network attempt to put such heavy emphasis on modern statistical models such as WHIP (Wins, Plus Hits Per Inning Pitched) and WAR (Wins Above Replacement) to evaluate a pitcher's value to a major league ball club and completely ignore the fundamentals of whether or not a pitcher is capable of fielding his position. In the long term, a pitcher's inability to field forces the shortstop and second baseman to play in close to compensate for the pitcher's lack of fielding and allows the opposing team to score runs out of ordinary balls hit over the head of infielders or through the box that they would have turned into outs if they could have played a little deeper.

Redlegs manager Birdie Tebbetts, a former catcher, was old school in regard to pitchers' fielding and assessed an automatic fine of twenty-five dollars for every ground ball or every base hit through the box that in his opinion the pitcher should have fielded. So it was fortunate for the Redlegs' hurlers of the middle 1950s that they had playing behind them such outstanding middlemen as Roy McMillan and Johnny Temple, who could move fast and far. Time and time again, McMillan and Temple would race behind second base on ground balls hit through the box, turning hits into outs and sparing the pitcher a fine.

The most amazing aspect of the McMillan-Temple duo was that it had been obtained by the Cincinnati Baseball Club at virtually no costs. Both players were signed when they showed up at tryout camps: McMillan in 1947 at Tyler, Texas, and Temple in 1948 at Mooresville, North Carolina.

When Roy McMillan was signed he was a softball player with almost no experience at playing baseball. He broke in with Tyler in 1947, but played most of the season with Ballinger, where he hit .275 and led the league in fielding. With Tyler in 1948 he led the league in fielding and hit .307. Branch Rickey saw McMillan play in 1948 and a story has it that he offered Cincinnati Reds general manager Warren Giles $40,000 for him, which he declined.

After having another great minor league season in 1957 at Savannah, where he hit for an average of .299 and had 170 hits while attempting to adjust to playing third base, Curt Flood received another late season call-up from the Cincinnati Redlegs.

On September 25, the Redlegs lost to the Chicago Cubs 7–5 at Crosley Field. In the fifth inning, after Don Hoak had doubled, Curt Flood was sent in to pinch run for him. Flood remained in the game playing third base and had two at bats. In the ninth inning with the Redlegs trailing the Cubs 7–3, Jerry Lynch led off with a home run to center field of Moe Drabowsky. Curt Flood then followed with a home run to left. It would be Flood's only major league hit playing for the Cincinnati Redlegs.

With the 1957 season in the rear-view mirror, Johnny Temple was beginning to consider employment options for when his career in the big leagues ended. So Temple turned his attention toward becoming a manager and signed on with the Pastora Milkers team in the Occidental winter league in Venezuela.

After Curt Flood had committed 41 errors at Savannah in the 1957 season, Redlegs general manager Gabe Paul thought that perhaps Flood could be converted into a second baseman and eventually replace Johnny Temple. So Paul asked Temple to take Flood to Venezuela with him and provide some instruction. However, Flood's stay in South America was short, as he was struck with dysentery.

Curt Flood later stated that as a coach, Johnny Temple was both pleasant and patient with him and was one of the few players or coaches who attempted to help him improve his game. But Temple was also realistic and recognized that Flood was never going to make it to the major leagues as a middle infielder.

Back in Cincinnati, Gabe Paul didn't really know what to do with his prize prospect. Vada Pinson was making steady progress in the minor leagues and Paul decided to give up on Curt Flood. It would be a huge mistake. On December 5, 1957, Paul traded Flood along with Joe Taylor to the St. Louis Cardinals for pitcher Willard Schmidt, Marty Kutynce and Ted Wieand.

Had Gabe Paul not traded Flood, in just a couple of years the Cincinnati Reds would have had an all-Oakland, McClymonds High School outfield consisting of Frank Robinson, Vada Pinson and Curt Flood, all All-Stars and hands down the best outfield in the major leagues and arguably one of the best of all time.

Curt Flood went on to play fifteen years in the major leagues, playing 1697 games in the outfield and six as an infielder (four games at third base and two games at second base). Flood would play twelve years with the St. Louis Cardinals, play in three World Series and finish his career with 1861 hits and a lifetime batting average of .293.

Of course Curt Flood would become as famous in baseball for his off-field activity as his on-field play. At the conclusion of the 1969 season, Flood was traded by the St. Louis Cardinals to the Philadelphia Phillies. In January 1970, disgruntled with the trade, Flood refused to report to the Phillies. Subsequently, he filed suit challenging legality of the reserve clause in players' standard contracts that literally made a player property of the club owner. Flood's case was heard in 1972 by the U.S. Supreme Court. In its ruling the Court by a 5–3 vote refused to overturn Major League Baseball's exemption from antitrust statutes. While Curt Flood had lost the first battle against the reserve clause, the players and the Major League Players Association would soon win the war.

In April 1972, just before opening day, a strike was called by Players Association director Marvin Miller. The strike lasted for thirteen days (April 1–13) and canceled 86 games. But the benefits the players gained were substantial. The agreement called for a $500,000 increase in the pension fund and for salary disputes to be held before an independent arbitrator, which ended the perpetual renewal rights of owners.

Then three years later in 1975 the reserve clause was again challenged by two pitchers, Dave McNally of the Montreal Expos and Andy Messersmith of the Los Angeles Dodgers, who declared themselves free agents after having played a full season without signing a contract. Without going to court, the Players Association and the owners came to an agreement that anyone with ten years' major league experience, the last five with a single club, could no longer be traded without the player's consent. Further actions would occur throughout the 1980s, effectively bringing the reserve clause to an end.

Five. Earl Lawson Gets Punched

Soon after Curt Flood's departure from Venezuela, Johnny Temple ran into trouble too and lasted just six weeks on the job. Temple's difficulties came within a four-day period. First he got in a heated argument with umpire Augie Guglielmo and was given a stiff fine by the league after he entered the umpire's dressing room and continued to argue with Guglielmo. A few days later he was fired by the Pastora club owner.

Temple received notice of his termination while he was dressing for the game in his Venezuelan hotel room when the bellboy appeared with an important-looking letter. Of course, Temple did not read Spanish so he had a friend read the letter to him. The friend opened the letter, glanced at it, then looked at Temple and said, "Goodbye, John. You have been fired."[9]

At the time the Pastora Milkers were in first place, but Latin American baseball was just as crazy then as it is now. The owner of the Milkers, a rather wealthy man, thought he should win every game and attempted to micromanage the team. On occasion he would even write out lineup cards before games and present them to Temple for his guidance.

The owner also bet heavily on the games and was very upset that a recent loss had occurred when ex-Redleg Jim Greengrass had been thrown out at the plate attempting to score the tying run from third base on a fly ball to the outfield in the ninth inning.

In another loss, Temple had started former major league pitcher Duane Pillette (New York Yankees, St. Louis Browns/Baltimore Orioles and Philadelphia Phillies) against the wishes of the owner. Pillette lost the game 3–1.

The owner decided he had enough of Temple and replaced him as manager with—of all people—Duane Pillette. Officially the club owner stated he fired Temple because he would not be able to participate if the Milkers got into the Caribbean World Series.

Temple did have his supporters in the front office, and four members of the Milkers' board of directors resigned over his firing. To show their appreciation for Temple, when he and his wife Becky and son Mike boarded a plane to return to the United States, they showered the family with gifts.

Overall, Temple felt that his six-week tour of duty as manager of the Pastora Milkers had been a positive experience. "I went down there for experience," said Temple, "and I found out I can manage men ... that's what I wanted to know. The first three or four games were the toughest. I was on edge then. But I settled down and got to the point where I could think two or three innings ahead."[10]

Later Temple was to say that his Venezuelan experience had given him a higher appreciation of some of the challenges Birdie Tebbetts had to confront. In turn he was sure that Birdie appreciated having a boss in Gabe Paul who didn't meddle in on-field decisions. Unfortunately the coming 1958 season would be Birdie Tebbetts's last as Cincinnati Redlegs skipper.

Six

Shake-Up in Cincy

When Birdie Tebbetts received his contract for the 1958 season he noticed that the attendance clause had been removed. Tebbetts was surprised and a little suspect of the ball club's motives. Since he had taken over as the Cincinnati Redlegs manager in 1954 there had been a clause in his contract that called for a bonus of $1000 for each 100,000 fans the Redlegs drew above 600,000 during the year. In 1956 Tebbetts took home a $5000 bonus when the Redlegs season attendance hit 1,125,928. In 1957 he took home an extra $4000 when the team drew a season total of 1,070,850. With a growing family and a mortgage, the bonus money came in handy for the Tebbetts household.

As he ruminated on the situation, Tebbetts reasoned that first and foremost baseball is a business and he thought that perhaps Powell Crosley, Jr., was planning to move the Redlegs to New York and take up residency in the Polo Grounds that the Giants had just abandoned at the end of the 1957 season for San Francisco. If that was the plan, it was certain that with both the Giants and Dodgers departing New York City for the west coast, the Redlegs would draw massive crowds in the city as the only National League entity.

In the spring of 1958, Powell Crosley, Jr., did threaten the city of Cincinnati with a franchise shift if he didn't get increased parking facilities around Crosley Field, but he never seriously considered relocation to the east coast. Nonetheless Crosley was aware of the fact that the Redlegs were a regional team, a Southwestern Ohio team, not just a Cincinnati team. Fans drove long distances from communities such as Columbus, Dayton, Washington Court House and Portsmouth in Ohio, as well as from Indianapolis, Indiana; Huntington, West Virginia; Lexington, Kentucky, and others to attend Redlegs home games.

Since the end of World War II the automobile had dramatically changed the urban landscape. The era of the neighborhood ballpark was over, as demonstrated by the Brooklyn Dodgers' departure from historic Ebbets Field, leaving behind one of the most loyal fan bases in the history of the game.

In Cincinnati, construction on an interstate highway (I-75) was planned just outside the confines of the Crosley Field centerfield wall. So Powell Crosley, Jr., seized the opportunity to bully the city fathers, complaining about the deterioration of the west end neighborhood around the ballpark and taking care to emphasize the fear factor of white fans who felt threatened parking their cars on the streets in the black neighborhood near Crosley Field. The Cincinnati City Council quickly responded by forming a Stadium Advisory Committee. The result was that property on two sides of the old ballpark (left field and first base line) was purchased and structures demolished to make way for parking lots in close proximity to a planned ramp coming off the interstate near the ballpark.

Hustling little Johnny Temple was now synonymous with "double play," playing alongside Roy McMillan to form the best keystone combination in the major leagues. Not only was he considered the best middleman in double plays in the major leagues, but he continued to amaze the opposition with his ability to shift in either direction very fast and throw while off balance.

But his .284 lifetime batting average was overlooked. While Temple was a model of consistency and did just about everything but hit home runs, it was also overlooked just how tough he was at bat against certain teams. A case in point was the Dodgers. In 1957 Temple had hit .354 against the Dodgers and battered lefty Johnny Podres for a .412 average. Temple also was the Redlegs' leading base stealer. In four seasons he had stolen 76 bases and only been thrown out 21 times, an average of .783. In the 1957 season, Temple, with 19 stolen bases, was the fourth leading base stealer in the league behind the Giants' Willie Mays (38), the Dodgers' Junior Gilliam (26) and the Cardinals' Don Blasingame (21).

Although Rogers Hornsby had been gone from the Cincinnati scene for over four years, there were those among the Redlegs faithful who were still questioning why the Rajah had ignored Johnny Temple in favor of weak-hitting Rocky Bridges.

The bond between Birdie Tebbetts and Johnny Temple had become solid. Tebbetts referred to him as a manager's ballplayer. Temple's mind was constantly in the ball game. It was during the 1958 season that *Cincinnati Enquirer* sportswriter Bob Husted boarded the Redlegs bus with the players bound for the airport after a tough loss on the West Coast. Husted

Six. Shake-Up in Cincy

sat down next to Johnny Temple, who was staring out of the window. As the bus rolled along, Temple said nothing, but he seemed to be preoccupied with something. Then suddenly he turned towards Husted and said, "Wasn't that a hellava way to lose a ball game?"[1] That was the mindset of Johnny Temple—he played every game as if it were his last.

The Cincinnati Redlegs began the 1958 season at Crosley Field with a 5–4 loss to the Philadelphia Phillies. Although Temple went hitless in the opener, he was about to embark upon a fine season.

When the Redlegs defeated the St. Louis Cardinals 5–2 on April 29, it was a milestone game for Johnny Temple—he hit the first home run of his career in Crosley Field. The blow, which traveled approximately 380 feet and cleared the left-center field wall, came off Cardinals left-hander Vinegar Bend Mizel. Following the solo poke as Temple completed the grand tour around the bases and entered the Redlegs dugout, Birdie Tebbetts said two words to him, "Forget it."[2]

Temple had tired of having outfielders play so close in when he was at bat. According to Temple, "If I dunked a single to right field I had to run like hell to prevent my being thrown out at first base. The opposition moved their outfielders in on me until I could see the whites of their eyes."[3] He had been using 32- to 34-ounce bats like most of his teammates. Then one day during spring training a year earlier, Clint Courtney, catcher for the Washington Senators, tossed Temple a 37-ounce bat; he tried it and liked it. Suddenly he was getting more wood on the ball and decided to order even heavier bats—40-once bats.

On June 14 the Redlegs were at Wrigley Field, and once again Birdie Tebbetts, ever the innovator, made a player switch in the field that led to another rule change. In the bottom of the second, Bobby Thomson led off for the Chicago Cubs with a single. Birdie Tebbetts, anticipating a sacrifice bunt, moved first baseman George Crowe to second base and Johnny Temple from second to first. Neither player switched his glove. The next batter for Chicago, Johnny Briggs, attempted to bunt but popped up. Temple sped in from first and caught the ball on the fly, turned and threw to first, where Crowe caught the ball for a double play.

Cubs manager Bob Scheffing protested the call, and when the play was not overturned, he announced that he was playing the game under protest. The Cubs eventually won the game 4–3 and Sheffing withdrew his protest. But the next day, National League president Warren Giles ruled that, when a first baseman switches to another position, he must discard his first baseman's mitt and use a fielder's glove.

Johnny Temple had consistently been hitting over .300 during the first few months of the 1958 season, and on June 27 he used his bat to defeat the San Francisco Giants 6–5 with a two-run walk-off triple in the bottom of the ninth.

At the All-Star Game break in 1958, the Cincinnati Redlegs were in fourth place, 3½ games back with a record of 37–37 and struggling to remain in the first division. The big sticks in the Redlegs batting order were underperforming: Frank Robinson (.249), Gus Bell (.252) and Ed Bailey (.249) collectively were hitting .250. Johnny Temple was hitting .308 and was one of the few players keeping the team in the pennant chase.

Following the ballot box–stuffing campaign by the Cincinnati fans for the 1956 and 1957 All-Star games, under the ruling of the commissioner, the 1958 game was the first in which the starting players would be selected by the managers, coaches and players. The results would yield some surprising and historical controversial results, suggesting that the personalities of players as much as their performance became an important factor in being selected by their peers.

After having had an unprecedented presence on the 1956 and 1957 All-Star teams, the Cincinnati Redlegs were nearly invisible in the 1958 game. The Redlegs' dynamic keystone duo of shortstop Roy McMillian and second Johnny Temple were not selected to start the 1958 All-Star Game or as reserve players on the squad. In fact, not one Cincinnati player was voted to a starting position for the 1958 squad and only two Redlegs were selected as reserve players, first baseman George Crowe and pitcher Bob Purkey. Neither player played in the game.

Roy McMillian was not selected because of the emergence of future Hall of Fame shortstop Ernie Banks of the Chicago Cubs. Furthermore McMillan was struggling at the plate. At the time of the voting by the managers, coaches and players, McMillan was hitting a paltry .208.

Although Roy McMillan would lead all National League shortstops in fielding in 1958 with a .980 average, twenty points higher than Ernie Banks, who led the league in errors for shortstops with 32, he would be buried in the dust of Banks's huge offensive output. Banks would lead the league in home runs with 47 and RBIs with 129.

Still, politics raised its ugly head in the player selections too. When the National League manager, the Braves' Fred Haney, announced the reserves, of course Milwaukee's favorite son Johnny Logan was picked as the back-up shortstop.

It was also surprising that the managers, coaches and players selected the Pittsburgh Pirates' Bill Mazeroski, who was hitting .272 as the starting second baseman for the National League, over Johnny Temple, who was hitting .308. Then when Fred Haney selected the reserve players for the team, he passed over Temple in favor of St. Louis Cardinals second baseman Don Blasingame, who was hitting .276. In the case of Temple it was clearly a double snub by both the managers, coaches and players in selecting the starting team, and Fred Haney in selecting the reserves.

In fairness to Fred Haney, it should be mentioned that he also passed on selecting his own second baseman Red Schoendienst as a reserve. In 1957, Red Schoendienst had hit .310 and led the National League in hits with 200. In 1957 Schoendienst, playing for the New York Giants and Milwaukee Braves, had become the first National League player to ever lead the league in hits when playing for two different teams.

Following the 1958 season, Red Schoendienst would be hospitalized for tuberculosis and lose a lung. But Schoendienst would make a gallant comeback and play parts of five more seasons between 1959 and 1963. He would be elected to the Hall of Fame by the veterans committee in 1989.

Following the 1958 All-Star Game, the Cincinnati Redlegs went into a steady decline. At Crosley Field the boo-birds were very active and Birdie Tebbetts was taking the brunt of their dissatisfaction every time he stepped out of the dugout onto the field.

On August 13 the Redlegs lost a double-header to the Milwaukee Braves and found themselves in last place with a record of 52–61 and 14½ games behind. During the double-header, booing by the fans had become overwhelming.

The fact was that the Cincinnati fans had been expressing their feelings from the stands with the Redlegs play for a few weeks and the full-throttle assault was taking a toll on Tebbetts. Following the second game of the disastrous Milwaukee double-header, Tebbetts met with general manager Gabe Paul and offered to resign. Paul had no intention of firing Tebbetts and told him to sleep on it. So Tebbetts went home and discussed resigning with his wife Mary, and although it meant the loss of a $40,000 a year job, she agreed that it was the best thing to do.

The following morning, at a press conference held in Gabe Paul's office in the Union Central Life tower downtown, Tebbetts resigned as Redlegs manager. In a prepared statement he told the press, "I am not resigning because of my feeling that I am not doing the job properly, but solely because, in my heart, I believe that it is better for Cincinnati baseball that someone succeed me."[4] So ended the reign of the 34th manager in the 83-year history of the Cincinnati Reds.

The relationship between Gabe Paul and Birdie Tebbetts had been cordial during his tenure as manager of the Redlegs, and Paul realized

Left to right: Redlegs brain trust, Powell Crosley, Jr. (owner), Gabe Paul (general manager) and Birdie Tebbets (manager), circa 1957 (Rhodes/Klumpe Reds Hall of Fame Collection).

that he himself had played a huge part in the Redlegs' sub-par performance. Still there was an apparent whiff of disagreement apparent between Paul and Tebbetts following his resignation. Gabe Paul told *Cincinnati Enquirer* reporter Lee Allen that the new manager of the Redlegs had to be an executive. "The man I want has to have experience as a manager," Paul insisted, "although not necessarily in the major leagues. I will be looking for a fellow who is an executive, and who will have an organization program for managing the players at his disposal."[5]

Reasonable speculation leads one to conclude that, as the 1958 season progressed with one bullpen failure after another, Birdie Tebbetts wanted to make a trade for relief pitching and Gabe Paul was against it. But Birdie Tebbetts was like most employees then and now: when they leave a job under some duress in order to secure a new position, they avoid burning bridges behind them. Tebbetts was cautious about protecting his future in baseball, and following his resignation he remained tight-lipped, taking great care to not criticize anyone in the Cincinnati organization. Eventually Birdie Tebbetts and Gabe Paul would have a working relationship together again with the New York Yankees and remain friends for the rest of their lives.

Although the fans in Cincinnati had come down on Birdie Tebbetts petty hard, they were divided in their feelings about his resignation; some were glad, some were sad. Some refused to blame Tebbetts for the Redlegs' lackluster performance, stating that Birdie couldn't do the hitting and pitching for the players. Others felt Tebbetts hadn't been emphasizing good fundamentals on the diamond and that his resignation was the best thing that could have happened to the team. There were even some fans still stuck in the Big Klu era who maintained the belief that the ball club had been in a steady nose dive since Gabe Paul traded Ted Kluszewski to Pittsburgh.

Speculation began immediately on who the new Cincinnati skipper was going to be. In early August, Gabe Paul and Powell Crosely, Jr., had been spotted having lunch at the 21 Club in New York with Leo Durocher and his wife, actress Laraine Day. So immediately the press and fans were advancing the notion that Durocher would soon appear in the Queen City. Other popular names for a successor to Tebbetts that began to circulate in the Cincinnati press and barrooms included Eddie Stanky, Pee Wee Reese and Bobby Bragan.

At the time of Tebbetts's resignation, owner Powell Crosley, Jr., had been vacationing in Alaska, so any serious discussion of who the Redlegs' new manager might be was put on hold.

Meanwhile, 61-year old coach Jimmy Dykes took over the club for the remainder of the season. Dykes had played twenty-two years in the American League and previously managed three teams in the junior circuit (Chicago White Sox, Philadelphia Athletics and Baltimore Orioles). Dykes publicly expressed his desire to be appointed permanently, but Gabe Paul preferred someone younger.

One of the first things that Jimmy Dykes did upon becoming interim skipper was to remove the take sign from Johnny Temple on the first pitch. Word had circulated throughout the league that Temple was customarily going to take the first pitch and perhaps the second. As a result, a few days later at Seals Stadium in San Francisco, in the fifth inning Giants starter Stu Miller grooved a first pitch to Temple that he hit out of the park. A stunned Miller stood on the mound as he watched Temple circle the bases. For Temple it was his third home run of the season. The Giants went on to win the game 4–3 in ten innings.

For the Redlegs it was their twenty-eighth one-run loss of the season and twelfth extra-inning defeat, dropping them 19½ games behind the league-leading Milwaukee Braves. Brooks Lawrence, ace of the 1956 staff, was now pitching in relief and was charged with his twelfth defeat of the season and ninth loss in a row.

The Redlegs did perk up and began to win more games under Jimmy Dykes, and by August 30 had taken over fourth place. Playing out the schedule under Dykes, the club had a record of 24–17.

Part of the Redlegs' successful climb into the first division was due to the pitching of two right-handers and a left-hander that Gabe Paul had acquired. In December 1957 Paul had traded southpaw Don Gross to the Pittsburgh Pirates for right-hander Bob Purkey, who would finish the 1958 season with an outstanding record of 17–11. Then Paul acquired left-hander Harvey Haddix from the Philadelphia Phillies in exchange for slugger Wally Post. Finally, a third of the way through the 1958 season on June 15, Paul acquired former National League MVP and Cy Young Award–winning right-hander Don Newcombe from the Los Angeles Dodgers. The combined mound work of Purkey, Haddix and Newcombe would bring a much-needed lift to the quality of the Cincinnati Redlegs' pitching in the 1958 season.

Although Don Newcombe spent more time bending his elbow in bars than he did on the mound, Big Newk could still pitch. When playing for the Dodgers, Newcombe had been open about his huge thirst for alcohol, often consuming large amounts of beer in the clubhouse following games. No one complained or cared that he was a functioning alcoholic because he was winning. But by the time he got to Cincinnati his addiction was taking more control over him and he attempted to hide his alcoholism. Even George Crowe, Newcombe's roommate, was unaware that he was an alcoholic. Newcombe would pitch batting practice for an hour, then run for an hour, working up a huge sweat in an effort to metabolize the alcohol in his system.

Although Don Newcombe had consumed his first beer in his hometown of Madison, New Jersey, when he was eight years old, he has maintained that he started drinking hard during his time with the Brooklyn Dodgers because he couldn't cope with the criticism from the press and fans that he was not able to win big games. Regardless of the fact that in 1956 Newcombe had a won-lost record of 27–7, won the MVP and Cy Young Award, because the New York Yankees beat him in the World Series, people said he choked. The psychological pain from the criticism was intense; he internalized his agony and attempted to drown it in a sea of booze. During the winter of 1956–1957, Newcombe refused to speak with anyone; he just played golf and got drunk. Within four years Don Newcombe would be out of baseball and drinking two fifths of whisky a day. At one point he even sold one of his World Series rings to get more alcohol.

In 1967 Don Newcombe promised his family he would change. He stopped drinking and has been a recovering alcoholic to this very day. Eventually Los Angeles Dodgers owner Peter O'Malley would buy back Newcombe's World Series ring for him and also hire him. In 1970 Don Newcombe became the Los Angeles Dodgers' community relations director and for fourteen years handled the team's alcohol and drug rehabilitation program. One player who benefited greatly from Newcombe's intervention in getting him sober and saving his career in 1980 was pitcher Bob Welch.

The other part of the Redlegs' successful move into the first division in 1958 was the spirited play of Johnny Temple. But on September 14, in the first game of a double-header with the San Francisco Giants, Temple suffered a hairline fracture in a small bone in his left ankle after colliding with Darrell Spencer and had to be removed in the second game. It was a season-ending injury for Temple, and Alex Grammas took over at second base for the remainder of the schedule.

Although he missed the final two weeks of the 1958 season, Johnny Temple led the Cincinnati Redlegs in hits with 166 and putouts with 395. He hit for an average of .306. His batting average was the second highest on the ball club behind right fielder Jerry Lynch, who hit .312, but who went to bat 420 times as opposed to Temple's 542 plate appearances.

The Cincinnati Redlegs finished the 1958 season in fourth place with a record of 76–78. Johnny Temple had been largely responsible for leading the Redlegs' surge toward the first division during late August and early September. In acknowledgment of the spark that Temple had ignited in the Redlegs' late-season comeback, the Cincinnati chapter of Baseball Writers Association named him the Cincinnati Redlegs' Most Valuable Player for 1958.

The Redlegs didn't finish higher in the 1958 standings due to two factors. First, they struggled in attempts to defeat the other first-division teams. Against pennant-winning Milwaukee the Redlegs finished with a record of 5–17; against second-place Pittsburgh they were 10–12 and third-place San Francisco 11–11. Second, with a sagging bullpen, the club was 22–32 in one-run games, and in extra-innings games they finished with a record of 7–13.

As the Redlegs struggled, their fans became disgusted with the club's poor performance. To show how they felt, they voted with their feet. In 1958 those parking lots that Powell Crosley, Jr., had lobbied Cincinnati City Council for remained for the most part empty as season attendance nose dived at Crosley Field to 718,582, a drop of 33 percent from 1957.

You didn't need to be a sportswriter or an experienced baseball front office executive.to understand the personnel problems on the 1958 Cincinnati Redlegs; they were apparent to everyone, even kids collecting baseball cards. The average fan was familiar with the club's deficiencies. The Redlegs lacked quality relief pitching, and their awesome power surge of a couple of seasons earlier had fizzled out; the Redlegs were no longer hitting home runs. The Redlegs' 1958 long-ball leader was Frank Robinson with 31 round-trippers. As a team the 1958 Redlegs hit just 123 home runs, second least in the league, and 98 fewer than they had hit as a team two seasons before when they tied the National League record.

Still there was hope for the Redlegs' future in the presence of two promising young players who were brought up from the minors that September: outfielder Vada Pinson and left-handed pitcher Jim O'Toole.

Vada Pinson was a speedy, hard-hitting outfielder, and it looked like he would be ready to take over center field from aging Gus Bell in the coming 1959 season. Frank Robinson who was a few years older than Pinson and would serve as his mentor.

Jim O'Toole, a left-hander with a good curve ball, grew up on the south side of Chicago, the son of a policeman. He had come to spring training with the Reds in 1958 and then was sent to AA ball at Nashville, where he achieved a record of 20–7 with 200 strikeouts and 23 complete games.

Six. Shake-Up in Cincy

In September, Jim O'Toole was called up to big leagues. He pitched one game on September 26 against the Milwaukee Braves opposing Lew Burdette, who was going for his 20th win of the season. O'Toole lost the game 2–1 when Frank Robinson wound up playing third base instead of Don Hoak and let a ball go through his legs that turned out to be the winning run. But O'Toole had gone head-to-head with the gritty veteran Burdette, giving up just four hits in seven innings, while striking out four. Burdette, on the other hand, had allowed nine hits in going the distance and struck out nine Redlegs.

Seven

A Deal That Sinks the Reds

Cincinnati Reds general manager Gabe Paul had his work cut out for him to make his 1959 team a lot more competitive than the 1958 club. Nonetheless the first order of business for Paul, Powell Crosley, Jr., and the Cincinnati Baseball Club, Inc., board of directors was to drop the silly Cold War appellation of Redlegs that the club had been using since 1954 and return to the team's historic name of Reds for the coming season.

Then Paul hired a new manager, 44-year old Mayo Smith, who had managed the Philadelphia Phillies in an undistinguished tenure, 1955–1958, winning 264 games and losing 283.

The next order of business for Gabe Paul was to do something about stopping the free-fall of the Cincinnati Reds' offensive statistics. The team's season home run production had fallen from 221 in 1956 to 187 in 1957 to 123 in 1958. Gus Bell had hit just 10 home runs and Ed Bailey 11 in the 1958 season. Two years before, Bell and Bailey had hit a combined 57 home runs, a figure that amounted to half of the team's entire home run production in 1958. During the same period between 1956 and 1958, the team's season run production had slipped from 775 to 747 to 695. In order to generate some offense, Gabe Paul reasoned that he needed another established power hitter and would make one of the worst trades in Cincinnati Reds history.

On January 30, 1959, Gabe Paul sent Smoky Burgess, Harvey Haddix and Don Hoak to the Pittsburgh Pirates in exchange for Frank Thomas, Whammy Douglas, Jim Pendleton and Johnny Powers. All that Paul did was fill in the missing pieces in the Pirates' lineup that would in two years make them World Champions while the Reds would receive nothing in return.

Frank Thomas was the key player in the deal. In the 1958 season, playing third base for the Pirates, Thomas had hit 35 home runs with 109

RBIs while hitting for an average of .281. But he brought with him a whopping contract of $40,000. Johnny Temple had been the highest paid player on the 1958 Reds with a contract calling for near $30,000.

But the Reds were getting damaged goods in the acquisition of Thomas. Before he signed his contract, Thomas informed Gabe Paul that he had a bad hand that wasn't healing. Thomas said, "He [Paul] told me not to worry."[1] The 1959 season would turn out to be the worst of Thomas's career as his offensive production would tank and he would he would hit just 12 home runs, have 47 RBIs and finish the season with a batting average of .225.

According to Thomas, "My hand was very, very sore. I had tears in my eyes every time I put any pressure on it and when I hit the ball on my fists it really jarred it."[2] Thomas, a native of Pittsburgh, said things were so bad at the plate that back home in the Steel City his kids were burning his bubble gum baseball cards.

Despite his disability and inability to perform at peak levels, Thomas never asked Mayo Smith to take him out of a game. He tried hard to become a member of the Cincinnati Reds and to develop friendships with his teammates, but most of them were standoffish with him. In regard to Johnny Temple, Thomas maintained that he was hard to get to know and while he gave 100 percent on the field, Temple tended to stay to himself off the field.

Thomas also didn't get to know Jim O'Toole very well, or relief pitcher Jim Brosnan, whom the Reds would acquire in June 1959 from the St. Louis Cardinals in exchange for Hal Jeffcoat.

No one got to know Don Newcombe because he lived in his own world. He didn't hang out with anyone, and after games he left the clubhouse quickly to get to one of his favorite watering holes.

The Cincinnati Reds opened the 1959 season with the Pittsburgh Pirates, so fans eagerly welcomed Smoky Burgess, Don Hoak and Harvey Haddix back to Crosley Field. Ted Kluszewski was still with the Pirates too. The Reds won the game 4–1, giving hope to their fans for the unfolding campaign, but by mid–May they were mired in the second division.

During the 1958 season the *Cincinnati Times-Star* had been acquired by its competing afternoon newspaper, the *Cincinnati Post.* Former *Times-Star* scribe Earl Lawson had been hired by the *Post* to cover baseball for the paper. One of the editors suggested to Lawson that he collaborate with one of the Reds players and ghostwrite a column for the paper. The idea was certainly nothing new. When Ted Kluszewski had been traded by the Reds to the Pirates the year before, he had agreed to write a column for the *Pittsburgh Press* called "Klu's Views." The column ran in the paper three times a week, and despite the fact that it was rather corny, not very newsworthy and rather gossipy, it was popular with the Pirates fans.

To the surprise of some at the *Post*, Lawson announced that he would like the Reds' Johnny Temple to write the column with him. Although the column would only pay $25.00 a week, Temple agreed to do it. The ghostwritten column was titled "Johnny-on-the-Spot," and like Kluszewski's blurb in the *Pittsburgh Press*, it was to be carried three times a week.

Earl Lawson had a gut feeling that Temple's ideas for the column might be controversial and he didn't let him down. On May 20 the Reds were in Los Angeles for a series with the Dodgers at the Coliseum. In the second game of a twi-night double-header won by the Reds 7–5, Frank Robinson was called out on strikes by home plate umpire Frank Dascoli to end the top of the ninth inning. A heated argument ensued and Johnny Temple got into the fray. As the jawfest continued, Temple asked Dascoli, "'You think you're Almighty, don't you?' To which Dascoli replied, 'Yes I do.'"[3]

Both games of the double-header with the Dodgers had been heated, somewhat emotional contests. There were players playing for both teams who had recently been on the other club. Former Reds Johnny Klippstein and Art Fowler were now pitching for the Dodgers. The second game at the Coliseum featured two starting pitchers who were former Ebbets Field icons: Carl Erskine, pitching for the Dodgers, and Don Newcombe, now pitching for the Reds. The Reds knocked Erskine out of the box in the top of the third inning while Newcombe pitched a complete game. On June 4, Carl Erskine would pitch against the Reds again at Crosley Field in relief of Denny McDevitt. It would be Erskine's last game and close out his twelve-year major league career, all with the Dodgers.

The umpires would throw three players out of the games during the double-header in Los Angeles. But Johnny Temple, who was not tossed out, would be the only player to be fined.

After the second game in Los Angeles, Johnny Temple was still irritated by Frank Dascoli's arrogant retort. The following day, when Earl Lawson asked Temple if he had any ideas for their next column, he suggested that they do one on umpires. Lawson agreed, wrote the column, then submitted it to Temple for approval. In the column Temple stated that he felt the umpires were "growing too sensitive and believed they were infallible."[4]

The result was that the column irritated the president of the National League, Warren Giles, and he fined Johnny Temple $75. Although Giles had sent Temple a letter informing him of the fine while stating that his newspaper column had no bearing on the matter, no one was buying it.

Earl Lawson wanted to run Warren Giles's letter to Temple in the newspaper alongside of his column. But when Temple conferred with Gabe Paul about the incident and asked if it would be all right to give Giles's letter to Lawson, Paul cautioned Temple to withhold it.

The fine against Temple was controversial and Gabe Paul suggested that he send a letter to Warren Giles explaining his side of the story. To that end, Temple sent a 330-word letter to Giles stating that he was being fined for doing nothing and that he felt he was being fined more for his remarks in the newspaper column than for his exchange with umpire Frank Dascoli.

Gabe Paul supported Temple by writing a separate letter to Warren Giles stating in part, "Please don't let anything Johnny wrote in his column have any effect on this, as it has no bearing on the report issued by Umpire Dascoli."[5]

When Giles issued a separate statement in which he indicated that Temple had been fined for his conduct and remarks with Dascoli and not for anything he wrote in the newspaper, the Reds' traveling secretary, John Murdough, who was witness to the dispute with Dascoli, stated that Temple did not use any profanity in the exchange.

At the time of the controversy, Johnny Temple was hitting above .340 and was tied for the lead in doubles in the National League with thirteen. The fine was paid and Temple continued to get base hits and continued to collaborate with Earl Lawson on his column while offering the public his often tantalizing and sometimes controversial opinions.

In his June 10 column, Temple would be so bold as to take a swipe at the National League's living legend Stan "The Man" Musial. Even if Temple's remarks were to be considered tongue-in-cheek, no one, be it sportswriter, baseball executive, opposing player, teammate, or fan, ever hinted of a disparaging word against "The Man." It was considered disharmonious to the game.

In the column Temple stated in part, "You hear lots of talk about Stan Musial being the 'nicest guy in baseball.' Me, I don't buy it. Don't get me wrong. I'm not saying Musial's not a nice guy. He is, but so are a lot of other fellows playing baseball. Maybe they should say Musial is the 'nicest rich guy in baseball.' When you're pulling down the money Musial has over the years, and you're blessed with his ability, it's pretty easy to be a nice guy. There's not much reason for a guy to be obnoxious when he's got health and wealth."[6]

But one "Johnny-on-the-Spot" column got Johnny called on the carpet by the Reds brass when he offered advice in the paper on how not to pitch to the Braves' Del Crandall. The Reds brass didn't take kindly to having unofficial scouting reports made public by a player.

On a road trip between May 8 and May 24, the Reds lost twelve out of eighteen games. The trip concluded with the Reds' being swept in a four-game weekend series with the Pirates. Slump-ridden Frank Thomas sat out three games of the Pittsburgh series with a jammed little finger on his throwing hand.

During the month of June, the Reds had once against lost more ball games than they won. Frank Thomas, both ailing and struggling, was hitting .229 and spending a lot of time on the bench. Outfielder Jim Pendleton took over at third base and back-up shortstop Eddie Kasko helped out once in a while. The Reds were becoming desperate for a third baseman. After huddling in his office for a few weeks attempting to devise a plan to fill the void, on July 1, 1959, Gabe Paul acquired veteran and former whiz kid, Willie "Puddin' Head" Jones from the Cleveland Indians for cash to fill the void.

As the month of July began, once again the Cincinnati fans were highly displeased with the Reds' performance and also with manager Mayo Smith. Some days the fans at Crosley Field acted more like the Paris mob than a crowd in a ballpark. The Reds players were not getting along with Smith either and talked about him behind his back. Jim Brosnan stated that he could never figure out how Mayo Smith got to be a big league manager. When Smith would come to the mound to say how he wanted a particular batter to be pitched to, Ed Bailey would tell him, "You don't know shit."[7]

Pitcher Bob Purkey said, "I liked Mayo, but I guess he was too easygoing. You lost a game, and it didn't seem to be important. Mayo would say, 'Well, we'll win tomorrow.'"[8]

Gabe Paul was getting restless with Mayo Smith and called former St. Louis Cardinals manager Fred Hutchinson, who had been let go by the Red Birds after the 1958 season. At the time Hutchinson was managing the Seattle club in the Pacific Coast League. Despite the fact that Seattle was in last place, Paul told Hutchinson that he might make a change. Hutchinson advised the Reds' general manager to not make a change. But Paul said, "The pressure was terrific in Cincinnati."[9] So Hutchinson agreed to take the job.

All this was taking place at the time of the first of the two 1959 All-Star Games. The Cincinnati Reds were in seventh place with a record of

Seven. A Deal That Sinks the Reds

35–45, 10½ games behind the league-leading Milwaukee Braves and 7 games out of the first division.

The Reds, however, were a better ball club than their won-lost record indicated. They had two of the top eight hitters in the league in their lineup: Johnny Temple was hitting .326 and Frank Robinson was hitting .323. Robinson was also second in the National League with 73 RBIs and had 18 home runs. Gus Bell was having a comeback year and by the All-Star break was hitting .263 with 11 home runs. Vada Pinson, playing in his first full season in the majors, was hitting .301 with 12 home runs. Willie Jones was by then playing third base and hitting .263. Even pitcher Don Newcombe was hitting .344 as a pinch hitter.

With the Reds' offensive resurgence, their dismal position in the standings at the All-Star break just didn't make sense, and while it may have been convenient for everyone to blame it all on Frank Thomas because he was only hitting .230, there was much more to the problem.

One of the Reds' most blatant weaknesses was once again the pitching. While Don Newcombe was the leading Reds starting pitcher with a record of 9–4, two of the starters were lagging: Bob Purkey was 7–9 and Brooks Lawrence 3–9. The bullpen was also struggling. The other weakness was lack of leadership from the dugout.

On July 8, Gabe Paul announced that Mayo Smith had been fired and that he had hired Fred Hutchinson. In his press release Paul stated, "Mayo was my personal choice as the Cincinnati manager and I deeply regret that things have worked out as they have."[10]

The first players' pension fund was established in 1947 when Major League Baseball was threatened by competition from the Mexican League. Then in 1954 a new pension agreement was negotiated by J. Norman Lewis assisted by two players, Ralph Kiner and Allie Reynolds. The agreement provided that the plan was to be funded by 60 percent of the radio and television proceeds of the All-Star Game and World Series and 60 percent of the net gate receipts of the All-Star Game.

Beginning in 1959 two All-Star Games would be played during the season and the practice would continue through 1962. The additional revenue generated from the second game was for the players' pension fund and for assisting needy old-time players, as well as giving a boost to youth baseball programs. Under the existing agreement with Major League Baseball, 60 percent of the gate receipts from the All-Star Game continued to be allocated to the players' pension fund. When the number of All-Star Games returned to one each season in 1963, the pension fund's share of gate receipts was increased to 95 percent and remained at that figure until 1967.

The first of the two 1959 All-Star Games was played in Pittsburgh on July 7. Johnny Temple was voted as the National League starting second baseman by the players, coaches and managers. It was the third time in his career that Temple had been voted as the league's starting second baseman. Frank Robinson and Vada Pinson were also chosen as reserves on the National League squad but would not appear in the game.

By now a lot of players and sportswriters were impressed with Pittsburgh Pirates' young second baseman Bill Mazeroski and felt that he was the best at the position in baseball. In fact, Mazeroski had won the 1958 Gold Glove for second baseman. But the mere suggestion that Mazeroski might be superior to him irritated Johnny Temple and he was vocal in expressing his dissatisfaction when he told a sportswriter, "Bill Mazeroski can't carry my glove."[11]

Temple's egotism on the matter was controversial and he was forced to expand on his assertion that he was a better second baseman than Mazeroski. Temple did acknowledge that Mazeroski was probably a better double play man than he. "I never saw a second baseman with quicker hands than Maz," said Temple. "I recognize talent when I see it. But I'd be defeating my own argument with Gabe Paul every year on contract if I conceded that Maz was better than I am. I believe I cover as much ground as Maz but maybe I'm not as spectacular. I like to believe that I get my share of the balls hit in my direction."[12]

Temple also admitted that while he didn't hit as many home runs as Mazeroski, he hit for a higher average and had more total bases than Maz. To that end, Temple was still smarting over being snubbed by his peers for selection to the 1958 All-Star squad and stated, "Do you know that last year when Maz was the All-Star second baseman, I was picked fourth? I was hitting .309 at the time, Maz was hitting .272."[13] Speaking in the third person, he concluded his remarks by stating he didn't believe that there were three second basemen in the league better than Johnny Temple.

An attempt to obtain a reply from Bill Mazeroski in regard to this historical assertion made by Johnny Temple was unsuccessful.

It is probably best to take Johnny Temple's historic boast in a context that looks at what each player, he and Mazeroski, contributed to the overall record of their respective teams during their careers rather than "*mano a mano*" (between the two of them). In other words, determine each player's value. Colin Wyers stated in *The Hardball Times* (January 22, 2009) that a player's value is determined by his contributions to his team based upon his on-field performance (hitting, running, fielding, pitching) in a neutral context.

Seven. A Deal That Sinks the Reds

Using such methods of comparison over the course of their careers would no doubt favor Bill Mazeroski with eight Gold Gloves and his epic game seven walk-off home run in the 1960 World Series. But at the time of Johnny Temple's boast in 1959, using the same methods of comparison would give Temple the edge.

It's really a classic "hot stove league" discussion in the same vein as who was the better all-round player: Jackie Robinson or Joe Morgan, Joe DiMaggio or Ted Williams, Mickey Mantle or Willie Mays, Bob Feller or Sandy Koufax, Johnny Bench or Yogi Berra, etc. One could Sabermetrics the issue of Temple vs. Mazeroski endlessly to quantify these arguments, yet in the end the only legitimate answer lies in the true sentiments of the fans.

Adding to the pre-game hype of the first All-Star Game in 1959 was a party held by the baseball writers the night before the game. One thousand people were in attendance at $15 a ticket. George Jessel was the toastmaster and former catcher turned broadcaster Joe Garagiola was the principal speaker. Johnny Temple, chosen as the National League's starting second baseman, was there in a dual role as a player and as a correspondent.

In regard to the affair, Temple wrote in his *Cincinnati Post* column "Johnny-on-the-Spot," "Heck! Even Richard Nixon, the vice-president turned out. The boys were still chuckling Tuesday in the clubhouse over Hank Aaron's introduction to Nixon. Ole Hank shook hands with him and then turned to someone and asked, 'Who's he?' Now I gotta' believe it when they tell me Hank never knows who he's hitting against."[14]

The Dodgers' side-armed hard-throwing right-hander Don Drysdale started for the National League and threw three perfect innings. Early Wynn of the White Sox started for the Americans.

Johnny Temple went to bat twice without a hit. In the bottom of the sixth inning with the score tied 1–1, Stan Musial pinch-hit for Temple, who was then replaced at second base by Bill Mazeroski, to the delight of the Pittsburgh hometown fans.

In the bottom of the seventh the Nationals scored twice to take the lead 3–1 on a double by Ernie Banks, then successive singles by Del Crandall and Bill Mazeroski.

In the top of the seventh the Pittsburgh Pirates' pint-sized reliever Elroy Face, 5'8" and 150 pounds, was sent to the mound by National League manager Fred Haney. Face had won 17 straight games in relief over a two-year period and was greeted by the Pittsburgh fans as he took the mound with a standing ovation.

Face proceeded to retire five straight batters, striking out two, but after two were out in the top of the eighth, the American League pounced on him, scoring three runs to take the lead 4–3, two of the runs coming on a bases-loaded double by the Baltimore Orioles Gus Triandos.

But the National League battled back and scored twice in the bottom of the eighth inning to regain the lead 5–4. One run was driven in by Hank Aaron, and what proved to be the winning run came on a triple by Willie Mays that hit the wall near the 436-foot mark in right field in spacious Forbes Field that scored Aaron. Don Elston of the Cubs then shut down the Americans in the top of the ninth.

The Cincinnati Reds started the second half of the 1959 season under new manager Fred Hutchinson by being swept in a three-game series with the San Francisco Giants at Crosley Field. The Reds closed out the month of July in seventh place with a season record of 47–55. Under Fred Hutchinson they won 12 games and lost 10 and were 14–14 overall for the month.

While the Reds' bullpen had been marginally improved with the addition of Jim Brosnan and Orlando Pena, they were still not winning many extra-inning games or close ones. The good news was that the team was scoring a lot more runs than they had a year ago.

Johnny Temple was still the Reds' leading hitter with a .328 batting average. Temple's 137 hits were second to Hank Aaron's 151 hits in the National League and more hits than any player in the American League but one, Nellie Fox. Frank Robinson was also continuing to have a fine season, hitting .321 with 89 RBIs, second in the National League. Vada Pinson was hitting .311 and Gus Bell .276. With Frank Thomas still on the bench and contributing very little to the team, Willie Jones continued to hold down third base, hitting .261 while being backed up by Eddie Kasko.

The second All-Star Game in 1959 was played on August 3 in Los Angeles. Having a second All-Star Game during the season was not without controversy and disliked by many fans and some players. Baseball Commissioner Ford Frick addressed the issue by stating, "The second All-Star Game is as much for the fans as the first. It's our only way to raise money for the pension plan and old-time players. But if it takes anything away from the first All-Star Game we'll discontinue it."[15]

Frick's defense of the second game did not preclude a few notable players from going on record expressing their concerns about holding two All-Star Games.

Stan "The Man" Musial, of the St. Louis Cardinals, a veteran of sixteen All-Star Games at that time, said: "It just didn't seem like the same game. The first game takes something away from the second."[16]

Johnny Temple went a little further with his remarks. "It's just another exhibition game in my opinion," said Temple. "I would like to point out that despite reports to the contrary, that the players voted against—not for—the second all-star game. We [the players] were told after the votes were in that we would have to go through with the second game as the radio and television rights had already been sold."[17]

The second All-Star Game in 1959 was played in the Los Angeles Coliseum with 54,982 on hand. The managers were not bound to start the same players chosen for the first All-Star Game in the second. Also some of the pitchers and reserve players were added to the roster for the second game not chosen to be on the first game roster.

A few players with injuries decided not to participate, such as the Braves' Eddie Mathews, who was nursing a hip injury; the Giants' Orlando Cepeda due to a wrist injury; and Baltimore catcher Gus Triandos because of an injured hand. Also Harvey Kuenn of Detroit and Gil McDougald of the New York Yankees sat out with ailments.

The starting pitcher for the National League was Don Drysdale of the Los Angeles Dodgers, who had started the first All-Star Game in Pittsburgh. Twenty-year old Jerry Walker of the Baltimore Orioles started for the American League. At the time Walker was the youngest starting pitcher in an All-Star Game. He would remain so until the 1986 All-Star Game, when 19-year old Dwight Gooden of the New York Mets was the starting pitcher for the National League.

The American League won the game 5–3 on home runs by the Yankees' Yogi Berra (a two-run shot), the Indians' Rocky Colavito and the Red Sox Frank Malzone. The other Americans run came on three errors by the Nationals in the seventh inning.

Two Cincinnati Reds played key roles in the National League's losing effort. The first was Johnny Temple, who led off for the Nationals in first inning by driving a pitch from Walker to left field that Ted Williams overran, letting the ball get by him and roll to the wall for a double. One out later, after taking third on a bouncing grounder by Ken Boyer, Temple scored on a sacrifice fly by Hank Aaron, pushing Yogi Berra aside as he crossed the plate.

In the fifth inning Jim Gilliam of the Los Angeles Dodgers would pinch-hit for Temple and draw a walk. Later in the seventh inning Gilliam would hit a home run.

Frank Robinson had been nursing an injured right thumb and been in a slump, not having a hit in his last twenty-three trips to the plate, and had not hit a home run since July 15. But Robinson insisted on playing and entered the game, replacing Stan Musial at first base, and hit a solo home run in the fifth inning off Early Wynn of the Chicago White Sox. Robinson also had two singles. The Cincinnati contingent of Johnny Temple and Frank Robinson wound up having four of the National League's six hits in the game and accounted for two of their three runs. Vada Pinson entered the game as a pinch runner for Joe Cunningham in the fifth inning.

On September 2 the Reds were in fifth place, 10½ games behind league-leading Milwaukee, and it was apparent that it was only a matter of time before they would be eliminated from the 1959 National League pennant race.

That day the fourth-place Pittsburgh Pirates, trailing Milwaukee by just 4½ games with an outside shot at the pennant, arrived at Crosley Field for a double-header with the Reds. But the Reds would quickly put a damper on the Pirates' pennant hopes by sweeping the twin bill, leaving them 7 games behind.

In the first game, the Reds defeated the Pirates 6–3 as Jim O'Toole pitched a complete game. Willie Jones delivered the "coup de grace" to the Bucs, hitting a three-run home run off reliever Elroy Face. Although Face gave up the homer he was not charged with the loss because starter Vern Law had put two men on. Vada Pinson and Frank Robinson had also homered in the game.

In the second game, Don Newcombe went the distance against the Pirates as the Reds beat Bob Friend 2–1. The winning run for the Reds came with two out in the eighth inning when Johnny Temple tripled and then scored on Vada Pinson's 44th double of the season.

Actually it was a bit surprising that the Pirates were still in contention so late in the season. The season had been a three-way battle for the top between the Braves, Giants and Dodgers. With eight games left on the schedule, the Giants had a two-game lead over both the Braves and Dodgers. The San Francisco front office was feeling so confident of winning the pennant that they were having a discussion about whether to play the World Series in cozy little Seals Stadium or attempt to play it in Candlestick Park, their new home, still under construction.

But the issue was solved on September 19 when the Dodgers swept a double-header from the Giants at Seals Stadium. The Dodgers moved into first place and held firm down the stretch. The Giants proceeded to lose seven out of their last eight games to the Cardinals and Cubs and finished in third place, three games behind the Braves and Dodgers, who finished in a tie for first.

Johnny Temple wasn't surprised that the Giants blew the pennant.

Seven. A Deal That Sinks the Reds

"I'm not mentioning names," said Temple, "but we could see some of those players getting too tense. And Daryl Spencer, their second baseman, obviously got tired. He seems to be the kind of player who starts off fast and then fades. I could tell by his movements that he was a mighty tired boy toward the end of the season."[18]

In fact the San Francisco Giants did make Daryl Spencer the fall guy for their stretch drive pennant collapse, and following the season traded him to the St. Louis Cardinals along with Leon Wagner for second baseman Don Blasingame.

Meanwhile the Braves were teetering, winning one day, losing the next, and on the final day of the season wound up tied with the Dodgers for first place with a record of 86–68.

Then the Dodgers polished off the Braves, winning the first two games of a planned best-of-three game playoff series. The Dodgers won the pennant after spending only 18 days in first place during the season, as compared to the Braves and Giants, who had each spent 86 days at the top of the standings.

The Reds finished the 1959 season in a tie for fifth place with the Chicago Cubs with a record of 74–80 (35–45 under Mayo Smith and 39–35 under Fred Hutchinson).

While the 1959 Reds had finished in the second division, they were a greatly improved ball club over the 1958 edition. In 1959 the Reds scored a major league leading 764 runs. The Reds also led both National and American Leagues in doubles (258), batting average (.274), and slugging average (.427). The Reds' pitching staff tied the Los Angeles Dodgers for most saves in the National League with 26. Lastly the Reds were once again hitting home runs and the team's production rose by 24 percent (161 to 123) over the 1958 club.

The 1959 season would be the best in Johnny Temple's major league career. He hit .311, with 8 home runs and 67 RBIs. In addition Temple set the Cincinnati club record for sacrifice flies in a season with 13, a mark that still stands.

Frank Thomas had a miserable season. He played in only 108 games, playing just 64 games at third base while hitting .225 with 12 home runs and 47 RBIs. Thomas was truly sorry that he had let the team down and let the Reds' fans down. While he experienced a large share of boos at Crosley Field, it was really Gabe Paul, not Thomas, whom the fans were most angry at. It had been Paul who hired Mayo Smith and traded Smoky Burgess, Don Hoak and Harvey Haddix.

Although the Pittsburgh Pirates finished in fourth place in 1959,

Smoky Burgess and Don Hoak had played well. Burgess had been an All-Star. On May 26 Harvey Haddix had pitched one of the greatest games in major league history, throwing a perfect game for twelve innings against the hard-hitting Milwaukee Braves, before losing the game in the thirteenth inning. Haddix, while an average starter, had been popular in his brief tenure in Cincinnati, and his incredible pitching performance had really agitated Cincinnati Reds fans still disgruntled with his trade to Pittsburgh.

Thanks to the generosity of Gabe Paul and the Cincinnati Reds, the pieces were coming together on the Pirates' puzzle for what general manager Joe Brown and owner John W. Galbreath saw as a pennant contender for the 1960s. The acquisition of Burgess, Hoak and Haddix, joining Pirates stars such as Roberto Clemente, Dick Groat, Bill Mazeroski, Vern Law, Bob Friend and Elroy Face, gave the Pirates a lineup strong defensively, offensively and on the mound. Joe Brown even attempted to add more power to his lineup by acquiring Roger Maris from the Kansas City Athletics, but was outmaneuvered by the New York Yankees, who were able to swing a seven-player deal with the A's on December 11, 1959.

In the case of the debacle that the Frank Thomas trade had become for the Reds, Gabe Paul knew that he had to do something to make sure that he could not be blamed or criticized later for not taking action. Paul needed to get Frank Thomas and his huge contract out of sight and out of the minds of the Cincinnati fans and press. Following the season, on December 9, 1959, Paul traded Thomas to the Chicago Cubs for veteran left-handed relief pitcher Bill Henry; Lou Jackson, an outfielder who had a cup of coffee in the major leagues; and Lee Walls, an outfielder who could also play third base if needed.

Former New York Yankees pitcher and future Hall of Fame member Waite Hoyt had been the Cincinnati Reds' primary radio broadcaster calling play-by-play action since 1942. The Frank Thomas for Bill Henry trade with the Chicago Cubs was very unpopular with Hoyt. The Reds were in bad need of pitching and Hoyt had told Gabe Paul they he could acquire Chicago White Sox pitcher Dick Donovan for Thomas but he turned the deal down.

In five seasons with the White Sox, Dick Donovan had posted a record of 67–49. He had been the fourth starter on the Chicago White Sox pennant-winning team in 1959 with a record of 9–10. Donovan would pitch in the American League for fifteen years, posting a career record of 122–99. His best year was with the Cleveland Indians in 1962 when he went 22–10.

Seven. A Deal That Sinks the Reds

In a letter to newly appointed Hall of Fame historian and longtime friend Lee Allen, Hoyt stated, "Guess by now you have digested all the 'ramifications' of the Henry deal. Although I cannot say we suffered too much—as Thomas is a negative character who isn't generally liked, and who must do it all in a big way to be of value. Of course, we didn't get a pennant in return, but we couldn't expect that. The sad note is that I hear we could have had Dick Donovan from the White Sox for Thomas—but as always I guess numbers appeal to Gabe more than specific quality."[19]

Upon acquiring Frank Thomas, the Chicago Cubs made an appointment for him with their team physician. Surgery performed on Thomas's hand revealed that tumors had been growing around a nerve.

As if the Frank Thomas fiasco weren't enough stress for Gabe Paul in the fall of 1959, he also had to deal with ghost of Ted Kluszewski, who came charging out the past to become a World Series hero in Chicago even though the White Sox lost the series to the Los Angeles Dodgers four games to two. Late in 1959 the Pirates had dealt Kluszewski to the White Sox. In the 1959 World Series, Big Klu hit .391 (9 for 23) with 3 home runs and had 10 RBIs. His ten RBIs were a record at that time for a six-game series. He also equaled three other records.

Kluszewski's old bosses Powell Crosley, Jr., and Gabe Paul were present for game one of the 1959 World Series at Comiskey Park when he hit two home runs, while going 3 for 4 and driving home five runs in an 11–0 rout of the Dodgers. That night in Cincinnati there was some subtle criticism of Gabe Paul about giving up on the former Reds home run king.

In December, still needing a third baseman, Gabe Paul approached Washington Senators owner Calvin Griffith and offered him $500,000 for 23-year-old slugger Harmon Killebrew. In the 1959 season that saw the Senators finish last in the American League, Killebrew had hit just .242 but tied Cleveland's Rocky Colavito as the league leader in home runs with 42. Griffith turned the deal down, forcing Paul and manager Fred Hutchinson to look inside the Reds' organization for someone to cover the hot corner in 1960.

Gabe Paul was still desperate for starting pitching too and he wanted a first baseman, so Frank Robinson, who had played 125 games at first in the 1959 season, could be returned to his natural position in the outfield.

On December 15, 1959, Paul shocked the entire Cincinnati community when, just before the midnight deadline for inter-league trades, he traded popular Johnny Temple to the Cleveland Indians for three players: pitcher Cal McLish, veteran second baseman Billy Martin, and minor league first baseman Gordy Coleman.

The trade of Johnny Temple was front-page news in Cincinnati and elsewhere—he was just 31 years old and had his best season in the majors in 1959 when he hit for an average of .311 and been named an All-Star for the third time. Johnny Temple was one of the most popular players to ever wear a Cincinnati Reds uniform. Furthermore, at that time Temple was getting national media attention. Two weeks after he was traded to Cleveland, a five-page article featuring Temple, "Roughneck At Second Base," written by Furman Bisher, was published in the January 1960 issue of *Sport* magazine.

In the eight seasons that Johnny Temple had been with the Cincinnati Reds he had played in 964 games, had 1054 hits, 15 home runs, 300 RBIs and hit for an average of .290, while he and shortstop Roy McMillan had become recognized as the best double play combination in the major leagues.

Although it has been more than a half century since Johnny Temple last donned a Reds jersey, his name still resonates among the all-time Cincinnati Reds batting leaders. Through the 2014 season Temple still had the 15h highest OBP (On Base Percentage), .372, in the history of the Reds franchise. Furthermore, Temple's .372 OBP is higher than the OBPs of some very elite players among Cincinnati Reds all-time team leaders, such as Barry Larkin .371, Ken Griffey, Sr. 370, Ken Griffey, Jr. .362, Ernie Lombardi .359, George Foster .356, Bid McPhee .355, Tony Perez .346 and Ted Kluszewski .302.

Johnny Temple was emotionally devastated by the trade to Cleveland. After spending eight summers in Cincinnati, Temple and his wife Becky had come to have great affection for the community and for the Reds' fans. Neither could ever see him putting on any other uniform than the Cincinnati Reds. Gabe Paul didn't even have the decency to call Temple after trading him. Instead he delegated the task to traveling secretary John Murdough. Recently Temple and his wife had bought a home in Tampa, Florida, where the Reds held spring training. Also Temple was operating a business in Tampa, so he was concerned about what effect his long-term absence would have on the enterprise. The Cleveland Indians trained in Arizona.

When Dick Forbes, sportswriter for the *Cincinnati Enquirer*, called Temple at his home, he found him in tears—sobbing over the phone, saying he could never understand why it was happening to him. Regaining his composure, Temple told Forbes, "It shook me pretty badly. Nobody knows how I feel about it. I don't see how anybody could leave Cincinnati and not feel sorry about it. There's bound to be some regret. Fellows like

Gus Bell, Joe Nuxhall, Roy McMillan and myself—we've been together all the way. I didn't want to be traded, but since I am, I'm glad it's to the other league so I won't have to play against my old teammates."[20]

In a farewell "Johnny-on-the-Spot" column published in the *Cincinnati Post & Times Star* on December 16, 1959, Temple thanked the Cincinnati fans, stating in part, "It will sure feel funny looking down and not seeing those red stockings. I always felt that if Mr. Paul wanted to improve the pitching, he'd have to trade either Roy McMillan or me. But I don't see why it had to be me. No matter where I go, I know that fans will never be nicer than you Red fans have been to me and my family. It seems to me there's a closeness between ballplayers and fans in Cincinnati that you never find any place else."

It wasn't surprising that the Cleveland Indians would give up three players for Johnny Temple. Indians general manager Frank Lane, sometimes referred to in the press and baseball circles as "Trader Lane," had a reputation for trading players.

During his tenure as a big league general manager with the Chicago White Sox (1948–1955), St. Louis Cardinals (1956–1957), Cleveland Indians (1958–1960), Kansas City Athletics (1961) and Milwaukee Brewers (1971–1972), "Trader Lane" would be involved in 241 deals involving 353 players. He traded players with reckless abandon. Many of the trades made no sense and would be considered some of the worst in baseball history.

No one was immune to Lane's compulsive penchant for trading ballplayers. In fact, no one was immune to his whims. While general manager of the St. Louis Cardinals, even though he would deny it, Lane attempted to trade Stan Musial to the Philadelphia Phillies for pitcher Robin Roberts. Apparently Cardinals owner Gus Busch had to intercede and block the deal.

Nonetheless Lane did succeed in trading Red Schoendienst, the second most popular Red Bird on the team, during his tenure at St. Louis.

In the 1950s comedian Bob Hope was a minor share owner in the Indians when he stated, "I'm afraid to go to Cleveland, Frank Lane might trade me."[21]

Lane hired Bobby Bragan to manage the Indians in 1958, but after half a season with a record of 31–36, he fired him and replaced him with Joe Gordon. When Lane called Bragan to inform him he was being let go he stated, "Bobby, I don't know how we are going to get along without you, but starting tomorrow, we're going to try."[22]

On paper the trade with the Reds didn't look that bad. Cal McLish had been the Cleveland Indians' winningest pitcher the past two seasons.

In 1958 McLish had been 16–8. In 1959 he had won 19 games and lost 8 with an ERA of 3.63 over 235⅓ innings—all tops on the Indians staff.

Calvin Coolidge Tecumseh McLish was part Indian. He had bounced around the major and minor leagues for fourteen years. At the age of eighteen in 1944 he broke into the National League with Brooklyn then went on to pitch for Pittsburgh and Chicago. But McLish had never been a winning pitcher in the big leagues and wound up pitching in the Pacific Coast League between 1952 and 1955 before returning to the major leagues in 1956 with Cleveland. But now McLish was 34 years old, raising the question of how long he could still pitch and at what level of competition. Cal McLish contended that he was traded because general manager Frank Lane had never liked him.

Billy Martin, whom most fans still associated with the New York Yankees dynasty of the early 1950s, was expected to take over Temple's position at second base. But Martin was also 31 years old, nearing the end of his career; his knee would occasionally give out on him and he was becoming a part-time player. In 1959 Martin hit .260 for the Indians but played in only 73 games, having had his jaw broken in August after getting hit with a pitch thrown by Tex Clevenger of the Washington Senators. Among other physical injuries Martin had endured during the season was a separated shoulder that occurred when he was fielding a bunt.

When asked by the press about the trade to Cincinnati, Billy Martin remarked, "So I'm out of the American League because [manager] Joe Gordon doesn't like me."[23]

The Cleveland Indians finished second in the American League in 1959, five games behind the Chicago "Go-Go-Sox." The New York Yankees finished third. Billy Martin felt the Indians should have won the pennant but were handicapped by the prejudice toward him held by manager Joe Gordon. Martin disliked that Gordon would pinch-hit for him at times he considered the wrong times. Gordon had tried to bench Martin but was ordered by general manager Frank Lane to put him back in the lineup. Martin was of the opinion that because Joe Gordon let his personal feelings toward him get in the way of his responsibility to manage the team correctly, it cost the Indians the pennant.

But Frank Lane felt that Joe Gordon was more than capable of evaluating the skills of second baseman. Lane stated, "Gordon, who played the position so well that he should know a second baseman when he sees one, rated Martin nothing more than a mouthy guy without ability. Anyway, it was either Gordon or Martin and I already decided on the manager."[24]

In his playing days Joe "Flash" Gordon was a nine-time All-Star. Gordon had taken over second base for the pre–World War II New York Yankees from Tony Lazzeri in 1938 and proceeded to become the American League MVP in 1942. Gordon played in five World Series with the Bronx Bombers, winning four rings. In the 1941 series when the Yankees defeated the Brooklyn Dodgers, Gordon hit .500.

In 1947, after playing in 1000 games and getting 1000 hits for the New York Yankees, Joe Gordon was traded to the Cleveland Indians for pitcher Allie Reynolds. At Cleveland in 1948, Gordon teamed up with Indians player manager-shortstop Lou Boudreau to play an integral part in bringing Cleveland its first pennant in twenty-eight years. For his part, Gordon hit 32 home runs and had 124 RBIs. The Indians then proceeded to defeat the Boston Braves in the 1948 World Series. In 1951 Joe Gordon retired after eleven years in the major leagues with time out for service in World War II. Gordon's 246 career home runs are still the American League record for a second baseman. In 2009 Joe Gordon was elected to Hall of Fame by the Veterans' Committee.

The wild card in the Cleveland-Cincinnati trade was 25-year-old first baseman Gordy Coleman. At 6'3" and 208 pounds, Coleman looked like a great prospect. In 1959 Coleman had led the Southern Association with a .355 batting average, hit 35 home runs and had 125 RBIs. He was a late season call-up by the Indians and hit for an average of .533, going 8 for 15.

At the time, Vic Power was playing first base for the Indians and had been selected to the American League 1959 All-Star squad. Also the Indians had 26-year-old Tito Francona, who was going to play behind Power. So Coleman was excited about going to Cincinnati, where he felt that he had a chance to play regularly.

At Cleveland, Johnny Temple would be joining an infield that was made up of Vic Power at first base, Woodie Held at shortstop and Bubba Phillips at third base, just acquired from the White Sox. When Frank Lane had taken over as general manager in Cleveland during the winter of 1957–1958 he inherited what one sportswriter referred to as a leaky infield consisting of Vic Wertz, Chico Carrasquel and Billy Harrell. The 1960 Indian infield promised to be second to none.

For some unknown reason National League president Warren Giles felt compelled to add his two cents to the volume of comments occurring throughout the baseball world in regard to the Temple trade. Giles was quoted as saying he thought that Cincinnati got the best of the deal because Temple was a good hitter but his fielding was overrated.

When Temple was advised of Giles's comments, he quickly sent off a telegram to him stating, "No one has ever overrated you as National League president."[25]

Frank Lane called Johnny Temple one of the best second basemen in baseball. "We didn't get him cheap. But getting him gives us a pretty damn good infield—the best one Cleveland has had for many years, both offensively and defensively."[26]

When asked about the players he gave in the trade, Lane stated, "We gave up a fine pitcher in McLish and a pretty good second baseman in Billy Martin, who will probably play second in Cincinnati. Naturally we didn't think Martin had all the ability that Temple had or we wouldn't have made the deal."[27]

The facts were that Johnny Temple had a .290 lifetime batting average and in exchange for him the Reds were getting Billy Martin, who had a lifetime batting average of .260. In regard to the loss of Temple, Gabe Paul remarked, "I hated to see him go. But our club was the best offensive team in the National League last year and we still finished in a tie for fifth place. We had to get pitching ... we had to gamble."[28]

The sad fact is that if Waite Hoyt's assertion was accurate that Gabe Paul could have got Dick Donovan from the Chicago White Sox for Frank Thomas—heads up—then he would not have needed to gamble. Paul would have got a quality pitcher for the Reds and at the same time been able to keep Johnny Temple and perhaps even keep his own job in Cincinnati.

Eight

Traded to Cleveland

The 1959 Cleveland Indians would be the franchise's last pennant-contending team for over the next three decades. The 1960 edition of the Indians that Johnny Temple would join was a team in disarray.

The decline of the Indians was greatly influenced by Frank Lane during his controversial tenure as general manager from 1958 to 1960. After arriving in Cleveland following the1957 season, "Trader Lane" quickly began to rearrange the Indians' roster by freely dealing the team's star players, such as future Hall of Fame pitcher Early Wynn, and young prospects such as outfielders Al Smith and Roger Maris.

Roger Maris had hit 14 home runs as a rookie for the Indians in 1957, then Lane dealt him to the Kansas City Athletics along with Dick Tomanek and Preston Ward for Woodie Held and Vic Power.

Early Wynn and Al Smith went to the Chicago White Sox for infielder Fred Hatfield and outfielder Minnie Minoso. During his nine years with the Indians between 1949 and 1957, Early Wynn had been a twenty-game winner four times and in 1954 led the American League with twenty-three wins, helping the Indians to capture the American League pennant.

During the entire 1959 season the Cleveland Indians had been locked in a heated battle for the American League pennant with the Chicago White Sox. The defending and perennial American League champion New York Yankees struggled throughout the 1959 season, plagued with injuries to many key players, and the sudden decline of the competitiveness of the Bronx Bombers was a total surprise to the entire American League.

Notwithstanding injuries to key players, a lot of the problems began when several Yankees players, including Mickey Mantle and Whitey Ford, began the season disgruntled, having received salary cuts from general manager George Weiss after winning the World Series in 1958. Weiss defended his action by stating that the ballclub needed to end the continuous spiral of Yankees pay raises.

Mickey Mantle had injured his shoulder in the 1957 World Series in a collision with the Braves' Red Schoendienst. Early in the 1959 campaign, Mantle reinjured the shoulder making a throw from centerfield. Then, in early May, he was hit by pitch during batting practice and suffered a chipped bone in his right index finger. Unlike past seasons when the Yankees needed a home run from Mantle, in 1959 he didn't come through. As a result of his injuries Mickey Mantle hit only .285, with 31 home runs and 75 RBIs in the 1959 season. It was Mantle's lowest batting average and RBI total since his rookie season of 1951.

Other key players, such as Gil McDougald and Bill "Moose" Skowron, suffered from back ailments. Although Skowron hit well when he played and finished with 14 home runs, he played in only 74 games. Also, dependable veteran right fielder Hank Bauer turned 37 years old and began to show his age at the plate, hitting just .238.

Then the Yankees' pitching collapsed. In 1958 "Bullet" Bob Turley had won the Cy Young Award with a record of 21–7; in 1959 he was 8–11 and appeared tired. While Whitey Ford finished the season with a record of 16–10, in the early part he was ineffective.

On May 26, 1959, after getting pounded by the Boston Red Sox 12–2 at Yankee Stadium, the New York Yankees had fallen into last place for the first time since 1940. Following the game, manager Casey Stengel was so frustrated when being interviewed by Leonard Shecter of the *New York Post* he wandered naked out of his office into the clubhouse and shouted to his players, "You want to know who's pitching tomorrow, ask Schecter. You want to know who's playing, ask Schecter. He's been running this club for three years. Yeah, Schecter."[1]

While the Yankees experienced a resurgence in June, winning 17 out of 23 games to pull within 1½ games of first-place Cleveland on June 20, during July they began to slip back down in the standings and never made another serious challenge to reach the top.

The end for the 1959 Yankees came in July when they lost three out of four games to the Chicago White Sox at Comiskey Park. A few days later Mickey Mantle hurt his right ankle and the Yankees finished with a record of 12–16 in July. The Yankees finished the 1959 campaign in third place, fifteen games out of first place.

The Chicago White Sox would take over first place in the American League on July 28 and would win their first season series with the New York Yankees (13–9) since 1925.

But the Cleveland Indians just kept challenging the White Sox for the lead, led by Rocky Colavito with 42 home runs, and Tito Francona, coming off the bench hitting for an average of .363 in 399 at bats with 20 home runs.

Tito Francona had played for three teams since coming up to the major leagues three years before the 1959 season. He was acquired by Frank Lane during spring training on March 21 from Detroit for Larry Doby. Francona's success was a surprise to everyone in baseball, prompting future Hall of Fame member George Kell to remark, "If somebody told you last March that Francona would be the best hitter in the American League, you'd be calling for the man in the white coat."[2]

On August 26, 1959, the Chicago White Sox were leading the American League by one game over the Cleveland Indians as the pennant stretch drive began. Straight ahead for the Indians was a crucial four-game series with the White Sox in Cleveland, August 28–30. Chicago swept the four-game series from Cleveland and opened a five-and-a-half-game lead.

Then on September 7, with the Cleveland Indians still hanging in there, the Chicago White Sox swept a double-header from the Kansas City Athletics to remain four and a half games in the lead.

With former Indians ace Early Wynn on the mound, the Chicago White Sox clinched the 1959 American League pennant on September 22, before 54,293 onlookers at Cleveland's Municipal Stadium with a 4–2 win over the Indians. For Early Wynn it was his twenty-first win of the year.

For the White Sox it was their first American League pennant in forty years, since the days of their founding father, Charles A. Comiskey, calling the shots. The jubilation in the Windy City was widespread and not just on the South Side. In celebration of the pennant, Mayor Richard J. Daley had all the civil defense sirens in the city activated.

With good pitching the Chicago White Sox had the ability to win close games, and by mid–September they had won 31 of 41 one-run games. Without Early Wynn's league-leading 22 wins, the White Sox would not have won the 1959 pennant.

During the 1959 season the Cleveland Indians had spent sixty-four days in first place. The Indians finished first in the American League in team home runs with 167 and first with a team batting average of .263 and first in team slugging with an average of .408, as opposed to the White Sox, who finished eighth in home runs with 97, eighth in slugging average with .364, and seventh place with a team batting average of .250.

The Indians didn't win the pennant because they couldn't beat the

White Sox when the two teams went head-to-head. The Indians finished the 1959 season with a record of 7–15 vs. the White Sox. The Indians had a superior season record against every other club in the league with the exception of the New York Yankees, whom they finished with an 11–11 record against.

Following the 1959 season, Indians general manager Frank Lane began to wheel and deal his players at a frantic if not neurotic pace. The acquisition of Johnny Temple on December 15 from the Cincinnati Reds for pitcher Cal McLish, second baseman Billy Martin and reserve first baseman Gordy Coleman was just the beginning of the numerous changes Lane would make on the Indians roster prior to the 1960 season.

Three days earlier Lane had traded outfielder Minnie Minoso, who had 21 home runs, 92 RBIs and hit .302 in the 1959 season, along with back-up catcher Dick Brown, left-handed pitcher Don Ferrarese and pitcher Jake Striker to the Chicago White Sox for catcher John Romano, third baseman Bubba Philips and first baseman Norm Cash.

When Johnny Temple joined the Indians, his journalism collaborative efforts with *Cincinnati Post & Times Star* reporter Earl Lawson in his column "Johnny-on-the-Spot" became an immediate concern of Frank Lane's as a result of pitcher/author Jim Brosnan's recent success.

Over the winter, Cincinnati Reds relief pitcher Jim Brosnan wrote an article for *Sports Illustrated*, published in the March 7, 1960, edition, about his one-sided contract negotiations in 1959 with St. Louis Cardinals general manager Bing Devine and the dull spring training ritual that manager Solly Hemus subjected the team to. Brosnan had been traded to the Reds from the Cardinals during the 1959 season and his article portrayed Devine as penny-pinching and Hemus as cartoon-like. Also Brosnan was so bold as to reveal the Cardinals signs in his article.

Harper & Brothers liked what they saw in the potential of Brosnan's writing style and offered him a contract to chronicle a whole season in a book. During spring training in 1960, Brosnan's first book, *The Long Season* was about to be published; it told the no-holds-barred story of his experiences in the 1959 season with the St. Louis Cardinals and Cincinnati Reds.

Jim Brosnan went on to author a second book a couple of years later, *Pennant Race*, and do many feature magazine articles. His style of sportswriting became a model for the glut of first-person sports memoirs that came on the book market throughout the 1960s and 1970s, such as *Ball Four* (Jim Bouton), *Veeck as in Wreck* (Bill Veeck, Jr.), *Out of Their League* (Dave Meggyesy), *Instant Replay* (Jerry Kramer) and many more.

Brosnan's style of journalism, using a diary format, was new for the sports genre, and the end product unnerved the baseball establishment. Many in baseball saw it as a violation of the major league's unwritten code that what happened in the locker room stayed in the locker room.

As a result of Brosnan's popularity, many front office executives wanted to nip the aspirations of other potential player-authors in the bud, but at the same time they didn't want to insult a group who might start buying ink in barrels. So in the spring of 1960 a rather strange relationship seemed to be developing, in which managers and general managers were suddenly advocating protection for newspaper baseball writer's rights.

Also there were some in the baseball community who were downright jealous and contemptuous of Jim Brosnan's work. Joe Garagiola, a former major league catcher turned broadcaster, had just penned a book, *Baseball Is a Funny Game,* that was released in January 1960, and he didn't like the competition that Brosnan's book created. In an effort to belittle the competition, Garagiola called Jim Bronsan "a kooky beatnik."[3]

As spring training began for the Cleveland Indians in March 1960 at Tucson, Arizona, general manager Frank Lane issued his first edict—no player on the Indians roster would be permitted to participate in any form of writing for newspapers or magazines. It was aimed directly at newly acquired second baseman Johnny Temple.

The previous season Johnny Temple had a ghost-written column that appeared in the *Cincinnati Post & Times Star*. Temple had received a similar offer from a Cleveland newspaper, but Frank Lane quickly stepped in to block it. Lane was convinced that a writing player was bound to make trouble. "The Cleveland club had plenty of trouble when Early Wynn did a newspaper column," said Lane, "and I don't want a recurrence. I told Temple he would do well to devote himself entirely to his second-base job and to leave the writing business to those who make a living out of it."[4]

Temple ungrudgingly took Lane's advice, and during spring training in Tucson he worked hard at getting adjusted to his new keystone partner Woodie Held. He had played eight seasons alongside the flashy Roy McMillan and it required a protracted break-in period to feel comfortable with a new shortstop. Long after other players had left the field for the showers, Temple and Held continued to work out at second base. Held practiced feeding the ball to Temple for the first out in a double play, learning how to make the soft toss of the ball right across the Cleveland letters on his uniform.

After the emotional crises triggered by being traded by the Reds had subsided, Johnny Temple began to envision his new task environment in

Cleveland as a possible opportunity. He was hopeful that he would get the recognition in the American League that he never got in the National League.

Temple still had supreme confidence and considered himself a team leader. "Every team needs a man to take charge," said Temple, "and I consider myself a take-charge guy. Every club has to have somebody on the field who can lead, somebody to take the initiative, somebody to take the blame and I understand they didn't have it here last year."[5]

But the reality was that Johnny Temple was still learning how to become team leader. He lacked gravitas (a very serious quality or manner).

A case in point occurred in the previous season when Temple had approached Cincinnati Reds outfielder Jerry Lynch and accused him of not hustling in a game at Los Angeles. After a line drive got by shortstop Eddie Kasko, attempting to make a diving catch, Lynch was slow reacting in the outfield and failed to back up the play. When the inning ended and the Reds players returned to the bench, there was Temple waiting for Lynch. He proceeded to berate Lynch, telling him that he if he wanted to lie down don't do it here.

Johnny Temple, 1960 (Cleveland Indians).

Temple's accusation infuriated Lynch and he challenged Temple to fight him. Once again as had happened numerous times before, teammates stepped between Temple and another player to restore order.

It wasn't just another case of Johnny Temple not being able to bite his lip. He simply failed to realize a basic fundamental of leadership: it is not necessary to humiliate someone in order to make your point. But Temple's fiery personality would just not allow him to separate combativeness from motivation when it came to being critical of a teammate, and as a result, he was always on the edge of leadership, not out in front of it.

Looking back at his days in Cincinnati and attempting to rationalize why he wasn't accepted as the team leader, Temple remarked, "I felt I was capable of taking charge, but I sensed that the fellows didn't think I was. I felt they didn't respect me enough."[6]

But it wasn't a case of teammates not respecting him. As a fellow ballplayer, they did. The problem was that Johnny Temple failed to recognize that leadership has boundaries and greatly depends on the team leader's being able to manage relationships between external and internal environments in such a way that permits fellow players to perform their individual tasks on the field in a highly functional capacity. Temple's self-appointed role on the team was not legitimate and rather disruptive. He was incapable of filling the gap in organizational leadership between the team's manager and team's players, or more plainly stated—he took it upon himself to act as the unofficial team captain of the Cincinnati Reds. But his teammates simply rejected his attempts to take charge and that created chaos.

Nonetheless Johnny Temple continued to attempt to take charge, using the only methods that he knew. In early April at Tucson, Temple was thumbed out of an exhibition game against the Boston Red Sox by home plate umpire Ed Runge after coming to the defense of Indians rookie Walt Bond. In the eighth inning, Bond ran by Red Sox first baseman Ron Jackson and Runge called him out for interference. It wasn't necessary to call interference because Jackson had caught the ball that Bond had popped up. But when Runge gave the signal for interference, it prompted Temple to get up on the top step of the dugout and yell at Runge, telling him to get off the kid.

Runge was outraged, ripped off his mask and asked Temple what he had said. Temple replied, "I said get off Bond. He's a young kid trying to make the ball club and you've been on him since the first day of spring training. An umpire's got no right getting on a kid. Leave him alone."[7]

Walt Bond also felt that Ed Runge had been treating him unfairly. Vic

Power told Bond to turn on Runge and speak his mind before he ran him out of baseball. Bond, who was 6'7" and 228 pounds, was impressed with Temple and expressed gratitude to him for coming to the defense of a rookie. Walt Bond would make the ball club in 1960 and go on to play for six years in the major leagues with Cleveland, Houston and Minnesota.

With opening day of the 1960 season less than a week away, Frank Lane once again gave in to his uncontrollable compulsion to trade players. On April 12 he traded first baseman Norm Cash to the Detroit Tigers for third baseman Steve Demeter.

Lane decided that young Norm Cash was expendable because he had Tito Francona. He had taken over for a slumping Vic Power at first base in early June during the 1959 season and proceeded to hit .361, playing in 122 games, at first in the outfield and as a pinch hitter. As a result, Francona even got a few votes in the AL MVP balloting. Casey Stengel had remarked that Tito Francona was one of five hitters in the American League in 1959 who kept the Yankees from winning the pennant.

In the short run Lane's decision to keep Tito Francona and trade Norm Cash worked fine. But over the long run the trade would prove to be one of the most boneheaded deals of Frank Lane's career.

Tito Francona would continue to play for Cleveland until 1965, then for the most part become a part-time player with St. Louis, Philadelphia, Atlanta, Oakland and Milwaukee (Brewers) for the rest of his fifteen-year major league career. Francona would be selected to one All-Star team, playing in two games, and would have a lifetime batting average of .272 with 125 home runs and 656 RBIs.

Tito Francona's son Terry Francona, born in 1959, would play in the major leagues for ten years and later become a manager. Entering the 2015 season, Terry Francona has managed fifteen years in the major leagues with the Philadelphia Phillies (four years), Boston Red Sox (eight years) and Cleveland Indians (three years), winning two pennants and two World Series titles with Boston (2004 and 2009).

Steve Demeter would play in exactly four games for the Cleveland Indians in 1960, getting two hits in twenty-three at bats before disappearing into the minor leagues, never to return to the majors again.

But Frank Lane wasn't done making deals, and on April 17, the day before the 1960 campaign began, he made a trade that shocked the baseball world and made headlines not just in Cleveland but across the nation. Frank Lane traded the Indians' biggest star, outfielder Rocky Colavito, to the Detroit Tigers for infielder Harvey Kuenn.

In 1958 Rocky Colavito hit 41 home runs and had 113 RBIs while hitting for an average of .303. In the 1959 season Colavito hit .257 with 42 home runs and 111 RBIs.

Harvey Kuenn had won the 1959 American League batting crown with an average of .353 and also led the league in hits with 198. Kuenn had also had 99 RBIs.

Rocky Colavito's 1959 contract was for $28,000, and over the winter he had been at odds with Frank Lane by asking for an increase to $45,000. He eventually signed for $35,000, but the contract negotiations had left him in Frank Lane's doghouse. The Detroit Tigers had a similar contract dispute with Harvey Kuenn, who wanted a $10,000 raise that would have put him in the range of $50,000 a year.

To the overwhelming majority of onlookers among the press and fans, the Colavito-for-Kuenn deal sure didn't look like a win-win situation. But for some strange reason Frank Lane saw a potential benefit to the Indians in trading home runs for singles and doubles, so he made the deal with Tigers general manager Bill DeWitt, Sr., to send Colavito to Detroit for Kuenn.

Ironically, Bill DeWitt stated in regard to the trade, "I have the highest regard for Kuenn's ability as a player, but we felt we needed more power and hope this trade will score more runs for us."[8]

At the time the trade was made on April 17, 1960, the Cleveland Indians were playing their final exhibition game of spring training in Memphis against the Chicago White Sox. Rocky Colavito had already hit a home run in the game and in his next at bat he hit a single and was standing on first base when manager Joe Gordon informed that he had just got his last hit for the Cleveland Indians as he had been traded to the Detroit Tigers.

Ironically the Indians' opening game of the 1960 campaign on April 18 was against the Detroit Tigers in Cleveland. So it was a surreal return to Cleveland for Colavito as he rode the Indians' team bus to the airport and boarded the Indians' plane for Ohio. Then, the next day at Municipal Stadium, he entered the visitors' clubhouse to join the Detroit Tigers.

In 1954 Rocky Colavito hit 21 home runs as a rookie and had become a fan favorite in Cleveland. He was considered a role model for youth: he went to church, signed autographs for the kids, didn't drink or smoke. His trade to the Tigers the day before the opening game of the 1960 season was highly controversial and angered Indians fans.

Still, "Trader Lane" was not done wheeling and dealing. Prior to the opening game, Lane traded pitcher Herb Score to the Chicago White Sox for pitcher Barry Latman. The fireballing lefty Score had never fully recovered from his tragic injury after being hit in the eye by a line drive off the bat of the Yankees' Gil McDougald in 1957. Regardless, the Cleveland fans had remained loyal to Score; some hoped and some prayed for his brilliance on the mound to return, even if he was now in a White Sox uniform. Score, who was Rocky Colavito's roommate on the team, was shocked by both trades.

A huge crowd of 52,756 fans, some curious, others confused, and many outraged over Frank Lane's trades, were in attendance at Cleveland's cavernous Municipal Stadium for the opening game of the 1960 season. Some fans hung Lane in effigy.

The Tigers won the game in 15 innings 4–2. Rocky Colavito went 0 for 6 for the Tigers, striking out four times and another time hitting into a double play. Norm Cash went 0 for 1. "I'll never forget the first game after the trade," Colavito said. "I was now with the Tigers, but we were playing Cleveland. And I thought that game would never end. I was never more nervous for a game."[9]

It was also Johnny Temple's first game with the Cleveland Indians, and he had 1 hit for 6 trips to the plate, while Harvey Kuenn went 2 for 7. But Kuenn pulled a hamstring in the game and the injury would hamper him the entire season.

The following day the Tigers defeated the Indians 6–4 and Rocky Colavito hit a home run in the fourth with two on off Jim Perry. Then Norm Cash homered in the eighth with what would be the deciding run.

On Tuesday evening, May 10, Johnny Temple played his first game at Yankee Stadium. In his first at bat in the fabled stadium he doubled down the right field line off Bill Short. Then his single off Ryne Duran in the top of the tenth inning scored Walt Bond with what proved to be the winning run, making the score 2–1. Temple's RBI hit was followed by a Harvey Kuenn single and Jim Piersall's three-run homer to make the final score Cleveland 5, New York 1.

The Tuesday game was the first of a scheduled three-game set with the Yankees. But the Wednesday game was rained out after a heavy downpour of fifteen minutes right before game time. While most of the Indians dressed in a hurry to take advantage of the day off in the big city, Johnny Temple lingered behind in the clubhouse.

Legendary *Newsweek* sports reporter Stan Isaacs was covering the New York Yankees. It had been Stan Isaacs, born in Williamsburg, Brooklyn, who swiped the 1955 Brooklyn Dodgers World Championship pennant that was displayed on the wall of the media room in the Biltmore Hotel in downtown Los Angeles during the 1959 World Series and brought it home to Brooklyn, where he considered it rightfully belonged.

With the rainout of the Indians-Yankees game, Isaacs seized the opportunity to chat with Johnny Temple and ask how he was adjusting to the American League after playing eighteen games in the junior circuit.

Temple remarked that after being traded to Cleveland, one of his brothers had reacted, "Any place but Cleveland." He felt that way because of Vic Power. "You see," said Temple, "they televise many of the games back to North Carolina. And when they watch Power and the way he plays they become infuriated." Vic Power had a tendency to showboat on the field but Temple skillfully avoided a direct reference to it. Temple went on to say that was the thing about Power: "When you played against him you became infuriated by him. When you play with him, you are infuriated by him."[10] Nonetheless, Temple felt Vic Power was the greatest first baseman he had ever seen, including Gil Hodges and Ted Kluszewski.

Temple continued by stating that Vic Power was a good guy and a positive influence on the ball club. In particular he mentioned how Power had befriended pitcher Jim "Mudcat" Grant and loosened him up. According to Temple, Grant came from "poor country Florida, where Negroes walk around bare-footed,"[11] and he was sensitive about being a black man.

When Isaacs asked Temple about how he was being accepted by his teammates in Cleveland, he stated that the camaraderie he was experiencing with the Indians was in stark contrast to that which he experienced with the Reds.

"When I get off the bus now, 10 or 11 guys want me to eat with them. It wasn't like that at Cincinnati for a long time. Guys wouldn't want to eat out with me because they were afraid I might insult the waiter."[12]

By May 25, Temple was hitting .262 and the Cleveland Indians were in second place with a record of 18–12. Although he was a career .290 hitter, Temple felt that being in the American League was like starting all over. "Every pitcher looks like Walter Johnson to me," said Temple. "I'll have to get acquainted with them."[13]

The dimensions of the ballparks in the American League were an adjustment for him as well. "The dimensions could mean a lot to a big hitter, especially one who pulls the ball," said Temple. "A lot of pop fouls are caught in, say, Baltimore and Cleveland, that would be out of the playing area in, say, Boston and Detroit."[14]

In mid–June the Cincinnati Reds met the Cleveland Indians in an exhibition game at Municipal Stadium. It was an opportunity for Johnny Temple to have a few words with some of his old Reds teammates and Cincinnati sportswriters covering the game. Earl Lawson was there and Temple told him that he liked playing in Cleveland, it was great playing behind a good pitching staff, but eventually he would like to live in Cincinnati again and possibly go into business. While he had received a couple of propositions he was not close to making a decision.

Temple had been out of the Indians lineup since being hit on the ankle May 21 in a pick-off play. The ankle was still swollen, so he played third base in the exhibition game. "Riding the bench, you know me," said Temple, "I'd go crazy. A few days I sit in the dugout. Then for a few days I try the bullpen, I smoke a lot of cigarettes. Looks like I'll be playing there [third base] for a while, the way the other guy's hitting."[15] The other guy Temple was referring to was Ken Aspromonte, who, since taking over at second base, was hitting .298.

But Temple's time riding the wood was minimal and by June 14 he was back in the lineup at second base as the Indians lost to the Baltimore Orioles 7–4.

At the All-Star Game break on July 10, the Indians were in second place, trailing the league leading New York Yankees by just 2½ games.

Once again two All-Star Games were scheduled to be played in the 1960 season; however, the format was changed by major league baseball to allow them to market the games with an illusion of being a double-header. The first game was to take place on July 11 at Kansas City and the second on July 13 in New York. While the first game in Kansas City was a sellout with attendance of 30,619 in little Municipal Stadium, the second game, played in the behemoth Yankee Stadium, was only about half full with 38,362 in attendance.

The Indians' Harvey Kuenn was hitting .305 and chosen to play on the Amer-

Johnny Temple, 1960 (Cleveland Indians).

ican League All-Star team. The Tigers' Rocky Colavito was hitting .255 with 17 home runs was not chosen.

Johnny Temple, as a newcomer to the American League, was not chosen to play in either the first or second All-Star Game. Although he was hitting .272 at the break, Temple was bypassed in favor of established American League second basemen Pete Runnels of the Boston Red Sox, who was hitting .321 and selected to start both games with the Chicago White Sox' Nellie Fox, who was hitting .264, as the back-up.

The fact was that Temple was glad to catch a break and not make the trek to Kansas City or New York. It was an opportunity for him to go down to Florida for a few days and be with his wife and son. Mike Temple was now eight years old. A left-handed hitter, he was playing Little League ball, and to the amazement of Temple was hitting the ball pretty well.

The National League won the first of the 1960 All-Star Games 5–3. Willie Mays led the attack with a single, double and triple to send the Nationals out to a 5–0 lead after three innings.

Bob Friend of the Pirates, who had been the starting pitcher for the National League, was the winning pitcher, throwing three scoreless innings. Elroy Face of the Pirates came on in relief in the sixth with the bases loaded and forced Luis Aparicio to hit into a double play, ending the Americans' only real scoring threat.

Two days later in New York, the Nationals defeated the American League again, this time by 6–0 margin. Once again it was Willie Mays with three hits who paced the Nationals, with Stan Musial coming off the bench in the seventh to hit a pinch-hit home run. The National League used six pitchers in shutting out the Americans; Vernon Law of the Pirates started and pitched two scoreless innings, followed by Johnny Podres, Stan Williams, Larry Jackson, Bill Henry and Lindy McDaniel.

An oddity existed in the 1960 All-Star Games as in both games the winning pitchers, Bob Friend and Vernon Law, were from the Pittsburgh Pirates. Vernon Law had also worked in relief in the first game, yielding no runs and two hits. The work of Friend and Law, combined with the relief pitching of Face in the first game—who pitched 1⅔ innings of relief, giving up no runs and two hits—meant that in the two 1960 All-Star Games, the three Pirates pitchers worked a combined 7⅓ innings and gave up no runs and only two hits.

Following the All-Star Game break the Indians started to slide backwards in the standings and by July 24 were in fourth place. As the losses mounted, Johnny Temple became frustrated.

On July 28 the Indians lost the first game of a double-header to the

Yankees in New York 4–0. It was the Tribe's fourth straight loss. Then, in the second game in the bottom of the first inning, Johnny Temple threw a temper tantrum.

The Yankees' Hector Lopez led off the inning against the Indians' Barry Latman with a single. Then Tony Kubek followed with a single, placing Yankees on first and second. Yogi Berra was next up and doubled home both Lopez and Kubek. Standing on second, Berra called time out to remove a shinguard he was wearing.

As Ken Aspromonte was hitting .311, John Temple was playing third base to make room for him in the Indians' lineup. When umpire Al Smith allowed Berra to call time out, Temple, believing that the umpire was being partial to the Yankees, stormed towards him, informing him that while he had just allowed Berra to call time out, he had denied the same to Indians shortstop Rocky Bridges, recently acquired from Detroit, who had asked for a time out when the ball had been returned to the infield following Tony Kubek's single. Smith said that he had refused Bridges's request because the ball was in play. As Temple ranted and raved on, Al Smith tossed him out of the game.

The Yankees went on to win the game 9–2, handing the Indians their fifth straight defeat. Cal Hubbard, the American League umpiring chief, was present at the game and later remarked, "Smith was right. We are trying to eliminate unnecessary delay of game."[16]

Frank Lane came to the conclusion that Indians needed a boost in starting pitching. On July 29 he bought Don Newcombe from the Cincinnati Reds for $30,000. While he was aware that Newcombe was no longer the pitcher he was during the period between 1949 and 1956, Lane felt that with his experience Newcombe might be of some help to the Indians.

Although he had been the Reds' winningest pitcher the year before, during the 1960 campaign Newcombe had been struggling. At the moment he had a record of 4–6 and had only completed one game in 16 starts, a 2–0 losing effort to Robin Roberts and the Philadelphia Phillies.

The move to Cleveland was not without controversy, as rumors had been circulating that Reds manager Fred Hutchinson was concerned that Newcombe's drinking was affecting his performance on the mound. Also Newcombe had suffered a groin injury during spring training that seemed to continue bothering him. Frustrated with his Cincinnati experience, upon arriving in Cleveland Newcombe stated that, "It's wonderful to be with a big league team again." When Newcombe's crack was mentioned to Reds coach Reggie Otero, he replied, "If Newk could finish only one of 16 starts in the 'minors' how can he expect to win in the majors?"[17]

Don Newcombe would pitch in twenty games for the Indians in 1960 and finish the season with a record of 2–3 (6–9 overall). Following the season he would retire from major league baseball after ten years with a career record of 149–90, having three twenty-game-winning seasons along the way, winning the MVP in 1956 and World Championship ring with the 1955 Brooklyn Dodgers.

The Cleveland Indians finished the month of July winning eleven games and losing seventeen. On August 3, 1960, the Indians, picked as a pre-season pennant contender, were in fourth place with a record of 49–46, and Frank Lane was considering firing manager Joe Gordon.

That same day, the Detroit Tigers, who had been picked in the pre-season to finish in the first division, were in sixth place with a record of 44–52 after losing 12 of their last 15 games, and general manager Bill DeWitt was considering firing manager Jimmy Dykes.

A few weeks earlier as a joke, Bill DeWitt had remarked to Frank Lane, "Why don't we make a really big deal? Let's trade managers."[18] It sure seemed like a plan to Frank Lane, so that is exactly what he and DeWitt did—they shocked the baseball world again by trading managers, Lane sending Joe Gordon to Detroit in exchange for Jimmy Dykes.

Veteran sportswriters were dumbfounded by the deal—it was unprecedented in the 84-year history of major league baseball. They simply chalked it up to the mind-set of Frank Lane and made jokes about putting managers on waivers like players before they could be traded.

At first Jimmy Dykes was reluctant to go along with the trade. But after pondering the matter, Dykes came to the conclusion that as he was almost sure not to be back with the Tigers the following season, he might as well try it. After all, he was taking over a fourth-place team after managing a sixth-place team.

Joe Gordon, on the other hand, had been having some explosive moments with Frank Lane during the season. Much of the trouble centered on the antics of Indians controversial and unpredictable outfielder Jimmy Piersall.

At one point Gordon had asked Lane to do something about Piersall. But Lane responded by telling Gordon that it was his responsibility to manage twenty-five players, not twenty-four.

Jim Piersall had a long history of bizarre behavior on the baseball diamond. By 1960 Piersall was 30 years old, a family man, married with seven children; eventually the family would grow to nine children. By then his zany antics on the baseball diamond were considered status quo by the fans and sportswriters. However, among major league umpires, managers and baseball executives, they served no purpose and were a constant source of agitation. There is no doubt that Joe Gordon felt relieved not to have to deal with Piersall's shenanigans anymore.

During the 1952 season, while playing for the Boston Red Sox, Jim Piersall had suffered a mental breakdown and was confined to Westbrook State Hospital in Massachusetts for seven weeks. In an attempt to cash in on his disability, Piersall authored an autobiography titled *Fear Strikes Out*, which was adapted for a television movie in 1955 and two years later was adapted into a major motion picture.

With all the publicity surrounding Jim Piersall's struggle with mental health issues, the fans took it as a license to harass him on the field and yelled insults at him in every ballpark in the American League. Of course, Piersall's penchant for ludicrous behavior on the field fueled the fans' abuse of him, and it became totally unpredictable when fans were going to react badly or just plain silly when he was in the lineup.

In December 1958, Jim Piersall was traded by the Boston Red Sox to the Cleveland Indians and his zaniness, and predictably the fans' reaction followed him from Fenway Park to Municipal Stadium.

But Piersall wasn't playing regularly in Cleveland and he had left his heart in Boston. Over the winter of 1959–1960 he had contacted Red Sox general manager Bucky Harris to see if he could make a trade to bring him back to Boston. However, Ted Williams had announced that 1960 was to be his last season. In Boston the front office planned to surround the season around that event, and bringing back Jim Piersall and his bizarre behavior didn't fit into their plans. The Red Sox brass still had vivid memories of his various stunts, including the day he climbed the flagpole at Fenway Park.

As it turned out for Joe Gordon and Indians, the 1960 season was a banner year for the oddball behavior of Jim Piersall. May 30, 1960, was to be a very troubling day for Jim Piersall at Comiskey Park. The Cleveland Indians were in Chicago to play a double-header against the White Sox. In the third inning of the first game, Piersall reached first base on a fielder's choice and then stole second.

Then with Harvey Kuenn hitting against Early Wynn, from his vantage point on second base, Piersall started to accuse home plate umpire Larry Napp of calling strikes on pitches that were outside. Napp ignored Piersall. However, second base umpire Cal Drummond came up from behind Piersall and told him to knock it off. Immediately, Piersall started to rant and rave at Drummond, who found his comments offensive and ejected him from the game.

With a fifteen-game hitting streak ended as a result of being tossed out of the game, Piersall went into a rage. He literally emptied the contents of the Cleveland dugout onto the field. It took the Indians' batboy more than ten minutes to retrieve all the bats, towels, batting helmets and balls. While the batboy was chasing all the equipment, Piersall went over to the White Sox dugout, grabbed a bucket of the groundskeeper's sand and emptied it onto the field.

When Piersall returned to the Indians' lineup for the second game, the fans began to taunt him and throw things at him. White Sox owner and president Bill Veeck had installed a $350,000 exploding scoreboard at Comiskey Park in which fireworks were set off each time a White Sox player hit a home run or the team won a game. When White Sox outfielder Minnie Minoso hit a line drive to center, Piersall remained rigid and let the ball sail over his head for a double. However, the White Sox public relations man thought that a home run had been hit and set off the scoreboard fireworks. All at once, after receiving the signal, the fireworks crew behind the scoreboard fired the ten mortars that contained bombs, rockets and firecrackers. This agitated Piersall because in the early days of the exploding scoreboard, players could be hit by a lot of flying debris from the explosions.

The final out of the game was a fly ball to Piersall in center field. At the same time he was fielding the ball, he was hit in the head by an orange thrown out of the stands. So he picked up the baseball and threw it at the scoreboard as hard as he could. Then he picked up the orange and threw it at the scoreboard. He had hoped to hit the glass portion of the scoreboard but missed.

Piersall's assault on the scoreboard upset Bill Veeck and he called him on the telephone expressing his displeasure. The American League fined Piersall $250 for the incident.

Just a couple of days before his antics at the Comiskey Park, Piersall had gone through a harrowing experience in Detroit. As he took the field at Briggs Stadium, Piersall was greeted by the fans with such taunts as "Jimmy the bug" and "When are they going to put you back in your straitjacket?"[19]

During the game, fans in the center field bleachers peppered Piersall with bolts and ice cubes, and zeroed in with paper clips shot out of slingshots. Every time he would go back on a fly ball, a fan would drop a firecracker on him. "When I caught the last fly of the game, a firecracker went off so close to me that the ball dropped into my glove through a cloud of smoke,"[20] said Piersall.

During the All-Star Game break in the 1960 season, Jim Piersall made fan abuse towards him a major issue at a meeting between the player representatives and owners. Harvey Kuenn, the spokesman for the player reps and Piersall's Cleveland teammate, demanded that the American League order its clubs to provide better protection for players.

American League president Joe Cronin assured Kuenn that he too had a genuine concern in regard to the reports that he had been receiving in his office about rowdy fan behavior. He said that on June 7, he had sent a communication to all the American League clubs emphasizing the potential harm that could come to players from objects being thrown from the stands. He reminded each that it was their responsibility to provide the protection necessary to eliminate such behavior.

The reasoning by the Boston Red Sox front office in their decision to not bring Piersall back was confirmed on July 23, 1960. The Cleveland Indians were playing the Boston Red Sox at Fenway Park when Jim Piersall, playing center field, went into a war dance to distract Ted Williams when he was at bat in the sixth and eighth innings. Piersall was ejected from the game and fined $100 by American League president Joe Cronin. It was Piersall's sixth ejection from a game in a season that was just barely past the halfway point.

With manager Joe Gordon traded to Detroit, Jim Piersall was now Jimmy Dykes's problem. When Dykes was asked how he intended to deal with Piersall, he replied, "I don't know. I don't know the man well enough to say now."[21] The fact was that Dykes's challenge to control the controversial centerfielder would be considerable.

Bill DeWitt was hopeful that Joe Gordon's aggressive style of managing would get results that the Tigers didn't get with Jimmy Dykes. Meanwhile Gordon became philosophical about the strange trade: "It's nice to know that when something happens in one place, you're wanted in another."[22]

In the one-game interim after the trade of Gordon to Detroit, Jo-Jo White managed the Indians to a win. But even when Dykes assumed the helm, the Indians continued to lose. Between July 24 and August 14 the Indians went 6–16, virtually eliminating them from the 1960 pennant race. The Indians finished the 1960 season in fourth place with a record of 76–78 (26–32 under Jimmy Dykes), 21 games behind the pennant-winning New York Yankees.

In 1959 the Indians had finished with the second highest attendance figure in the American League with 1,497,976 fans going through the turnstiles. In 1960 that figure dropped to 950,985, sixth largest in the league out of eight teams. On opening day 52,756 fans had been on hand at Municipal Stadium. But going forward in the 1960 season the Cleveland Indians had only one other large crowd like the one on opening day when on June 26, 52,621 packed the stadium for a double-header with the New York Yankees.

The trades engineered by Frank Lane yielded no benefits for the 1960 Indians. In regard to the arguably irrational trades that Frank Lane had made of Cal McLish, Billy Martin, Minnie Minoso, Herb Score and Rocky Colavito, Indians pitcher Mudcat Grant probably said best what was on all the Cleveland players' minds.

"I don't know what Lane was thinking about," said Grant. "There was no way we could make up for the loss of 200 RBIs and a 19 game winner. We got Johnny Temple from Cincinnati and he wasn't a bad ballplayer, but he wasn't worth McLish and Martin and had only a couple of years left."[23] It should also be pointed out that Cal McLish had beaten the New York Yankees five times during the 1959 season.

Rocky Colavito would spend four seasons with Detroit, 1960–1963. In 1961 he would hit a career-high 45 home runs for the Tigers. In 1964 Colavito would be traded to Kansas City, where he would hit 34 home runs. Colavito would hit a total of 173 home runs before returning to Cleveland in 1965 nearing the end of his career.

Harvey Kuenn hit .308 in 1960 for the Indians, but played in only 126 games after pulling a hamstring in the opening game. At the end of the 1960 season, Kuenn would be traded to the San Francisco Giants for Johnny Antonelli and Willie Kirkland. But Kuenn would never again be the great hitter that he had been in the American League during the 1950s.

Returning to the Chicago White Sox in 1960 where he had played from 1951 to 1957, Minnie Minoso would lead the American League in hits with 184 while batting .311, an average not equaled by any player on the Indians' roster. He would also have 20 home runs and 105 RBIs that year. A native of Cuba, when he came up to the White Sox in 1951 Minnie Minoso was the ninth black player in major league baseball. A three-time Gold Glove winner, in 1980 he was elected into the Chicago Sports Hall of Fame.

Norm Cash would become the regular first baseman in Detroit for the next fourteen years and hit 373 home runs for the Tigers. In 1961 Cash would win the American League batting crown with an average of .361. A four-time All-Star, Cash would finish a seventeen-year major league career with 377 home runs, 1091 RBIs and lifetime batting average of .271.

Roger Maris would be traded by the Kansas Athletics following the

1959 season to the New York Yankees, where in 1960 he would be named the American League MVP after hitting 39 home runs and leading the league in RBIs with 112. In 1961 Maris would hit 61 home runs, breaking Babe Ruth's single-season record of 60. This record would stand until the 1998 season, when Mark McGwire hit 70 home runs and Sammy Sosa hit 66. Between 1960 and his retirement in 1968, Roger Maris would play in seven World Series with the New York Yankees and St. Louis Cardinals.

As for Frank Lane's trade with the Cincinnati Reds, he had given up the ace of his 1959 pitching staff, Cal McLish, who had a record of 19–8 in 1959, and got no hurler in return. But McLish would fail miserably at Cincinnati. He would wind up in the bullpen and finishing the 1960 season with a 4–14 record, suffer the wrath of the Crosley Field boo-birds and be run out of town, traded to the Chicago White Sox over the winter.

Gordy Coleman would become the regular first baseman at Cincinnati for the next few years and hit 26 home runs for the 1961 National League Champion Reds. In all, Coleman would play for eight years in Cincinnati. With his beaming personality following retirement as a player, Coleman would become the head of the Reds speakers' bureau for several years.

At the time Johnny Temple was traded by Cincinnati to Cleveland he was regarded as one of the finest second basemen in baseball. As the decades of the 1960s, 1970s and 1980s past by, Temple's legacy would become clouded and rusty, prompting one highly respected baseball author, Peter Golenbock, to offer a huge historical understatement in regard to Temple. In his 1994 biography of Billy Martin, *Wild, High and Tight: The Life and Death of Billy Martin*, Golenbeck stated that when Martin was traded as part of the McLish deal, Cleveland received an over-the-hill infielder in Johnny Temple.

The facts were that while Johnny Temple's legs weren't what they use to be, in 1960 he did a pretty good job in Cleveland for being an alleged over-the-hill infielder. Despite the fact that he played in only 98 games due to injuries, he had a 19-game hitting streak and finished with a batting average of .268.

In contrast, Billy Martin became controversial and a huge embarrassment to the front office in Cincinnati as well as a bust on the field, playing in just 103 games and hitting .246. Martin would be traded to Milwaukee over the winter.

A brawler his entire career, Martin didn't change his personality because he had put on a Reds uniform. In a game against the Philadelphia

Phillies that summer, Reds Cuban relief ace Raul Sanchez had hit three Phillies batters in a row. When Phillies manager Gene Mauch came charging out of the dugout to complain, Martin intercepted him, thinking he was going after Sanchez. At that moment Martin was blindsided with a sucker punch from the Phillies' 6-foot-8-inch pitcher (and Boston Celtics forward) Gene Conley and knocked to the ground. Martin proceeded to get up from the ground and punch the towering Conley in the neck before peace was restored.

Martin's next bout came on August 5, 1960, when he was involved in another fighting incident that would lead to a threat on his life. The Reds were playing the Chicago Cubs at Wrigley Field when rookie left-hander Jim Brewer threw a pitch behind Martin's head. Martin had actually been hit on the arm with the pitch, but the umpire said that it had hit his bat and called it a foul ball. Martin had been beaned by Tex Clevenger the previous season and publicly vowed that any pitcher who threw at him in the future would pay a price. Brewer's next pitch was wide outside. Martin swung at the ball and flung his bat toward the mound, acting as if it had slipped out of his hands. Brewer had to jump over the bat. Martin waited for someone to retrieve the bat, but when no one did, he began walking toward the mound to get the bat. Brewer was yelling and Martin always maintained that the Cubs pitcher asked him if he wanted to fight. Believing that he was about to get punched as he approached the mound, Martin decided to make a pre-emptive strike and punched Brewer in the jaw, knocking him to the ground.

Immediately players from both benches came charging onto the field. Someone kicked Cal McLish in the stomach. So McLish then punched Brewer several times. The left side of Brewer's face had been caved in and he was immediately taken to the hospital.

Billy Martin was fined $500 and suspended for five games. A few years later Martin was sued for $1,040,000 by the Chicago Cubs and Jim Brewer. The case took several years and several hearings to reach a judgment handed down on January 29, 1969. Brewer was awarded $10,000 and $12,000 in legal fees. The judgment kept Martin in debt for several years.

In addition, an interested party outside of baseball believed that Billy Martin had taken a cheap shot at Jim Brewer and threatened revenge. On September 1, 1960, Martin went to the FBI office in Cincinnati and produced the following letter which had been sent to the Cincinnati Reds' front office addressed to "Mr. Billie (Horse Face) Martin," postmarked Fort Scott, Kansas, and bearing a return address of Kansas City, Missouri.

8/20/60

> Horse Face Martin—you do have a face like a horse—you pulled the most cowardly trick which you pull where ever you have an oppertunity when the Cub pitcher asked you if you wanted to fight. You said No Sir I came after my bat the he took you at your no good word, relaxed and turned, then you took your cowardly swing at him. All this you know, but I do want you to know some time your gona meet a guy like me who in life has encountered a couple of bums like you. they pulled the same trick under different circumstances. they both got their Belly Cut Wide Open a hole big enough to put a cantaloupe in—And both like you yelled Cop like you. I do hope you return to Kansas City as I will see that we meet some way or other as I would enjoy converting you. & give you an oppertunity to swing on me, and me the Oppertunity of Sliceing you down in the Gutt. Please hurry as I am anxious to meet you—Love.
> Cincinnati is the only Major League Club who wanted you now they don't—[24]

Billy Martin believed that the anonymous letter constituted a violation of the Extortion Statute. However, after both the Cincinnati and the Kansas City offices of the FBI investigated the matter, United States Attorney Wilbur G. Leonard of Topeka, Kansas, disagreed and declined any prosecution status.

To protect Billy Martin, the letter and original envelope were placed in an anonymous letter file in the Bureau's Kansas City office. No subsequent threatening letters were ever received in the matter.

By the end of the 1960 season the Cincinnati Reds had had enough of Billy Martin's antics, and on December 3, 1960, they sold him to the Milwaukee Braves for cash.

A month later on January 3, 1961, Frank Lane quit as general manager of the Cleveland Indians. The following summer he would be hired by Charles O. Finley as the general manager of the Kansas City Athletics. While the organizational marriage of Lane and Finley would be a perfect match for the two whimsical screwballs who would accomplish nothing in Kansas City, the damage Lane left behind in Cleveland would take decades for the franchise to recover from.

In Cincinnati there was also fallout from the Johnny Temple trade as the fans felt Gabe Paul had been bamboozled by Frank Lane. The failure of Cal McLish to win and the antics of Billy Martin caused general manager Gabe Paul to see the writing on the wall. Although Paul owned a considerable amount of stock in the Reds, he resigned at the end of the 1960 season to become the general manager for the planned entry of the expansion Houston Colt .45s team into the National League in the 1962 season.

Following World War II the city of Houston, Texas, became a boomtown. Between 1950 and 1960 the population of the city rose by 57 percent from 596,163 to 938,219. By 1970 the city's population would exceed one million inhabitants and continue to grow. Houston had become the headquarters of NASA, and with the expansion of the ship channel, it was now under the spotlight of international attention and potential investors. The voters in the county of Harris had even approved a $20 million bond issue to build an air-conditioned domed stadium to be ready for use by 1962.

Quietly, civic, civil rights and business leaders in the community had got together for a meeting at the "whites only" Rice Hotel, and in just one day they agreed to end racial segregation in public accommodations in the city of Houston.

In the center of all of this civic progressive thinking and movement, the Houston Sports Association had been formed. The association consisted of five members of the city's business community: former UPI sports reporter George Kirksey; Craig Culliman, Jr.; Judge Roy Hofheinz; R.E. Smith; and K.S. "Bud" Adams, who would eventually own the Houston Oilers (later the Tennessee Titans) NFL football team. For several years the Association had been pursuing a major league team for Houston by attempting to buy the St. Louis Cardinals, Philadelphia Phillies or Cleveland Indians.

When Branch Rickey's plans for creating the Continental League were abandoned, the National League awarded Houston one of two planned expansion teams, the other going to New York, which the National League had abandoned in 1958.

Hired by George Kirksey, Gabe Paul was charged with putting the franchise's front office together, hiring scouts, signing free agents and players, as well as organizing the minor league affiliates.

While Paul set about expediting his new duties with enthusiasm and diligence, after a short time he tired of the politics in dealing with the Association's over-zealous members and the micromanagement of his business decisions by Judge Roy Hofheinz. So when the Cleveland Indians offered Paul the job of general manager, on April 26, 1961, he quickly packed his bags and skedaddled out of Texas pronto.

In Cleveland, Gabe Paul would renew his association with former Reds manager and coach Jimmy Dykes and former Reds second baseman Johnny Temple. Both would be a little skeptical about the reunion.

Following the Tigers' dismal sixth-place finish in the 1960 season, Bill DeWitt left Detroit to become the new general manager of the Cincinnati Reds.

There is a post-script event to the 1960 season of which it is absolutely sure that Johnny Temple took notice—but never remarked on publicly—as Maz proved to Temple that he could indeed carry his glove.

Bill Mazeroski had quite a year in 1960 playing second base for the

Pittsburg Pirates. He led the National League for second basemen in putouts (413), assists (449), double plays (127), total chances per game (5.8) and fielding average (.989).

On October 13, 1960, the Pittsburgh Pirates defeated the New York Yankees in game seven of the World Series on a ninth-inning walk-off home run by Bill Mazeroski. It was the Pirates' first World Championship in thirty-five years and Mazeroski's homer instantly made him a legend in major league history and a hero to everyone in the Steel City for decades to come. Mazeroski's iconic World Series home run would eventually carry him into the Baseball Hall of Fame.

Nine

A Fading Star

As spring training for the 1961 season loomed on the horizon, Johnny Temple was beginning to consider his options for when he hung up his glove. He was now 32 years old, bald, and a nine-year veteran of the big leagues.

In 1960 during his first spring training with the Cleveland Indians at Tucson, Arizona, Temple was shown a dude ranch that was for sale by former big league outfielder Hank Leiber, New York Giants (1933–1938, 1942) and Chicago Cubs (1939–1941). After he spoke with his wife Becky and took her to view the property, the two decided to buy it and make plans to operate it.

The property has long since been subdivided and today is dotted with half-million-dollar homes and modest apartments. But at the time the Temples occupied it, the Rancho Del Jefe was situated on eighty acres at the foot of the Rincon Mountains with the Catalinas rising in the background to form a majestic backdrop. The property was enhanced by the proximity of the scenic Saguaro National Monument, a veritable forest of cacti with a maze of trails for horseback riding.

Speaking about the property in early 1961, Temple remarked, "We just fell in love with this country. You know I haven't been off the ranch since I arrived home in early October."[1]

As spring training drew near, Temple, along with his wife and son Mike, was working sixteen hours a day, busy preparing the ranch for a planned November opening, hopeful of attracting the family trade. They had renovated all the ten units and at the moment bookings were pretty solid for the period between December 1961 and February 1962. The string of horses on the ranch was being cared for by a real cowboy by the name of Dee Williams, who had met the Temples when they stayed at the 49ers Ranch. Williams quickly developed a rapport with the Temples and agreed to join them when they took over the Rancho Del Jefe.

The Temples' ranch also included other amenities such as shuffleboard courts, horseshoe pits, a dance hall, a game room and a heated swimming pool. So at the moment it appeared that Johnny Temple had found a post-season career to support his family.

Nonetheless, spring training for the 1961 season was fast approaching, and reporters were interested in speaking with Temple about what caused the Cleveland Indians to nose dive in the 1960 American League pennant race after the first of July.

"We collapsed then because of two things," said Temple. "The inexperience of our pitching staff caught up with us and more important, the team lost its pride. Players started to think more of individual records than team records."[2]

Also Temple coyly made a reference to the trades that Frank Lane had made prior to the 1960 season as being a factor in the Indians' poor showing: "There's nothing wrong with the Indians that keeping players around long enough to get acquainted with the fans won't cure."[3]

As for the coming 1961 season, the baseball writers were less than enthusiastic about the Indians' chances of taking the American League flag. While they felt that the Indians' infield and outfield were outstanding with seven veterans, including Vic Power, Johnny Temple, Woodie Held, Bubba Phillips and John Romano, along with Jim Piersall and Tito Francona, who had established himself after having a solid season, the question mark was if their pitching would be strong enough for them to overcome the New York Yankees in the coming pennant chase.

The most reliable starting pitcher for the Indians in 1960 had been Jim Perry, who finished with a record of 18–10. Four other starters had finished with ERAs above 4.00, including Gary Bell, who had won five of his first six starts before developing a shoulder hitch that he was unable to shake the rest of the season.

While there had not been the wholesale trades of Indians players as had happened prior to the 1960 season, Frank Lane had made one significant trade before departing Cleveland that everyone felt had the potential to be beneficial to the Tribe. In early December, Lane had attempted to correct his error in the Harvey Kuenn for Rocky Colavito trade by sending Kuenn to the San Francisco Giants for veteran left-hander Johnny Antonelli and outfielder Willie Kirkland, who had hit 57 home runs in the past three years.

Most of the experts seemed to agree with the opinion advanced by *Sports Illustrated* that if Gary Bell and Johnny Antonelli had big years, the Indians could win the pennant. If they didn't, they wouldn't.

As spring training was winding down, a reporter informed Johnny Temple that last season Frank Lane had offered to trade him to Kansas City for Jerry Lumpe, but was turned down. Temple's reply was, "Is that so? Well, Lane is now the general manager of Kansas City. Why don't you call him and ask him whether he would make the same trade now? I'll bet he wouldn't."[4] In the 1960 season Jerry Lumpe played in 146 games at second base, shortstop and third base for the Athletics and hit .272 with 8 home runs and 69 RBIs.

As a result of his ankle injury in May, Temple held the opinion that last season had turned out to be a nightmare. His batting average sunk to .268, the lowest it had been since his rookie year in 1954. When he returned to the lineup in June after healing his ankle, Joe Gordon put him at third base, partly because his replacement at second, Ken Aspromonte, was hot at the plate and doing a credible job in the field.

"It didn't take me long to find out I was no third baseman,"[5] said Temple. He felt he had made a fool out of himself in Baltimore when twice chasing foul balls he fell on his face. "You get a different perspective at third. You should have heard the riding I got from the Baltimore bench. I felt like walking off the field. I was never so embarrassed in my life."[6]

When it came to second baseman, it was clear that the one Temple liked the best at the position was Temple. "Aspromonte did a good job for us, but at top speed," said Temple, "he is not the second baseman that I am even at three-quarter speed. As a result we were hurting at two positions."[7]

During the off-season Ken Aspromonte had been put on the expansion draft list by the Indians and taken by the Los Angeles Angels. So Temple was assured of being back at his second base position in the 1961 campaign. Little could Temple have ever imagined that Aspromonte would return to Cleveland in the coming season, but that is exactly what would happen on July 3, when the Indians purchased Aspromonte from the Angels on waivers.

While Cleveland prepped for the 1961 season in Tucson, a large number of observers in camp were talking about the blazing fastball being thrown by Indians 18-year-old southpaw prospect Sam McDowell.

Manager Jimmy Dykes, speaking with reporters, remarked in regard to McDowell, "Fast as hell. Other day he threw two wild pitches in one inning. They hit the backstop and came back past the catcher as fast as they'd gone by him. Frank Lane offered $100,000 for McDowell."[8]

Johnny Temple was paying attention to McDowell too. "He has fantastic natural ability," said Temple. "But no head. I mean, he has the wrong idea about pitching. He has a great fast ball and great curve, the best in camp. But when I went over to watch him warm up the other day, and what was he working on? Knucklers, sliders, screwballs—everything but his fast ball and his curve."[9] Temple asked McDowell what he was doing. His reply was that he was working on his pitches. "You got to have six or seven pitches to make the majors,"[10] said McDowell. Temple looked at McDowell and told him point-blank, "Keep it up, and you won't have any pitches at all."[11]

At the end of spring training, Sam McDowell was optioned to the Salt Lake City Bees of the Pacific Coast League. It would be another season before Sam McDowell would become part of the Indians' roster. But shortly after coming up for good in 1962 he would become known to American League batters as "Sudden Sam," a moniker pinned on him by a *Cleveland Plain Dealer* beat writer. Although McDowell never threw a no-hitter, he would go on to become a six-time All-Star and lead the American League five times in strikeouts between 1965 and 1970. McDowell would play in the major leagues for 15 years and finish with a lifetime record of 141–134 and have 2453 career strikeouts. His career strikeout record places him as 35th best of all time. But it should be pointed out that only four other pitchers who had shorter careers than McDowell are ahead of him on the all-time strikeout list. Had he pitched only a couple of more years, "Sudden Sam" McDowell would have finished much higher on the all-time strikeout list.

The Indians began the 1961 campaign on April 11 with a 9–5 win at Detroit with Jim Perry on the mound. Tigers starter Jim Bunning had been driven from the mound by Cleveland when they scored six runs in the second inning.

The first half of the season Detroit held down first place with Norm Cash, Al Kaline and Rocky Colavito having great years. For a while it looked like Cleveland was going to challenge the defending American League Champion New York Yankees and Detroit Tigers for the pennant as the Tribe held down first place between June 7 and June 16. Then Cleveland lost 9 out of 11 games, fell into third place, and never recovered. Following the 1961 All-Star Games, the Yankees, led by the epic assault on Babe Ruth's season home record by Roger Maris and Mickey Mantle, took charge of first place for the rest of the season.

The Cincinnati Reds had gotten off to a poor start in the 1961 season and at the end of April found themselves in last place in the National League with a record of 6–10. New vice-president and general manager Bill DeWitt, Sr., reasoned it was time to make some changes.

Nine. A Fading Star

On December 3, Billy Martin had been sold to the Milwaukee Braves. As far as the Reds' fans were concerned, it was a case of "good riddance."

Nonetheless, the Reds needed a second baseman. To fill that void, and no one knows why, DeWitt drafted a 30-year-old career minor leaguer by the name of Jim Baumer off the Pittsburgh Pirates' roster. Baumer was a former Chicago White Sox bonus baby who hadn't played in the major leagues since 1949, when he played in eight games. So Baumer started the season at second base for the Reds but couldn't cut the mustard, and by April 26 wasn't hitting his weight with a .136 batting average.

After consulting with manager Fred Hutchinson, Bill DeWitt traded All-Star catcher Ed Bailey to San Francisco for second baseman Don Blasingame and catcher Bob Schmidt. At the time Bailey was hitting .308 and the move was unpopular with Cincinnati fans. Hutchinson had managed Blasingame in St. Louis and was confident of his abilities. Still, a lot of fans and sports scribes felt that the Reds had just given the pennant to the Giants.

The trade was also unpopular with Bailey's old Reds teammate Johnny Temple as well. Harry Grayson, a sportswriter from the *Cincinnati Post & Times Star* who had known Temple from his days with the Reds, caught up with him in New York and asked him to comment on the trade.

"The Giants got the top man in the business in Bailey," said Temple. "Many baseball men consider Del Crandall the best catcher in the National League, but I'll take Bailey ahead of anybody in the game. That goes for all departments handling pitchers, receiving, throwing, hitting and bunting."[12]

As for the players the Reds got in return for Bailey, Temple called catcher Bob Schmidt a minor leaguer. Always eager to critique other major league second basemen, Temple stated, "Blasingame couldn't throw a lick in Arizona this spring. It looked like he had a bad arm. As a second baseman, Blasingame is a good offensive ballplayer, period."[13]

The fact was that as soon as Bill DeWitt arrived in Cincinnati he began to remake the Cincinnati Reds. After shipping Billy Martin to the Braves, his next move on December 5 was to engineer a three-way trade sending All-Star shortstop Roy McMillan to the Milwaukee Braves for pitchers Joey Jay and Juan Pizarro. DeWitt then traded Pizarro to the Chicago White Sox for third baseman Gene Freese.

Both those trades would pay huge dividends for the Cincinnati Reds in 1961. Between June 15 and July 19, the Reds would win 21 out of 28 games and open up a five-game lead over the San Francisco Giants.

Joey Jay would finish the season with a record of 21–10, while Gene

Freese hit 26 home runs. The Reds never really had a permanent keystone combination in 1961 as Don Blasingame, who hit only .222, shared the second baseman position with Elio Chacon, and Eddie Kasko, a younger version of the departed Roy McMillan, shared shortstop with Leo (Chico) Cardenas.

Still, with Jim O'Toole winning 19 games, Bob Purkey 16 and Vada Pinson hitting .343, second highest average in the league behind Roberto Clemente, while Frank Robinson won the National League MVP honors having one of the best seasons in his career, hitting .323 with 37 home runs and 124 RBIs, the Reds won the 1961 National League pennant.

At the time of the first All-Star Game break on July 9, the Cleveland Indians were in fourth place with a record of 47–39.

Johnny Temple was hitting .288 and selected to play in the All-Star Game. It was the fourth time that Temple had been selected to play in the All-Star Game. He had been selected in the National League with the Cincinnati Reds (1956, 1957 and 1959) and now in the American League with the Cleveland Indians (1961).

The fact that Temple was an All-Star in both the National and American Leagues is no small achievement. While Johnny Temple was the first player to achieve that distinction, going forward he would be joined by a very elite circle of players in that regard.

In the eighty-one years that the Major League All-Star Game has been played between 1933 and 2014, 1707 players have been selected to represent either the National or American League in the midsummer classic. Among those 1707 players, fewer than 40, or 2 percent of those selected, have represented both leagues in the All-Star Game during their careers. Those who have for the most part are Hall of Fame members, future Hall of Fame members or recognized stars of their era, players such as Hank Aaron, Dick Allen, Vida Blue, Jim Bunning, Miguel Cabrera, Roger Clemens, Ken Griffey, Jr., Rich (Goose) Gossage, Randy Johnson, Johnny Mize, Graig Nettles, Phil Niekro, Frank Robinson, Nolan Ryan, Johnny Sain, Curt Schilling, Jim Thome and Dave Winfield. Of course there are a few marginal players included in the list, such as Bob Boone, his son Bret Boone, and Leo Cardenas.

One of the players named above, Rich (Goose) Gossage, holds the record for representing the most teams in All-Star competition—four. In 1975 Gossage was a member of the American League squad representing the Chicago White Sox. In 1977 Gossage was on the National League team representing the Pittsburgh Pirates, in 1978 and 1980 was once again a member of the American League team representing the New York Yankees, and finally, Gossage represented the San Diego Padres on the 1984 and 1985 National League teams.

While Major League Baseball continued to hold two All-Star Games in 1961, they returned to playing the games a couple of weeks apart. The first game in 1961 was played on July 11 at San Francisco. But it was clear that many were tiring of the two All-Star Games, which was evident by the mere handful of sportswriters who were in attendance for the game.

The game was won by the National League 5–4 in the bottom of the tenth inning on a single by Roberto Clemente after Willie Mays had doubled, scoring Hank Aaron.

While a record seven errors were made in the game (American League 2, National League 5), Johnny Temple made the best play of the day. In the top of the fourth inning, Braves second baseman Frank Bolling smashed a torrid liner over second. Temple, running to cover second, leaped into the air and caught the ball with one hand as the momentum of the ball knocked him to the ground.

Temple was hitless in three at bats for the Americans. With the score tied 3–3 in the top on the ninth inning, Jim Gentile pinch-hit for Temple and struck out.

A sportswriter inquired of Temple if he still wore his shinguard to protect his leg mutilated in a domestic fire back home in North Carolina when he was a teenager. Temple replied, "I keep it well hidden. Enemy runners that slide into me, tell me what hard bones I have."[14]

Neither of the Yankees' sluggers, Mickey Mantle or Roger Maris, did much at bat in the game. Mantle struck out twice and sprained his wrist while batting. Maris was held to a single in four trips to the plate. Furthermore, in the second inning Mantle had lost Roberto Clemente's fly ball in the sky and it dropped for a fluke triple.

The second All-Star Game in 1961 was played on July 31 at Boston. The game wound up in a 1–1 tie, the first tie in All-Star Game history, when rain began to fall after the ninth inning. The only run scored by the Americans came on a home run by Rocky Colavito in the first inning. The Nationals scored their only run on a single by Bill White in the sixth that drove in Eddie Mathews.

Appearing in what would be his last All-Star Game, Johnny Temple went 0 for 2 at bat. He had been an All-Star four years and played in six games. At the plate he had two hits in 15 at bats, including one double, for a batting average of .200. He had one RBI. In the field, Temple was perfect for six games, making no errors in 22 total chances for a fielding average of 1.000. Also he made one double play.

In the 1961 season, Jim Piersall continued to be the object or victim of yet more episodes of abnormal fan behavior, some which resulted in on-field combat that grabbed major league headlines.

Some of the trouble was created by Piersall himself. On June 25, he touched off a huge brawl with the Detroit Tigers when he charged the mound in pursuit of pitcher Jim Bunning in the fifth inning of the first game of a double-header at Municipal Stadium. Piersall charged Bunning after being hit by a pitch on the shoulder. As Piersall was being subdued by his teammate Vic Power, players emptied out of both benches and a melee began. When order was restored, Piersall, Johnny Temple and Bob Hale were ejected. The only injury resulting from the fracas was a spike wound suffered by Bunning from his wresting match with Piersall.

Fans throwing objects at a player from the stands is very dangerous act, but when fans come onto the field to confront a player, it constitutes a high degree of escalated fan violence.

In late August a fan jumped out of the stands at Municipal Stadium in Cleveland and ran towards Jim Piersall, who applied a swift kick in the pants for the invader. "I made up my mind that the next guy who tried it would really be sorry," said Piersall. "I don't mind the name-calling, but lately they have been throwing things and I'm not going to be a clay pigeon for those guys."[15]

Late in the season Johnny Temple would come to aid of Piersall again in a memorable incident of fan nonsense. The Cleveland Indians had lost nineteen straight games at Yankee Stadium. September 10, 1961, was a hot, humid 90-degree day in New York City and the Yankees were on the verge of sweeping a five-game series with the Indians. The day would turn out to be one of the most turbulent in the history of Yankee Stadium.

Going into the first game of scheduled double-header, Roger Maris had hit 56 home runs, Mickey Mantle 52, and 57,824 fans were packed into Yankee Stadium to watch them edge closer to Babe Ruth's all-time season home run record.

Johnny Temple led off in the first game with a double off Whitey Ford and then scored on a single by John Romano.

A brawl nearly took place in the fifth inning when Yankee pitcher Jim Coates, who had replaced Ford, hit Vic Power with a pitch. Power stood at the plate and in his imperfect English told Coates what he thought about it. As Power took his base, the Yankees fans gave him a very heavy dose of the Bronx cheer. When Coates attempted to pick Power off and nearly hit him again, he bristled, and now the fans really gave it to him. The harassment went on the entire game.

Coates said later that he was simply trying to pitch Power inside. But Johnny Temple had a different take on the matter. "That Coates is in the same class as Don Drysdale," said Temple. "When the count is 0–2, see where the ball goes. Right at somebody's head. All lousy pitchers do that. He shouldn't be wearing a Yankee uniform."[16]

Jim Piersall's father had just died of a heart attack on September 5. There had been a close bond between Piersall and his father. He had deeply resented his father's portrayal (played by Karl Malden) in the movie *Fear Strikes Out* as an overbearing, dominating influence causing his psychological difficulties.

With two outs in the bottom of the seventh inning of the first game, Mickey Mantle was on first and John Blanchard at bat. Suddenly two youths jumped out of the right field stands, charged onto the field and headed in the direction of Piersall in center field. Without hesitation, Piersall stood his ground; he threw his glove down and squared off, throwing a left hook at one of his attackers that connected, sending him sprawling on the outfield grass. Then he turned on the second attacker, who decided to make a hasty retreat, and kicked at him, just missing his backside.

Meanwhile, scrappy little 160-pound Johnny Temple and six-foot-seven-inch, 237-pound Walt Bond rushed to Piersall's aid, joined in the fray and got in a few punches on the intruders before the stadium police arrived on the scene and arrested the youths.

When play was resumed, Jim Piersall ended the inning by making a spectacular catch of a fly ball near the auxiliary scoreboard to the right of the bleacher wall while colliding with teammate Willie Kirkland. The huge Yankee Stadium crowd cheered Piersall wildly.

The two youths—James McInerty, Jr., 18 years old, of Bayport, Long Island, and Robert Mendez, 17, of Ronkonkoma, Long Island—were taken to night court and held on $50 bail awaiting Adolescent Court in the morning. At police headquarters McInerty was asked why he went after Piersall. He replied, "I've been watching Piersall on TV and he antagonizes me."[17]

The first game ended in a 7–6 defeat for the Indians. Neither Maris nor Mantle hit a homer.

Manager Jimmy Dykes decided to keep Jim Piersall, Johnny Temple and Walt Bond on the bench for the second game to protect them from the rowdy crowd at Yankee Stadium. Ken Aspromonte, who was hitting .224, as opposed to Temple's .280, started at second base.

As expected, the Yankees' fans got heated up again in the second game. The nonsense began in the sixth inning. Following a walk issued to

Elston Howard by Indians pitcher Jim Perry and a single by Bill "Moose" Skowron, Clete Boyer hit a Perry fast ball that disappeared in the shadows of left field and appeared to have gone into the bullpen. Actually the ball had caromed off the grandstand rail at the 402-foot mark. Boyer, not aware of the fact that the ball was in play, slowed up as he neared third, and with a series of relays begun by Chuck Essegian, he was called out at third base by umpire Frank Umont. At first, umpire Charlie Berry had wrongly signaled that the hit was a home run.

While two runs had scored, the crowd felt like they had been robbed by the umpire's call and went crazy. For seventeen minutes, even when play was resumed, thousands of fans threw everything they could get their hands on—paper cups, beer cans, articles of clothing, hot dogs, wet balls of newspapers—onto the field and into the press box. The mayhem continued until the eighth inning, and even then a few hundred fans refused to cease fire.

New York manager Ralph Houk actually played the game under protest. Of course there was no need for such an action as the Yankees won handily, defeating the Indians 9–3 and extended their winning streak to twelve games. In the game Mickey Mantle hit his 53rd home run of the season. The best that Roger Maris could do was stroke two singles in the double-header and remained stalled at 56 home runs.

The loss left the Indians in fifth place, 28½ games behind the Yankees. It was just part of a total collapse in the second half of the 1961 season for Cleveland as they lost 61 out of the final 101 games to finish in fifth place with a record of 76–78. Jimmy Dykes was fired before the last game of the season.

On October 1, the last day of the season, Roger Maris connected off Boston's rookie pitcher Tracy Stallard for his record-breaking 61st home run. After hitting his 54th home run, Mickey Mantle, affected by injuries and an infection, had to sit out most of the rest of the season. The New York Yankees went on to win the 1961 American League pennant and defeat the Cincinnati Reds four games to one in the World Series.

When a reporter from *The Sporting News* caught up with Johnny Temple on his dude ranch in Arizona and asked why the Indians collapsed in July, he was only too happy to offer his opinions, but maybe too eager in the minds of the Cleveland front office.

Attired in cowboy garb, compete with a Stetson hat and boots, Temple put his feet up on an ottoman and with candor remarked that, when the Indians were just a half game out of first place, only 17,000 fans showed up at Municipal Stadium. "It kind of took something out of the players to be treated like that in their home city."[18] Once again, as he had done prior to spring training, Temple assailed the frequent trades, stating, "Cleveland is hurting as a baseball town because its players are a bunch of strangers as far as the fans are concerned."[19] Lastly, Temple felt that departed manager Jimmy Dykes's modus operandi of naming his starting lineup the day spring training opened and playing that lineup throughout the six-week exhibition schedule added to the Indians' collapse, as it caused players to peak too early. As a result, according to Temple, players were worn out by midsummer.

Temple was also angry at the press because according to him, someone had misquoted him in a Cleveland newspaper as saying he wouldn't mind being traded to Los Angeles so he could be near his dude ranch in Arizona.

Gabe Paul, who had taken over as general manager at Cleveland after bolting the expansion Houston Colt .45s after a couple of months on the job, decided to make some changes on the Indians' roster for the 1962 season.

When asked if he thought that Gabe Paul might trade him, Temple replied that he wanted to stay in Cleveland, but Paul had traded him before, so he wouldn't be surprised if he traded him again.

But one of Gabe Paul's first off-season moves on October 5 was to trade embattled outfielder Jim Piersall to the Washington Nationals for pitcher Dick Donovan, outfielder Gene Green and shortstop Jim Mahoney.

While Temple was sorry to see Piersall go to Washington—stating that not many players will climb fences like him—he believed that the acquisition of Dick Donovan was a positive move for the Indians, calling him one of the toughest pitchers in the league. Temple also stated, "If we can come up with some catching help for Johnny Romano, then I think we'll really be a contender."[20] It seems that Temple never considered the old adage, "Be careful of what you wish for."

On November 16, 1961, the day after Johnny Temple's remarks on the state of the Cleveland Indians were published in *The Sporting News*, Gabe Paul traded Temple for the second time in three years. This time Temple went to the Baltimore Orioles for three players: first baseman Ray Barker, journeyman catcher Harry Chiti and minor leaguer Art Kay.

When Gabe Paul had traded Johnny Temple from Cincinnati to Cleveland at the end of the 1959 season, the move had triggered an emotional crisis for Temple. He had thought he was set for life in Cincinnati. But his second trade by Paul in two years to Baltimore infuriated him as he believed that he was being undervalued and felt the move was personal.

Temple remarked to the press that he might retire: "I don't mind being traded, but how could he trade me for Harry Chiti?"[21]

Temple certainly had a point. Harry Chiti had been knocking around the major leagues for parts of eleven years and had never distinguished himself as a big league receiver. The fact was that Chiti would not play one game for the Indians, and in April 1962 Gabe Paul would sell him to the expansion New York Mets franchise, where he would appear in fifteen games before ending his career.

It is not really known whether or not Johnny Temple talked himself out of Cleveland in his *Sporting News* interview, or if it had any influence at all on Paul's decision to deal him to the Baltimore Orioles. Still it seemed on the surface that some sort of personality conflict existed between Gabe Paul and Johnny Temple. Probably what Temple failed to realize was that although he played in 129 games and hit .276 in the 1961 season, the fact was that he was now 34 years old (or actually older) and his legs were shot. One sportswriter stated that Temple looked like he was running on a trampoline. Also his $40,000 a year salary no longer made him an asset when the Indians performed profit and loss analysis on their players.

Nonetheless there is more than a hint of Gabe Paul's having a spiteful streak in his personality recorded in various sources. One such incident involves Gabe Paul's reluctance as a member of the Hall of Fame's Veterans' Committee to vote for catcher Ernie Lombardi's induction to the Hall.

Johnny Temple, 1962 (Baltimore Orioles).

In his autobiography *Birdie: Confessions of a Baseball Nomad*, Birdie Tebbetts recalls that when he was selected to join Gabe Paul on the Veterans' Committee, he believed that Ernie Lombardi was being treated unfairly and decided to lobby for his admission to the National Baseball Hall of Fame. At his first meeting as a member of the committee, Tebbetts gave an impassioned speech on the late catcher's qualifications in consideration for induction.

Nine. A Fading Star

Reasons being advanced for keeping Ernie Lombardi out of the Hall of Fame were such as he got momentarily knocked out at home plate in the 1939 World Series when the Yankees' Charlie Keller's knee hit him in the groin at home plate, causing him to drop the ball. By the time Lombardi recovered, Joe DiMaggio had scampered around the bases and slid across the plate with a second run. Lombardi had actually recovered from Keller's shot in his grapes, retrieved the ball and attempted to tag DiMaggio. But DiMaggio made a slide that no one had ever seen before: twisting his body to the first-base side, he hiked his lead foot into the air and it went over Lombardi's glove. As it turned out, the Yankees swept the Reds in four games in the series; the play at home plate would be memorialized in baseball annals as "Lombardi's snooze," and he would be mocked for the play the rest of his career. Later Lombardi attempted to commit suicide and later in life suffered other mental problems, but all this seemed superficial to Tebbetts as by the time of his death the catcher was at peace with himself.

The facts are that Ernie Lombardi was the one of best hitting catchers of his generation, having a lifetime batting average of .307. Lombardi's lifetime batting average is better than some very elite catchers in the history of the game, such as Johnny Bench (.267), Yogi Berra (.289), Gary Carter (.262), Carlton Fisk (.269) and Gabby Harnett (.297).

Lombardi played in the major leagues for seventeen years and won two National League batting titles, while playing a pivotal part in leading the Cincinnati Reds to back-to-back National League pennants in 1939 and 1940. Slow of foot, if he could have run just a little bit faster, Lombardi would have probably won another couple of batting titles.

Birdie Tebbetts would eventually be successful in getting the Veterans' Committee to vote for the induction of Ernie Lombardi, but it took a while, until 1986.

Gabe Paul's reason for voting against Lombardi's admission to the Hall of Fame was personal. Following the first vote on Lombardi that Tebbetts forced the committee to take, he had coffee with Gabe Paul and he asked him how he voted. "Out of respect for you I did not vote," said Paul. "I could not vote for that man." Tebbetts then inquired, "You did not vote for him because of your dislike of him in your days as the Reds' traveling secretary."[22] It was a fact that Gabe Paul did not deny.

Meanwhile, out at the Rancho Del Jefe, Johnny Temple was continuing to make the transition from second-sacker to cowpoke. To complement the eighty acres on his ranch that he owned, he was now leasing an additional 6000 acres on which 300 head of cattle roamed. He was entering the construction business, so it appeared that he didn't need baseball to keep bread and butter, or steaks as the case seemed to be, on the table.

Temple had bought the dude ranch in Arizona for $125,000. He also owned 18 acres of speculative land on a highway outside of Tampa, Florida, for which he had paid $33,000 in cash. In addition he had invested about $5,000 with two hundred other ballplayers in a corporation that bought apartment buildings and rented them to mostly black families.

But Temple had also made some investments by that time that went bust. One in particular was a $10,000 investment he had made in a laundromat. It was a harbinger of things to come.

The first game that Temple played in as a member of the Baltimore Orioles was a wild affair. It was opening day in the Bronx, April 10, 1962, with the Orioles poised to take on the World Champion New York Yankees. Although the Yankees were the reigning champs of major league baseball, and Roger Maris and Mickey Mantle had grabbed mega-headlines all over the country the previous season in their pursuit of Babe Ruth's all-time season home run record, a sparse crowd of only 22,978 showed up for the 1962 opener at Yankee Stadium.

In the 1961 season Roger Maris (61), Mickey Mantle (54) and Bill "Moose" Skowron (28) had hit a combined total of 143 home runs as the Yankees shattered the all-time team season home run record of 221, held jointly by the New York Giants and Cincinnati Reds, by clouting 240 round trippers.

In the 1962 opening game all three, Maris, Mantle and Skowron, hit home runs to lead the Yankees in a 7–6 come-from-behind win over the Orioles.

Johnny Temple went 3 for 5 in the game and hit a home run off Yankees starting pitcher Whitey Ford in the top of the third inning to give Baltimore a 2–0 lead. But Orioles starter Billy Hoeft failed to hold the lead as he gave up a two-run inside-the-park home run hit by Moose Skowron to the deepest part of center field in the fourth inning and then served up a three-run homer to Roger Maris in the fifth inning. By the sixth inning both starters, Ford and Hoeft, were taking showers.

In the top of the sixth the Orioles fought back, scoring a run when Jerry Adair drove home Brooks Robinson to cut the Yankees' lead to 5–4. Then Baltimore retook the lead 6–5 in the top of the eighth.

The outcome of the game was settled in the bottom of the eighth when Mickey Mantle homered, then Elston Howard doubled and scored on a single by Skowron to make the score 7–6.

In top of the ninth Ralph Terry was relieved by Louis Arroyo after giving up a leadoff single to Johnny Temple. Arroyo then got the next two batters out before Jim Gentile reached base on an error. But Jackie Brandt then popped up to Bobby Richardson to end the game.

While Temple's inaugural game with the Orioles had been memorable, by the time of the All-Star Game, he was no longer in the starting lineup and for the most part was regulated to the role of pinch-hitter. Orioles manager Billy Hitchcock had decided to move Jerry Adair from shortstop to second base, and let Marv Breeding and Ron Hansen battle it out for the shortstop position.

Johnny Temple, 1962 (Baltimore Orioles).

On August 11, 1962, although he was hitting a respectable .263 as a parttime player, the Orioles decided that they didn't need his $35,000 a year salary and sold Johnny Temple to the expansion Houston Colt .45s for cash.

Moving around from team to team was starting to annoy Temple, and to be traded to an expansion team greatly affected his ego. He was ready to go home and so told Houston manager Harry Craft. But the Colt .45s manager asked Temple to stay awhile. Instead, he announced that he would not return for the 1963 season. "I love this game," said Temple, "but it's a grind for me now. I've slowed up just as much as any guy my age would ... however, I'm still faster than most of the players around today."[23] But Temple slightly kept the door ajar for a return by quickly adding that the odds for his return were 90–10.

Temple added that while he had been an All-Star three times in the National League and one time in the American League: "Nobody remembers that. They remember me as the guy who hit a sportswriter [Earl Lawson] in Cincinnati."[24] In fact, there was some validity to that assessment of his legacy.

The whole can of worms created with the Earl Lawson incident in

1956 had suddenly been reopened during the 1962 season when another Cincinnati Reds player socked the *Cincinnati Post & Times Star* scribe in the jaw. This time the assailant was Reds outfielder Vada Pinson, who was angered by a column Lawson wrote criticizing his fielding. The incident had taken place on June 20 in the Reds' clubhouse at Forbes Field prior to a night game with the Pittsburgh Pirates. The two were riding on the team bus from the hotel to the ballpark when an argument was instigated by Pinson over the article. When they entered the clubhouse, Pinson asked Lawson if he had been serious when he wrote the article and he replied that he had. With that, Pinson hit Lawson with a left hook. Lawson attempted to fight back but was restrained.

Lawson wasn't hurt by the blow, and he and Pinson made nice around the batting cage prior to the game. While Lawson said he held no grudge toward Pinson, he also remarked, "I'm a little tired of getting hit all the time by ballplayers." Then he added, "Temple hit harder."[25]

For six years Johnny Temple had been trying to forget his impulsive assault on Earl Lawson and was also hoping that the media would forget as well. Now, with the Vada Pinson incident, every sportswriter in the country who did a piece on it for their paper felt compelled to tie the Pinson fracas together with a mention of the Temple episode.

A few days after arriving in Houston, Johnny Temple took over the second base position from Joey Amalfitano and attempted to provide some team leadership to the Colt .45s as they struggled in their first year of existence. He said that Houston was a better club than they thought they were and were at least fifty percent better than the second-year expansion Washington Nationals.

Reflecting on his development as a major leaguer, Temple remarked, "The guy who helped me the most was Red Schoendienst." He said: "The easiest way you can do the job is the best way. He didn't mean to loaf. But when I had to make a tag I aimed it right for the runner's teeth. When I had to throw to first I threw right at his head. Everybody hated me. In the league even Robin Roberts told me he hated me, and I didn't think Roberts could hate anyone."[26]

The last weekend in August, Johnny Temple returned to Cincinnati and Crosley Field for the first time since being traded to Cleveland three years earlier. A double-header was scheduled between Houston and Cincinnati for Sunday, August 26. On that date the Reds were in contention for the pennant with a record of 81–51, 4½ games behind the league-leading Los Angeles Dodgers and 2 games behind the second-place San Francisco Giants.

The Colt .45s won the first game 2–1, beating the Reds' fire-balling right-hander Jim Maloney.

The second game was tied 4–4 in the top of the ninth inning when Johnny Temple reminded everyone that he was still one of the best contact hitters in the major leagues. With two outs and the bases loaded, Temple hit a single, driving home two runs to provide the winning margin of 6–4 as the Colt .45s swept the double-header from the Reds.

The loss of the double-header left the Reds 5½ games out of first and they never recovered, finishing the 1962 season in third place.

The Houston Colt .45s finished their inaugural season in in the National League in eighth place with a record of 64–96, coming out on top of the Chicago Cubs and New York Mets in the expanded ten-team league.

In the 1962 season, Johnny Temple hit .263 in 78 games for the Baltimore Orioles and .263 in 31 games for the Houston Colt .45s.

In November that year, Temple was named in a $25,000 civil suit filed in Arizona Superior Court in Tucson by Lamar Cotton, a real estate developer. In the suit, Cotton, the plaintiff, alleged that he was beaten and kicked to a state of near-unconsciousness by forty-three-year-old Bernard Allor while in the office of his attorney Charles Gatewood, and that Temple participated in the assault by blocking escape routes. Both Allor and Temple's wives were also named in the suit.

While the incident was mentioned in several out-of-state newspapers, it is not clear what the central issue was other than some sort of fracas had occurred during a business meeting.

The suit was never adjudicated. Temple was cleared of all charges on April 15, 1964, by the Superior Court of the State of Arizona, in and for the County of Pima, because the case had been on the inactive calendar for more than two months and never prosecuted.

As the off-season progressed, Temple stuck to his decision to retire from baseball. But following a conversation with Colt .45s manager Harry Craft, then checking himself into a hospital and having his leg operated on, Temple began to detect that strong addictive quasi–new car scent of spring training in the air. It was too persuasive, and Temple reported to the Colt .45s' spring training camp in Apache Junction, Arizona, four days early.

When asked about his decision to delay his retirement, Temple stated, "The way we played the last six weeks helped me change it and I had an operation this winter that has made my legs feel good again after years of trouble with them."[27]

Johnny Temple, 1963 (Houston Astros).

Although Temple didn't know how many games he would be capable of playing, he determined that players he had played with, such as Roy McMillan and Don Hoak, were still playing every day, so why shouldn't he give it a try?

Of course the question was raised of just how much Temple would play. Over the winter, the Colt .45s had acquired two-time American League batting champion and infielder Pete Runnels, who could play first and second base, from the Boston Red Sox. Also the club had decided to take a long look at twenty-one-year-old rookie second baseman Ernie Fazio.

As it turned out, Temple played in 100 games in the 1963 season, including playing 97 games at second base and one at third base, and finished with a batting average of .264. Temple finished with a batting average that was higher than both Pete Runnels at .253 and Ernie Fazio, who hit .184.

Since he first came up with the Reds in 1952, Johnny Temple had problems with umpires. Over the course of his major league career it is estimated that he had been thrown out of two to three games a year, costing him in the area of $1300 in fines.

It seemed as if Temple started every game mad and stayed that way. "I have to beef," said Temple. "I have to kick and scratch. That's the way I am. I was born that way. Once on our farm I saw my dad hit one of our mules right between the eyes. He sprained his wrist and couldn't work for two weeks."[28]

The 1963 season found Johnny Temple in one umpire batting episode after another. By July he had been fined three times for run-ins with umpires. After being fined $25 for an incident with an umpire in Chicago on June 17, Temple, who previously had been fined $100 and $50 by the league office, remarked, "I need a $75 fine now to hit for the cycle."[29]

At one point Temple publicly accused the National League umpires of a conspiracy against him. "I'm no crybaby," said Temple. "But there are six or seven umpires in this league who are out to get me. When we were in Cincinnati, a guy told me he heard one umpire say he was going to get me—and I can get this man to testify to that."[30]

Temple's accusations of a conspiracy brought a swift response from National League president Warren Giles, who demanded an explanation. Coming to the conclusion that he was unable to prove a conspiracy against him, Temple sent an apology to the league office through the Colt .45s publicity department. In part he remarked, "If my statements in the clubhouse after Sunday's game were offensive in any way to the National League office, I apologize. I had no intention of embarrassing the league's office or impugning the integrity of the league's umpires."[31]

Still, Temple did have one significant moment of glory on the field that last season playing for Houston. On August 4 he broke up Johnny Podres's no-hitter with a single in the ninth inning as the Los Angeles Dodgers defeated the Colt .45s 4–0.

The Houston Colt .45s finished their second season in the National

League in ninth place with a record of 66–96. At the end of the 1963 season, Houston handed Johnny Temple his unconditional release and offered him a job as a coach in their farm system.

Temple was no longer in the dude ranch business. He and his family now called Houston their home. So while he considered the .Colt 45s' offer, Temple decided to take the family back to North Carolina for the holidays.

But soon after, Temple got an unusual offer from the Cincinnati Reds, and bitten by the nostalgia bug of returning to the Queen City where he had enjoyed the greatest success during his playing career, Temple would be unable to refuse it. Suddenly he had delusions that the Cincinnati Reds job, no matter how insignificant in stature, would be his start toward advancing to a major league manager's job. The reality was that anyone could have told him he was about to go down a dead-end street.

Ten

A Complicated Return to Cincinnati

On December 13, 1963, the Cincinnati Reds signed Johnny Temple as a coach. While the thirty-four-year-old Temple was elated by the opportunity to return to Cincinnati, he quickly made it known that coaching was fine, but he didn't want to play. During the later stages of the 1963 season, Temple had once again experienced problems with his legs. "I hope I don't have to play anymore,"[1] said Temple. "I enjoyed my two years with the Colts and I hate to leave, but this is the start toward what I hope will wind up in a major league managing job."[2]

During the years that Temple had been playing in Cleveland, Baltimore and Houston, some changes had taken place in the Cincinnati Reds' front office.

Former general manager Gabe Paul was now serving in that position in Cleveland. Also, longtime Cincinnati Reds owner Powell Crosley, Jr., had died.

In 1961 William (Bill) O. DeWitt, Sr., had left the Detroit Tigers to become general manager of the Reds. Then, after winning a pennant his first year in Cincinnati, in October of that year DeWitt and a few others bought the ball club from the estate of Powell Crosley. So Bill DeWitt was now both president and general manager of the Cincinnati Reds.

Reds manager Fred Hutchinson had told Bill DeWitt that he wanted Johnny Temple back in a Cincinnati uniform. While Hutchinson personally liked Temple and would enjoy hanging out with him occasionally on the road, there were a couple of other reasons why he wanted him.

First, Fred Hutchinson believed that if he were activated, Temple, being a good contact hitter, could be a benefit to the club as a pinch hitter.

Second, Hutchinson convinced DeWitt that Temple could be a role model for Pete Rose, the Reds' free-spirited 1963 National League Rookie of the Year. Fred Hutchinson was telling the press, "I think Johnny can help Pete a lot."[3] The fact was that Hutchinson had a hidden agenda. What he really wanted Temple to do was separate Rose socially from the black players on the team.

Johnny Temple was familiar with Pete Rose. When Rose was a student at Western Hills High School in Cincinnati in the late 1950s, he spent some time around Crosley Field. Rose's uncle Curley Smart was a clubhouse helper for Chesty Evans, the Reds' clubhouse custodian. So Rose would come out to the ballpark and play catch during pre-game practice.

"Pete use to play catch with me and Roy McMillan," said Temple, "when he was 13 or 14 … hanging around. He was a tough little monkey then. You could tell he had a lot of heart. He was always asking questions about baseball, too."[4]

Bill DeWitt was receptive to Hutchinson's suggestion of offering Temple a job because he had become agitated by the fact that Pete Rose only hung out with the black players on the Reds: Frank Robinson, Vada Pinson, Tommy Harper, et al. In fact, during Rose's rookie season DeWitt had called him in for a conference at the club's offices in downtown Cincinnati and very bluntly asked Pete why he was hanging out with just the black players on the team.

Rose told DeWitt that since he joined the team the white players on the Reds had not exactly accepted him with open arms. But the black players had befriended him. The trouble began when Rose replaced popular starting second baseman Don Blasingame in the lineup. The Reds had veterans in all of the starting positions, and according to Rose, the players didn't want a rookie on second base.

There was no doubt that when Rose replaced popular veteran Don Blasingame in the lineup, it had annoyed a lot of his Reds teammates, and consequently they gave him the cold shoulder. But Pete Rose was also partly responsible for any disconnect with his teammates as he was aloof with them. Furthermore, from day one upon joining the team, Rose marched to the beat of a different drummer in regard to team protocol. His constant hustle and his habit of running out bases on balls bothered many of his teammates who considered it overkill.

During a spring training exhibition game in 1963 against the New York Yankees, Rose drew a walk and took off for first base in a gallop. Mickey Mantle and Whitey Ford, seated next to each other on the Yankees bench, began to chuckle, and Ford dubbed Rose "Charley Hustle." It was a moniker that would stick.

Prior to coming to Cincinnati in a trade with the San Francisco Giants in 1961, Don Blasingame had replaced future Hall of Fame second baseman Red Schoendienst in the St. Louis Cardinals lineup and was an All-Star in 1958. Then after coming to the Reds he played a pivotal role in Cincinnati's winning the 1961 National League pennant. Blasingame had also married former major league catcher Walker Cooper's daughter, a former beauty queen, and both were extremely popular with other players and their wives.

First baseman Gordy Coleman was the last player still on the team that had come to the Reds in the 1959 trade with Cleveland that included Cal McLish and Billy Martin in exchange for Johnny Temple.

In regard to Pete Rose, Coleman asserted that following a road game, the Reds' team bus would pull up to the hotel and a lot of the veteran players would go one way and the brash rookie Rose, the other.

More often than not, the veterans on the team would not see Rose after the games on the road. He very seldom rode the team bus to the hotel, a strange streak of independence for a rookie in the big leagues. Usually Rose showered after games and then met the girls who were waiting for him. Most of them were far from being something to write home about. Then the next day Rose would bore his teammates by relating his exploits with the women while they rode the team bus to the ballpark.

Also it was a source of huge irritation for a lot of the veteran players, mainly Don Blasingame and third baseman Gene Freese, that Rose, being a local kid, had a considerable fan following in Cincinnati. At home games hundreds of over-zealous, very boisterous rooters from Rose's old neighborhood in Sedamsville and the surrounding areas of Western Hills packed Crosley Field and cheered for him as if he were Joe DiMaggio.

The only players on the team who weren't standoffish with Rose were black players such as Frank Robinson and Vada Pinson. According to Pinson, "Here was this kid who wanted to be a major leaguer more than anything in the world. But he was so raw, he just didn't know how. Frank Robinson and I took a little time to show him. Dressing. Tipping. Basics like that. No big deal. Just a little kindness to a youngster."[5]

While no one had to teach Pete Rose how to hit, he lacked in the social graces and needed guidance. Part of the problem was the environment that he had grown up in. Pete was raised along the Ohio River on the west side of Cincinnati in the gritty little neighborhood of Sedamsville near the Anderson Ferry. That area of Cincinnati, which snakes along the banks of the Ohio, at the time Rose was growing up was filled with cafes that featured open bookmaking and was just a ferry ride across the river from northern Kentucky, which in the 1950s featured casino style gambling, prostitutes and an abundance of seedy night life controlled by the Cleveland syndicate.

Other than playing sports himself or watching his father Harry Rose play semi-pro football, family activities for Pete Rose and his family were limited. They included dinner at the Trolley Tavern, a popular but dowdy fish fry restaurant along River Road, or an afternoon spent at River Downs Race Track on the far-east side of Cincinnati.

Author Roger Kahn, writing in *Pete Rose: My Story*, stated that while Pete was growing up he ran with a crowd known as the River Rats and "all those kids knew about beer schooners and sports books before they were fifteen years old."

The River Rats were not hard-core delinquents in the classic sense of the organized street gangs that we know of today controlling drug trade in the ghettos of Chicago and Los Angeles, nor did they remotely resemble the romanticized Jets and Sharks street gangs of *West Side Story*. It is even highly doubtful that any of Rose's youthful associates would have been familiar with the street lexicon of the 1950s or be familiar with a basic term of the culture such as "to rumble." The River Rats were just a bunch of dysfunctional kids from low-income working-class families who hung out together and shared an ethos that lacked worldly direction, goals and motivation. Other than for those in sports and gambling, role models in that Cincinnati river bank neighborhood were few or nonexistent.

Pitcher Jim O'Toole stated, "Pete was a hometown kid and he had to prove himself to us. Don Blasingame had his best year in 1962 and he should have never lost his second-base job. As a pitcher, I didn't like that Rose couldn't make the double play like Blasingame."[6]

It also bothered O'Toole that Rose appeared so unsophisticated. "I didn't like that he talked like a hillbilly. He wasn't very educated."[7]

Jim O'Toole told Rose that the white players would accept him if he stopped hanging out with Robinson and Pinson. At the time there was a lot of jealousy on the Reds toward Robinson and Pinson because they had the biggest contracts and seemed to be comfortable with each other's company, ignored their teammates socially, and didn't care what they thought about them.

Although major league baseball had been integrated for sixteen years by the time Pete Rose came up to the Reds, racial assimilation on major league teams was slow in evolving and it wasn't just because white players

Ten. A Complicated Return to Cincinnati

were reluctant to socialize with black players. The same held true for many black players. There was a cautious approach to off-field socialization between white and black players. The overwhelming majority of white and black players didn't room together and didn't go out to eat together.

In the middle and late 1950s before being traded to Cleveland, Vic Power, a native of Puerto Rico, was a popular black first baseman with the Kansas City Athletics. His best friend on the Athletics at the time was a white player, third baseman Clete Boyer. When Power began to hang out with Boyer he was castigated by Harry "Suitcase" Simpson, Bob Trice and Hector Lopez, the other black players on the Athletics. Lopez was Power's roommate. All three felt that black players should stick together. Simpson called Power an "Uncle Tom" for befriending Boyer.

Frank Robinson and Vada Pinson were making a big leaguer out of a young, socially challenged Pete Rose. "Baseball is all Pete ever talked about," said Robinson. "It's all he ever wanted to do ... or dreamed about. Baseball, baseball, baseball."[8]

Author/pitcher Jim Brosnan was with the Cincinnati Reds between 1959 and 1963. According to Brosnan, during spring training in 1963 the only thing he noticed about Pete Rose was how tight and long he wore his uniform pants. "I had never seen anyone do that except for Frank Robinson."[9]

Also according to Brosnan, there was a stripper in Pittsburgh who was popularly known as a "star fucker." At first she ignored Pete Rose because he wasn't a star. But when she realized that he was the only one on Reds team she could get, she went out with him. She also brought along a blonde who was sleazier than she was. Here was Rose, stated Brosnan, standing between them looking like a little brat. "He went out with both of them. No one was jealous."[10]

Robinson and Pinson began to influence Rose off the field as well as on. Rose stated in his book *My Prison Without Bars*, that just before the Reds' first West Coast road trip in his rookie season, he put away his blue jeans and T-shirts and started to dress like a big leaguer and bought some nice sports jackets, slacks, dress shirts and ties. "You should've seen the looks when I drove back to the old neighborhood in my lime green Corvette, dressed in a suit and tie. Nobody could believe it was me,"[11] said Rose.

Of course there were others who held a different opinion in regard to the hazing and snubbing of Rose by his Reds teammates. Dave Bristol, who managed Rose in the minors and later was his manager with the Reds, believed, "Just Pete's personality sometimes could cause that. Freese and

Blasingame were toward the end of their careers. That kind of hazing in baseball at the time was common they always gave a rookie a hard time. Hey, Rose took Blasingame's position. I'd be mad too, wouldn't you?"[12]

The race issue aside, Bill DeWitt believed that Rose was a player who had to be protected; he took his comments seriously about being snubbed by veterans on the team and was swift in taking action. So DeWitt removed both Freese and Blasingame from the Reds roster.

During the 1963 season Gene Freese was sent down to the minors with the Reds' AAA affiliate San Diego. Later on November 26, 1963, Freese was sent to the Pittsburgh Pirates for cash. He continued to play in the major leagues until the end of the 1966 season.

Don Blasingame had played in only 18 games for the Reds in the 1963 season before being sent to the Washington Senators in exchange for cash. Blasingame continued to play in the major leagues until being released by Kansas City on September 7, 1966. He finished his 12-year major league career with a .258 lifetime batting average and a .977 lifetime fielding average.

But Blasingame was about to begin his second baseball career and became associated with Japanese baseball for the next sixteen years. In 1967 Blasingame went to Japan and became the second baseman for the Nankai Hawks for three years. From 1970 to 1977 Blasingame was a coach on the Hawks. Then in 1978 he became a coach for the Hiroshima Carp. In 1979 and 1980 he managed the Hanshin Tigers. Then in 1981 and 1982 Blasingame returned to the Carp as manager. His lifetime record as a manager in Japanese baseball was 180–208–28 (ties are played in Japan).

Don Blasingame's legacy in Japanese baseball is that he was one of a handful of American players and coaches who changed baseball in Japan by introducing a more firebrand style of play that included arguing with umpires, having pitchers throw brush-back pitches, and instructing runners to slide hard into second base in attempts to break up double plays.

At the Reds' spring training camp at Tampa, Florida, during March 1964, Johnny Temple began his transition from player to coach. When Fred Hutchinson presented him with a fungo bat and a stopwatch, a newspaper photographer quickly snapped a picture. As the Reds' pitchers ran in the outfield, Temple sat down on a nearby bench for rest. Grinning, Temple remarked that he hadn't got used to the fact that he could sit down anytime he wanted to.

Temple was glad to be in a Cincinnati uniform once again. He wasn't issued the familiar number 16 on his uniform that he had worn with the Reds during the 1950s when he and Roy McMillan were making those breathtaking double plays. That number was now being worn by All-Star shortstop Leo Cardenas. Instead Temple was issued uniform number 5, which in a few years would be issued to a 19-year-old catcher by the name of Johnny Bench, who would wear that number all the way to the Hall of Fame and retire it. "This has always been my team," said Temple. "Even when I was in the other league I followed the Reds closely through the newspapers."[13]

Temple was in a Cincinnati uniform because Fred Hutchinson had told Bill DeWitt that he wanted him, but what wasn't clear to everyone was just what Temple's responsibilities were on the ball club. When a reporter asked him about that very thing, he remarked, "Hutch has told me I'll have responsibilities. And if it were a job without responsibilities, I wouldn't be here."[14]

At the moment all that Fred Hutchinson was saying in regard to Temple was that he planned to use him a few times as a pinch hitter in some of the exhibition games and that he was confident that he would be a great help to Pete.

The informal inclusion of Temple on the coaching staff without a defined role was disconcerting to the other Reds coaches, Dick Sisler, Jim Turner and Reggie Otero. They tended to look at the Temple hiring with a jaundiced eye.

Towards the end of spring training, Frank Robinson developed a groin infection and was sent ahead to Cincinnati to be treated at Christ Hospital. However, by opening day Robinson was in right field for the Reds as they lost to the Houston Colt .45s by a score of 6–3.

Immediately following the game, manager Fred Hutchinson left for Seattle to enter a hospital for a checkup. In January, Hutch had been diagnosed with lung cancer.

On April 21, when the Reds made their first road trip of the season to Houston, Temple went to his residence there to pick up a few things that his wife Becky said she would like to have in Cincinnati. When Temple arrived at the house he found that thieves had broken in and looted it. Among the items taken were three television sets. One of the televisions, according to Temple, weighed 1200 pounds. The thieves even went up on the roof and took the special antenna that was necessary for color television reception. Other items stolen were most of Becky's jewelry and winter clothes, the family's silverware, three shotguns, and a rifle, and the liquor cabinet was cleaned out. All of the stolen items were insured. Ironically, Temple's insurance agent was Howie Pollet, former major league pitcher who was then the pitching coach for the St. Louis Cardinals.

As the still-young 1964 season progressed, Pete Rose became entangled in the eternal web of the sophomore jinx. On May 31, Rose went 0 for 8 in a double-header with the St. Louis Cardinals. With the Reds struggling in fifth place with a record of 21–21 and Rose struggling with a .215 batting average, Fred Hutchinson benched him and inserted Bobby Klaus at second base.

Both Bill DeWitt and Fred Hutchinson were far from being geniuses at social engineering, and both were afflicted with what we call today generational racism. Nonetheless they believed that Pete Rose had marquee potential, which translated to revenue for the ball club. But in order to cash in on Rose's star potential they needed to cultivate his social demeanor, and do it without the influence of the black players acting as his tutors, which was a source of embarrassment for both. And there was also the on-field issue; they also needed to get Rose out of his slump.

They had signed Johnny Temple with a mission to tutor Rose on and off the field. Temple was to be Rose's roommate and social mentor. On the field it was hoped that Temple could help Rose improve his mechanics around second base and help him to feel more comfortable at the plate. Temple's charge was a daunting task because of the complexity of Rose's personality.

But Bill DeWitt and Fred Hutchinson deemed him creditable for the task. Over time Johnny Temple, raised in a backwater town in North Carolina, by his own initiative had become socialized into solid middle-class American values. Temple knew what star quality meant in a player. He was cognizant of the fact that, if you were considered a star on the playing field, you had to continue to project that persona off the field to be taken seriously.

While a fiery contemporary such as Billy Martin often acted like a thug off the field, when Johnny Temple took his uniform off and donned his Ivy League suit, he left his feisty and fiery demeanor on the ball field, and in public demonstrated a quiet dignity about himself. He dressed well and spoke with a subtle eloquence. Temple was a regular at Toot's Shor's restaurant when the ball club was in New York and fit in well with the establishment's high-profile newsmen, celebrities and ballplayers such as Walter Winchell, Jackie Gleason, Mickey Mantle and Casey Stengel. Temple was cognizant of the fact that a positive public appearance also meant cash flow potential in the form of product endorsements.

Temple was ever so dapper that he covered his progressively balding head with a toupee. A few years earlier Temple had invested in two toupees at $500 each. The rug Temple wore was almost undetectable. He showered

Ten. A Complicated Return to Cincinnati 157

in it and wore it to bed. "Even barbers don't know," remarked Temple. "I once had a barber who started cutting my hairpiece until I straightened him out. I had to tell him where the hairpiece ended and my hair started."[15] Even Temple's golfing partners in Texas and his son Mike, now thirteen years old, were not aware that he was wearing a hairpiece.

Some other follically challenged major leaguers, such as Dick Groat and Bobby Schantz, had tried hairpieces, but abandoned them.

After Rose's rookie season, manager Fred Hutchinson told *Cincinnati Post* sportswriter Earl Lawson: "Pete's turning into a nigger. I need to do something to get him away from the blacks."[16] Hutchinson told Lawson about his off-field agenda for Temple in guiding Rose, "I'd want him to go out to dinner with Pete on the road ... polish him a little."[17]

Temple's charge for Rose was confirmed by second baseman Billy Moran, who played seven years in the major leagues (1958–1965). Later Moran remarked that Johnny Temple told him that Fred Hutchinson wanted him to make sure he did two things with Pete Rose: make sure "Pete Rose didn't hang around with black players and that Rose learned how to use a fork when he ate."[18]

At first Pete Rose was thrilled to have the opportunity to have a close association with Johnny Temple, one of his boyhood Redlegs heroes. During Rose's final season in the minors in 1962 playing with the Macon Peaches, a reporter from the *Macon Telegraph* asked Rose who his hero had been on the hometown Cincinnati Reds when he was growing up. His answer was a bit of surprise to the reporter: it wasn't Big Ted Kluszewski, Roy McMillan, or Frank Robinson, who joined the Reds when Rose was 14 years old in 1956. It was none other than Johnny Ellis Temple. So assigning Temple as Rose's mentor seemed like a good fit.

Temple began his quasi-Emily Post tutorials of Pete Rose, approaching the task with a strategy of counseling him in a fatherly way when they went out to eat. When Temple got around to the touchy subject of Rose's relationship with the black players on the team, he gingerly told Pete that he didn't have the respect of the white players on the team. Without hesitation Rose defended his actions, telling Temple he would do what he wanted and that the black players were his friends.

As Johnny Temple attempted to work with Rose on the field, he was convinced that Rose should be getting more hits and not be in the horrible slump he had been experiencing. He attempted to get Rose to bunt more often in an attempt to pull the third baseman in, then slap the ball by him. He also told Rose to relax on the field, not try to tag big outfielders on the eyes—just give them a sweeping tag.

Although Temple had hit over .300 three times in his major league career, when it came down to seeking advice on how to start getting hits again and shake his slump at the plate, Rose ignored Temple. He preferred to call his uncle Buddy Bloebaum. It had been Bloebaum, while a scout for the Reds, who convinced Phil Seghi, then farm director for the club, to give Rose a tryout. According to author Roger Kahn writing in *Pete Rose: My Story*, Bloebaum told Pete he was swinging the bat defensively. He said to lower his hands and attack the ball.

Regardless of how sincere Johnny Temple's intentions had been in helping Rose, his mission was failing. Soon Rose started to pull away from Temple, even avoid him altogether. According to Temple he didn't see Rose much late at night. "I couldn't go to the places Pete went. They were too lowbrow. I couldn't stay with him. I tried to take him to better places, but he wouldn't go."[19]

What Bill DeWitt and Fred Hutchinson had failed to consider in their attempt to create a bond between Johnny Temple and Pete Rose was the fact that friendships are reciprocal circumstances, not asymmetrical. Friendships are not casual psychotherapy sessions. There just wasn't any way that such an authoritarian approach to achieving behavioral changes with the hardheaded Rose were going to produce positive outcomes. In a very short time the Pete Rose social experiment had become a total failure.

Then on June 19, Temple's worst fear was realized—the Reds announced that as he had been signed as a free agent, he was being placed on the active list. The Reds were in the pennant race, holding down third place with a record of 33–27, three games out of first. Fred Hutchinson planned to use Temple as a pinch hitter.

On June 22 at Crosley Field, Temple made his first appearance in a game against the San Francisco Giants as a pinch hitter for pitcher Sammy Ellis. He hit an easy pop-up to Giants first baseman Willie McCovey as the Reds went down to defeat 6–2.

Temple would have six at bats in the 1964 season with no hits and two walks. On July 14, Johnny Temple made his last major league appearance as a player. He pinch-hit for reliever Billy McCool and drew an intentional walk from Houston pitcher Hal Woodeshick as the Reds beat the Colt .45s 6–5.

The next day, July 15, the Reds defeated the Houston Colt .45s to move within 4½ games of the league-leading San Francisco Giants. Prior to the game, the Reds had given Johnny Temple his unconditional release as a player to make room for catcher Don Pavletich on the roster. As with all unconditional releases, the player has to pass on waivers without any other club clamming him. As Temple was thirty-five years old, he breezed right through the waivers process with no takers.

Catcher Johnny Edwards had hurt his arm and it was necessary to open a roster spot in order to bring Pavletich up from the San Diego farm club of the Pacific Coast League. Temple would still be able to work with the players prior to the games, but would not be in uniform or on the bench once play started.

The fact was that no one was really paying attention to Johnny Temple or what he was doing, or supposed be doing, with the Reds. Furthermore, other than sportswriter Earl Lawson and a few friends of Temple's, no one was aware of his subterfuge tutorial of Pete Rose. As Temple traveled with the team, sportswriters were more interested in his toupee than his duties with the Reds. They started to refer to Temple's false hair as the finest toupee in the majors. Temple was philosophical about his toupee: "If you have a tooth missing, you replace it, don't you?"[20]

The scheme hatched by Hutchinson and DeWitt to bring Temple back to Cincinnati for the purpose of sophisticating Pete Rose had turned out to be ridiculous and had accomplished nothing but providing fodder for historical controversy. For decades afterward, in interviews with the press, with authors, on the radio and sometimes just talking to anyone who would listen to him, Pete Rose never missed a chance to cast himself as a victim in the illogical and twisted thought process of Bill DeWitt when he was a young player on the Reds.

By late August the Reds were still in the pennant race, now chasing the Philadelphia Phillies for the league lead. By this time manager Fred Hutchinson was in the hospital attempting to battle his cancer, and Pete Rose was back on the bench still battling the sophomore jinx, hitting .256. Chico Ruiz had been filling in at second while Rose sorted out his difficulties at the plate by himself.

During that time Temple had been working out in a pre-game workout around second base when Chico Ruiz came up to him and started asking questions. Temple told Ruiz that from what he had been reading and hearing he was doing all right without making any changes. Later Temple remarked that he had been accosted by acting manager Dick Sisler, who told him that Bill DeWitt had called down and told him to tell Temple to leave Ruiz alone. Temple was infuriated by the remark and called DeWitt on the telephone, who told him that Sisler had called him. So it became a "he said-he said" situation with no resolution.

Since spring training, Johnny Temple had been shunned by the other

Reds coaches and it had embittered him. Temple felt that the other coaches viewed him as an extra coach, a threat to their job security. He told Cincinnati sportswriter Earl Lawson, "I'm no donkey. I won't be treated the way I have been."[21] It was another Pete Rose–Don Blasingame episode among the coaches. Every time someone on the Reds felt that his job was in jeopardy, he resorted to the juvenile tactic of giving the other guy the cold shoulder.

The Reds were gearing up for the stretch drive, seven games behind the Phillies, and problems were in abundance. In addition to the problems with Fred Hutchinson's health, the sophomore jinx dogging Pete Rose, and potential morale problems being created by Johnny Temple's presence in the clubhouse, the ace of the Reds pitching staff, Jim Maloney, was ailing with a sore right shoulder and All-Star leadoff hitter Vada Pinson was hitting .257, 52 points below his lifetime average.

Assistant general manager Phil Seghi felt it was time to be proactive. While he couldn't do anything about the problems of Rose, Maloney and Pinson, he could attempt to shore up morale on the team. So Seghi approached Johnny Temple with an alternative. The Reds could terminate his employment with the club, or he could continue special scouting assignments at the major league level. Either way he would be paid until the end of the season. Seghi wanted Temple to return to his home in Houston and scout teams from there—out of sight, out of mind.

General manager Bill DeWitt went public with his remarks, putting a little spin on Temple's release by telling everyone that they had wanted Temple as a player: "Temple was taken on as a free agent last December at the insistence of manager Hutchinson. Hutch felt at the time that he could help us as both a player and adviser to Pete Rose. We signed him as a coach because we didn't have room on our playing roster at the time. But we wanted him chiefly as a player and we were disappointed when we learned he wasn't in condition to play."[22]

The fiery Johnny Temple considered the Reds' offer to return to Houston and scout an insult, feeling like the Reds' front office and coaches were sending him into exile. While he ultimately decided to return to his home in Houston, it was not to perform scouting assignments for the Reds. Prior to Friday evening's game on August 28, ironically with the Houston Colt .45s, Temple arrived at Crosley Field and entered the clubhouse to clean out his locker. Before arriving at the ballpark, Temple had consumed a couple of drinks.

When Temple entered the clubhouse, coach Reggie Otero was one of the first persons he encountered. Otero was not aware of the fact that

Temple had just terminated himself from the Reds organization. Otero slapped Temple on the back and playfully asked him how he was doing.

Already agitated, Temple took a swing at Otero, who retaliated by swinging at Temple, landing a haymaker that cut his face underneath the right eye. It turned out to be a four-punch fight, with Otero rapidly throwing three of the punches. Of course, as is the custom in baseball brawls, players rushed to separate the two combatants.

By the following morning the Cincinnati newspapers had chronicled the clubhouse commotion in detail on the front page.

That evening as Reggie Otero came onto the field, the Houston players began yelling at him, "How did Temple ever miss connecting with your big schnozzola?"[23]

It was a sad ending. Johnny Temple had been an All-Star second baseman with the Reds. He and shortstop Roy McMillan had formed one of the premier double play combinations in the major leagues during the 1950s. Overall, Temple had played thirteen years with Cincinnati, Cleveland, Baltimore and Houston. He had a .284 lifetime batting average and 1,484 hits. His lifetime fielding average was .973.

Now Temple was walking out of the Reds' clubhouse a battered man, both on the outside as well as the inside. Later that evening Temple called his old friend Earl Lawson and told him, "Twelve years ago, I walked into Crosley Field a topnotch professional ballplayer. I'm going out like a bum—beat up, nothing to do, and nowhere to go. I'm through with the game."[24]

The Cincinnati Reds' front office was greatly concerned that the confrontation between Temple and Otero might cause a division between the players on the team when unity was essential to making a final drive for the pennant. So after the Friday night game was called off due to inclement weather, a players' meeting was quickly called. Acting manager Dick Sisler headed up the meeting, but Phil Seghi persuaded the ailing Fred Hutchinson to attend. Many of the players voiced their opinions on what should be done—Bob Purkey, Frank Robinson, Joey Jay, Jim Maloney and Joe Nuxhall. They were all noncommittal to Johnny Temple and advanced their collective belief that winning games was the paramount issue.

It was not surprising that Joe Nuxhall, who had been a longtime teammate and friend of Johnny Temple going back to the minor leagues, would turn his back on him. A couple of years before, Nuxhall had been sent down to the minors and had to fight his way back to the major leagues. He was now thirty-six years old, nearing the end of his career, and knew it was dangerous to take a stand that would be unpopular with the front office. It was simply a case of rational action by Nuxhall, but nonetheless a gutless act.

Temple maintained he had been cut from the Reds by committee; that earlier in the week there had been a meeting among the coaches and they came to the conclusion that he wouldn't be able to get in shape sufficiently to be of any help in the stretch drive. In Temple's words, "They decided I was bad for the ball club."[25] Then Phil Seghi told him there was no spot for him on the coaching staff. Two days later a calmer Temple accepted Phil Seghi's offer to act as a scout for the Reds for the remainder of the season, working out of his home in Houston.

On September 21, after 150 games played in the 1964 season, the Philadelphia Phillies led the National League pennant race by 6½ games with 12 games to go. But the Phillies would go into a September swoon and begin a ten-game losing streak. They would lose ten out of their final twelve games and blow the pennant in one of the most famous late-season collapses in major league history.

The Phillies' rapid fall created a frenzied stretch run, with Cincinnati, St. Louis and San Francisco all in hot pursuit, taking the pennant chase down to the final hours of the 1964 season. Plans were even being drawn up by the National League office for a four-way playoff.

The pennant was decided on the final day of the season when the Philadelphia Phillies defeated the Cincinnati Reds and the St. Louis Cardinals defeated the New York Mets to win the flag. The Reds finished in a second-place tie with the Phillies, one game behind the Cardinals.

The attempted nurturing and socialization of Pete Rose into the major league mainstream by the Cincinnati Reds' front office was now officially at a close. There would be no more Johnny Temple–like tutors in his future. Pete Rose would have to adapt to the big leagues in his own way.

Rose played in 134 games in the 1964 season, finishing with a .269 batting average and 139 hits. But from that point on in his career, Pete Rose would not have fewer than 176 hits in a season until the strike-shortened season of 1981. Over the next fifteen seasons Rose would win three National League batting titles and have ten 200-plus-hit seasons. Pete Rose would finish his playing career in 1986 having eclipsed Ty Cobb as the major league all-time hits leader with 4,256 hits.

If Rose had not agreed to a lifetime ban with major league baseball in 1989 after evidence surfaced of his having placed bets on the Reds while managing the team, it is certain that he would have long ago been enshrined in the Hall of Fame in Cooperstown.

It had been a heart-wrenching experience for everyone connected with the Reds to watch Fred Hutchinson deteriorate before their eyes while battling his cancer as the 1964 season progressed, until he formally turned the reigns over to acting manager Dick Sisler on August 14.

Later Pete Rose was to say of Hutchinson's presence that season, "We saw Hutch go from 220 pounds to 140 pounds with the cancer and he never once complained. Tough. Really tough. More than baseball tough. He'd come into the clubhouse to conduct meetings and after a while, looking at Hutch was like looking a skeleton. But I'll tell you this. That skeleton was in charge."[26]

On November 12, 1964, both Pete Rose and Johnny Temple lost a true friend in Fred Hutchinson as he succumbed to his cancer peacefully in Bradenton, Florida.

Following his release by the Cincinnati Reds in 1964, Johnny Temple was never again offered a job in major league baseball, and his life began to slowly descend into darkness and desperation.

Eleven

The Tragic Fall of Johnny Temple

Following the pitiable experience of his return to Cincinnati and with his major league career clearly behind him, Johnny Temple and his family settled down in Houston.

One universal perk of playing in the major leagues then and now is that the experience provides a degree of fame for every player to secure employment opportunities when he hangs up his spikes. In May 1965, Temple became a radio show co-host on KTRH AM. The show was called Bradley's Bullpen, aired nightly from 10:15 to 11:00 p.m., and featured Temple fielding questions via telephone calls from fans.

By the late 1960s, Temple had moved over to television in Houston and became the sports director for Channel 11 KHOU-TV.

At the time Temple started at KHOU, the station had the smallest viewing audience in the huge and still growing Houston market. The station's news and sports department was a bare-bones operation. According to Richard West writing in the *Texas Monthly*, in May 1974 there was not much more than four stools and a gum-and-paper-clip-assembled set in the studio. "KHOU's production gaffes became instant fodder for cocktail jokes. At times key members of the engineering and production staff at KHOU had been employed no more than two weeks. High school kids ran highly complex equipment because management would not spend the money for professionals."[1] The station was using eight-year-old archaic 40-pound cameras and sound gear. Furthermore, the station spent only about $100,000 a year to promote all departments, which at the time was about 60 percent less than competing stations' expenditures.

Salaries were lower at KHOU as well. While Johnny Temple was being paid $25,000 a year as a sportscaster, his contemporary Bill Enis at KPRC was earning $50,000 a year.

In 1961, KHOU news anchor Dan Rather hired Ron Stone to be his replacement, joining fellow anchorman Dick John. The hiring of Stone was the first step toward the station's becoming competitive. Dan Rather eventually joined CBS and became a national news figure.

By the late 1960s, with Stone and John as anchormen, Sid Lasker doing the weather and Johnny Temple handling the sportscasting, KHOU's ratings began to soar. The task was accomplished on little more than the personalities of Stone, John, Lasker and Temple.

In his television reports, Johnny Temple talked sports rather than read from wire dispatches. With his outspoken, acid-dripping style of broadcast journalism, Temple's twice-a-day sports reports attracted a huge audience. In just a few months the station's ratings jumped from third to first. This was no small accomplishment—Temple was competing for viewers in a three-station block in the nation's fifth largest TV market.

No one was spared from Johnny Temple's wrath in his broadcasts. Jack Gallagher, a sportswriter for the *Houston Post*, wrote in one of his columns, "Johnny Temple has an unlisted home phone number: and I can understand why. The way the outspoken sportscaster picks his opponents, he needs a red telephone with a direct line to the SAC bomber base in Omaha."[2]

One of his favorite targets was massive Houston Oilers tackle Ernie (The Big Cat) Ladd. In 1967, Ladd, at 6'9" and 315 pounds, with 20" biceps and size 18 shoes, was the largest player in the AFL. That did not deter little Johnny Temple from heaping criticism on Ladd. Temple said of Ladd during one of his shows, "Every time Ernie makes a tackle the Houston management should call time out, run out on the field and give him a $100 bill. That seems to be the only way to get to the man—with money. That's all he cares about."[3]

Ernie Ladd played 112 consecutive AFL games within eight years with the San Diego Chargers (1961–1965), Houston Oilers (1966–1967) and Kansas City Chiefs (1967–1968). During his later years in the AFL he also became a wrestler. He would become the only man ever elected to the AFL Hall of Fame and World Wrestling Entertainment Hall of Fame.

Ladd was aware of Temple's criticism and when he came to Houston for a wrestling match, Temple telephoned him for an interview. Ladd immediately told Temple, "I don't need you." The fiery Temple shot back, "I don't need you either."[4]

In the early 1970s, Johnny Temple would be replaced as sports director at KHOU-TV by Ron Franklin, who would later move on to ESPN and become involved in a highly publicized wrongful termination suit that alleged his involvement in making sexist comments to a colleague.

Temple's sports gig in Houston had lasted for seven years. During that time KHOU, owned by Corinthian Broadcasting Company, whose parent company was Dunn and Bradstreet, saw the value of the station rise from $10 million to $44 million.

Temple and his family had led a productive and prosperous life in Houston. The family lived in lovely home and his son Mike was attending Texas A&M.

During Temple's tenure at KHOU, various individuals started coming to him with business propositions. So he entered into the recreational vehicle business—campers, boats, motorhomes, etc. His partner served as the business manager and Temple handled public relations. But bad luck seemed to doom any enterprise that Johnny Temple entered. The recreational-vehicle company had tax problems—proper withholding taxes were not maintained, and proper Social Security payments not made. Then a fire destroyed the business and Temple was to learn that the insurance policy covering the business had been voided for nonpayment of premiums. It was a mess of gargantuan proportions.

The land that the Temples owned was situated on the Katy Freeway (Interstate 10), on which construction began in the late 1960s. Today I-10 is the major east–west Interstate Highway in the southern United States. In the state of Texas, I-10 runs east from Anthony at the border with New Mexico, through El Paso, San Antonio and Houston to the border with Louisiana in Orange, Texas, covering a stretch of just under 879 miles.

So the government took what it wanted via eminent domain to build the freeway, while the Temples paid a small fortune in legal fees to lawyers in an attempt to retain their property rights. The banks also took a huge chunk of the Temples' resources as collateral in the recreational vehicle store to rescue their floor plans. Eventually the banks foreclosed on the business, giving Temple and his partner no time to sell off their remaining inventory. In the process, Temple lost everything, his home and business, including about $125,000 in equity in the land and $105,000 worth of stock.

The majority of Temple's investments had been speculative. He liked those types of investments. "It's like stealing a base," said Temple. "If you don't take a chance, you'll never make it."[5] In one such venture he bought 18 acres of speculative land on a highway outside of Tampa for $33,000 in cash. The investment never panned out.

Eleven. The Tragic Fall of Johnny Temple

In 1972 Johnny Temple and his family packed up and returned to the hometown of his wife, Becky Sheely Temple, in Ballantine, South Carolina. The family moved in with Becky's parents while they tried to get their feet back on the ground.

At first Temple attempted to get back into baseball, but no one would talk to him. Ever since the Reggie Otero incident, no one in any major league front office would return his calls.

Part of the problem, according to Becky Temple, was that baseball people had always mistaken his fierce pride and determination for arrogance. For some reason, because of his rural North Carolina background, Temple had always felt it necessary to prove himself to everyone that he belonged at the major league level.

Whatever the front office or public perception of Temple had been, Becky Temple steadfastly maintained that at home her husband had never been anything but a wonderful, thoughtful and loving father and husband to Mike and her.

After a while Temple got a state job and the family moved into an apartment. He became an assistant to John West, governor of South Carolina from 1971 to 1975. His salary was $17,500 a year and he wrote speeches for Governor West, U.S. Senator Strom Thurmond and others, but mostly worked in the civil disaster preparedness department.

That job didn't last long because Temple developed a drinking problem and was fired. Also Temple's supervisor had discovered that he had duplicated $30 worth of expense vouchers over a three-year period. He was not prosecuted or allowed to make restitution.

The entire affair made no sense for an employee making his salary to steal $30 from the state. Becky Temple always maintained that there were other reasons why her husband was fired, but she refused to elaborate. It has been speculated that the real reason Temple was fired was that he had stumbled across some irregularity in the state's business practices.

The drinking problem that Johnny Temple acquired was highly uncharacteristic of his personality traits. He had always deplored any sort of substance abuse. When he was playing ball, only rarely did he go out and hoist a few brews with teammates following games. According to his wife, at one time she had a serious drinking problem when Temple was still playing ball, and he got her the best professional help available.

The loss of the state job devastated Temple and he went into an emotional tailspin. He became deeply, perhaps clinically depressed and going forward never seemed to be able to completely overcome his mental state.

According to Becky Temple, Johnny began to change into someone she hardly knew.

Then suddenly the couple was confronted with judgments from all over in the Houston business fiasco. Becky went to work to help support the family and pay off as much money they owed as possible, but the constant harassment that Temple was experiencing began to take him down deep mentally.

Eventually Temple took a job in a warehouse for $2.30 an hour. Then bad luck for Temple escalated still further when he contracted pneumonia that left him with a weak lung.

By June 1975 Temple and his wife Becky were living in retirement in Lake Lure, North Carolina. Becky had persuaded her father to buy the couple a small cabin in the mountains where she felt the climate would be conducive to Johnny's recovery. Twenty-five years earlier the Temples had honeymooned in Lake Lure and fell in love with the community.

Over time, Major League Baseball and the Players Association, despite the pettiness of Los Angeles Dodgers owner Walter O'Malley, who did the bidding for the powerful owners, and the lack of leadership by Commissioner Bowie Kuhn, a pension plan had been developed that for many years had been filled with controversy. By 1975 based on revenues from major league All-Star Games to fund it, former players and coaches who had completed at least five years of service were eligible to receive funds upon reaching the age of 50 or up.

Although his actual age has never been established, by 1970 Johnny Temple was claiming that he was 50 years old and was receiving a player's pension of $437 a month on which he and his wife were attempting to make ends meet.

Becky Temple used to cringe when she received one of those "what's Johnny doing now" interview calls. Still, Temple fielded the calls and always put a positive spin on his circumstances, having too much pride to even suggest that he and his wife needed assistance.

When Jack Murray of the *Cincinnati Enquirer* called, Temple told him:

> One of the things that really hurts me—I was probably the best second baseman the Reds ever had until Joe Morgan, but I'll be remembered for taking a punch at Earl Lawson, who was my best friend in sportswriting and still is.
> Earl's a dear man.... Earl and I never discussed that and I'm sure he's sick of hearing about as I am. We exchange Christmas cards and look forward to them."[6]

When a reporter for the *Asheville Citizen-Times* caught up with Temple, he asked about the couple's relocation to Lake Lure. Temple stated,

"We've often thought and talked of Lake Lure over the years and of the wonderful, warm people up here. It was always tucked away in our minds to settle here and now we have our own place on this beautiful lake and are really enjoying it."[7] Temple also said that he was hoping to get involved with the recreation program in the area.

The fact was that Temple and his family were hurting and in dire straits financially. But Temple's fierce pride would have never allowed him to admit publicly that he was broke and needed financial assistance or that he desperately needed employment.

Becky's father had told her that she could come home anytime she wanted, but she was deeply devoted to Johnny and the thought of leaving him was unthinkable. She vowed to be with Johnny as long as God would permit her.

In late 1975, Thomas Mains, a real estate developer in Lake Lure, was attempting to buy the Asheville franchise in the Southern League. If successful he planned to install Johnny Temple as general manager. Unfortunately Mains lost the bid to Jimmy Crockett of Charlotte, who bought the ball club and moved it there. If Mains had been successful, he may have provided Johnny Temple with the most important job of his life and prevented the former All-Star from entering in to an astonishing association with low-life activity.

Then, in July 1976, Becky's mother had open-heart surgery. A week later she suffered a massive stroke. Becky went to Columbia, South Carolina, to assist her parents. She was there for three months and worried constantly about Johnny's being alone up in the mountains. As it turned out, her fears were warranted.

On Friday morning, November 4, 1977, the sports world was shocked to learn that Johnny Temple had been arrested at his home in Lake Lure, North Carolina, as part of a theft ring and charged with grand larceny.

Unlike current and former professional football and professional basketball players who seem to make headlines frequently with jail sentences, it has always been a rare occurrence when a former major league baseball player is sent to prison. Not even one of the eight Chicago White Sox players who conspired with gamblers to fix the 1919 World Series ever saw the inside of a jail. Of course, there have been some exceptions; Denny McLain and Pete Rose both did time in federal prisons. It was a severe shock to the sports world to consider the possibility that Johnny Temple might be facing hard time in a North Carolina slammer.

Newspapers across the country carried the story of Johnny Temple's arrest. The *Cincinnati Enquirer* carried the story on the front page, sandwiched between articles on the U.S. House of Representatives rejecting a proposed compromise by the U.S. Senate on funding abortions for poor women and the United Nations General Assembly approving a resolution condemning hijacking of commercial airliners.

Although Temple had not been a major star during his playing days in major league baseball, his plight was major news. Not just every news reporter in North Carolina wanted to talk with him, but scores of reporters from every major newspaper in the country. So the telephone continually rang and rang in Temple's Lake Lure home, but no one answered it.

The community of Lake Lure, North Carolina, was shocked by the news. For a time, Temple had been a councilman in the town and also worked in the recreation department.

Temple was one of a group of eight men, also including two former policemen and a councilman, charged with breaking and entering and larceny in connection with three tractors and a bulldozer worth $60,000. Temple was freed on $10,000 bond awaiting trial. If convicted he could be sentenced to forty years in jail.

Speculation about Temple's level of involvement ran wide and rapid. Some newsmen in North Carolina suspected that he was the ringleader and that the thefts had been going on for years. The MO of the ring was that they stole farm equipment and then sold tractors to farmers in western Carolina at bargain prices. One policeman interviewed by a local paper stated that as far as he knew, Temple was unemployed. "But he never looked like a guy who needed money. He lived in a pretty nice house."[8] Of course, the home that the Temples lived in was owned by Becky's father.

Whatever the façade the Temples had created, they were destitute. With her husband facing potential jail time, Becky Temple decided it was time to go public with a plea for support, both financial and moral.

She wrote letters to *The Sporting News* and to Earl Lawson, who was still writing for the *Cincinnati Post*. In her plea Becky stated that writing the letter was the most painful and heartbreaking endeavor that she had ever undertaken. She further stated that Johnny was very ill and since his arrest an unbelievable chain of events had occurred that had nearly killed her husband and herself.

Admitting that they were broke and destitute, Becky Temple pleaded with Temple's former fans, major league baseball and the sports world in general for relief. "I simply have no where else to turn," she bluntly stated. "None of our friends can offer us anything but consolation which is appreciated, but is not enough. I must add that there are very few who offer even that. Most of them want to pretend they never even knew us. The fans though, liked Johnny. Would they have compassion for him now? And can we reach them? We are so very, very desperate. Please try."[9]

On December 5, 1977, a true bill charging Temple with breaking and entering and larceny was returned by a grand jury in North Carolina.

No one really knew how many thefts had taken place, and there was wide speculation that Johnny Temple was the ringleader. As the State Bureau of Investigation continued to look into the case, Temple saved himself from prosecution when he turned state's evidence and the charges were dropped. He immediately went into seclusion under police protection while Becky and Mike remained in Columbia, South Carolina.

In February 1977, Temple testified for the state against his co-defendants, and they received jail sentences of four to seven years. As part of his agreement with the state, Temple agreed to testify as a state witness in two other counties in related cases.

With the heat off and left with a tainted legacy, Johnny Temple attempted to rebuild his life by doing whatever was available to him. During his major league career, Johnny Temple had appeared on twenty-five baseball card editions. So as the sports card hobby business began to boom in the early 1980s, Temple began to appear at baseball-card shows. While Temple was never able to turn the baseball card signing business craze into a perpetual cash cow like major stars such as Mickey Mantle, Willie McCovey and Pete Rose did, it helped provide a modest living. Occasionally Temple would enhance his profile by making an appearance at an old-timers' game.

In September 1993 it was discovered that Johnny Temple had been suffering from pancreatic cancer. He died at the age of 66 on January 9, 1994. At the time of his death, Temple was at the home of his only son Mike, who was employed as an assistant sheriff. A few days later a memorial service was held in Bethel Lutheran Church in White Rock, North Carolina.

While Johnny Temple had become estranged from his son for several years, by the time of his death the two had mended fences. Michael Temple probably knew him better than anyone and offered these thoughts in his epitaph: "He really was a wonderful human being. I think if I had the opportunity to hand-pick a father, I would have picked him."[10]

Afterword

As a post-script to the Johnny Temple story, it should be mentioned that although Temple died from pancreatic cancer, it was never determined if his longtime use of smokeless tobacco when playing baseball had been a contributing factor.

Studies by the American Cancer Society have indicated that smokeless tobacco can cause cancer of the mouth, tongue, cheek, esophagus, stomach and pancreas.

The death of former San Diego Padres Hall of Fame outfielder Tony Gwynn on June 16, 2014, from salivary gland cancer brought a renewed focus to the dangers associated with the use of smokeless tobacco that is still a common practice in major league baseball. Gwynn was a longtime user of smokeless tobacco.

The death of Tony Gwynn also renewed interest in the plight of Bill Tuttle, who died on July 27, 1998, after a long battle with oral cancer. Tuttle was a former major league outfielder who played for eleven years (1952–1963) with the Detroit Tigers, Kansas City Athletics and Minnesota Twins. Tuttle was another longtime user of smokeless tobacco. As Tuttle struggled with the disease, he required five operations that took over fifty hours to complete. As a result of the procedures, he lost most of his face, which had to be reconstructed using skin from other areas of his body. Until his final days Bill Tuttle worked tirelessly as a critic and educator on the dangers of smokeless tobacco, speaking to major league and minor league teams and children of all ages.

A 1999 survey revealed that thirty-three percent of rookies starting in major league baseball had tried smokeless tobacco. As of the 2014 season there were several high-profile major leaguers using smokeless tobacco, including Terry Francona, manager of the Cleveland Indians; Josh Beckett, pitcher, Los Angeles Dodgers; David Oritz, designated hitter, and Dustin Pedoria, second baseman of the Boston Red Sox.

Appendix A: Temple Among His Peers

Player	Years Played	Games	Hits	HRs	BA	RBIs	Errors	FA	AS	HOF
Johnny Temple	1952–1964	1420	1484	22	.284	395	181	.973	4	No
Ken Aspromonte	1957–1963	475	369	19	.249	124	70	.963	0	No
Bobby Avila	1949–1959	1300	1296	80	.281	465	138	.978	3	No
Gene Baker	1953–1961	630	590	39	.265	227	106	.964	1	No
Don Blasingame	1955–1966	1444	1366	21	.258	308	141	.978	1	No
Frank Bolling	1954–1966	1540	1415	106	.254	556	136	.982	2	No
Nellie Fox	1947–1965	2367	2663	35	.288	790	209	.984	12	Yes
Jim Gilliam*	1953–1966	1956	1889	65	.265	558	204	.973	2	No
Jerry Lumpe	1956–1967	1371	1314	47	.268	454	124	.980	1	No
Billy Martin	1950–1961	1021	877	64	.257	333	109	.975	1	No
Bill Mazeroski	1956–1972	2163	2016	138	.260	853	204	.983	7	Yes
Charlie Neal	1956–1963	970	858	87	.259	391	124	.971	2	No
Bobby Richardson	1955–1966	1412	1432	34	.266	390	150	.978	7	No
Red Schoendienst	1945–1963	2216	2449	84	.289	773	186	.982	10	Yes

Notes:
    AS—indicates number of years player was elected or selected to NL or AL All-Star team.
    HOF—indicates if player is elected to the National Baseball Hall of Fame.

*Statistics for Jim Gilliam include having played 1046 games at 2B, 761 games at 3B, 224 games in the OF and 2 games at 1B.

Appendix B: All-Star Game Statistics

Hitting

Years	Games	AB	Hits	2B	3B	HR	RBI	BA	SLG%
4	6	15	2	1	0	0	1	.200	.267

Fielding

Years	Games	Outs	TC	C	Errors	DP	FLD %
4	6	129	22	22	0	1	1.000

Appendix C:
Major League Career Highlights

4-time All-Star, 1956, 1957, 1959 (NL), 1961 (AL)

Hit over .300 in 1954, 1958, 1959

Tied for league leadership in walks (94), 1957

Led NL second basemen in putouts, 1954, 1955, 1958

Led NL second basemen in assists, 1956

Led NL second basemen in double plays, 1955

Tied for 4th place All-Time Cincinnati Reds season leader in singles: 157, J. Temple (1956); 157, P. Rose (1976)

15th place All-Time Cincinnati Reds career OBP: .372

Inducted into Cincinnati Reds Hall of Fame in 1965

Chapter Notes

Introduction

1. Hank Zureick, publicity director, Cincinnati Reds. "Johnny Temple," Johnny Temple clippings file, National Baseball Hall of Fame Library.
2. Jack Murray, "Temple and His Temper," *Cincinnati Enquirer*, September 19, 1976, p. C11.

Chapter One

1. Furman Bisher, "Roughneck at Second Base," *Sport* 29, no. 1 (January 1960): 38.
2. Mickey Herskowitz, "Veterans Came the Hard Way," *Houston Post*, April 23, 1963, Sec. 3, p. 2.
3. Bruce Wehrle, "Temple Was a Real Baller," *Davidson County (NC) Dispatch*, January 12, 1994.
4. Herskowitz, "Veterans Came the Hard Way."
5. Unknown author, Johnny Temple clippings file, National Baseball Hall of Fame Library.
6. Furman Bisher, "Roughneck at Second Base," *Sport* 29, no. 1 (January 1960): 40.
7. Ibid., 39.
8. Earl Lawson, "Tobacco-Chewing Youth Is Apple of Eye of Redleg Coach Benny Chapman," *Cincinnati Times-Star*, March 3, 1952.

Chapter Two

1. William A. Cook, *Waite Hoyt: A Biography of the Yankees Schoolboy Wonder* (Jefferson, NC: McFarland, 2004), p. 155.
2. Lawson, "Tobacco-Chewing Youth," March 3, 1952.
3. Earl Lawson, "Youngster Is Getting His Hits Regularly: Sewell Is Disgusted," *Cincinnati Times-Star*, March 18, 1952.
4. Ibid.
5. Earl Lawson, "Gabby Temple Now Talks with Bat," *Cincinnati Times-Star*, May 4, 1954.
6. Ibid.
7. Charles C. Alexander, *Rogers Hornsby: A Biography* (New York: Henry Holt, 1995), p. 277.

Chapter Three

1. "Bad to the Bone: Branch Rickey," The Deadball Era, www.thedeadballera.com/BadBoneRickey.html.
2. Dave Anderson, Sports of the Times, "Gabe Paul, Baseball's Old Trader," *New York Times Online*, April 4, 2002, http://www.nytimes.com.
3. Author's telephone conversation with Chuck Harmon, March 9, 2011.
4. Earl Lawson, "Temple and Bridges Are Putting All They Have on Line for Managerial Nod," *Cincinnati Times-Star*, March 25, 1953.
5. Earl Lawson, "Shrinking Violet? No," *Cincinnati Times-Star*, February 10, 1954.
6. Ibid.
7. Earl Lawson, "Gabby Temple Now Talks with Bat," *Cincinnati Times Star*, May 4, 1954.
8. Danny Peary, ed., *We Played the Game: 65 Players Remember Baseball's Greatest Era, 1947–1964* (New York: Hyperion, 1994), p. 259.
9. Associated Press, "Rough, Tough Johnny Temple of Redlegs Is Throwback to Bygone Days in Baseball," March 26, 1954.

10. Ibid.
11. Ibid.
12. Birdie Tebbetts with James Morrison, *Birdie: Confessions of a Baseball Nomad* (Chicago: Triumph, 2002), p. 123.
13. Ibid.
14. Associated Press, "Logan, Reds in Brawl," September 4, 1954.
15. Furman Bisher, "Roughneck at Second Base," *Sport* 29, no. 1 (January 1960): 36–40.
16. Ibid.
17. Harry T. Paxton, "The Redlegs' Miraculous Twins," *Saturday Evening Post*, August 3, 1957, p. 22.
18. Clark Nealon, "Fiery Johnny Temple Predicts Colts to Be on the Move in '63," *Houston Post*, March 10, 1963.
19. Hank Aaron with Lonnie Wheeler, *I Had a Hammer: The Hank Aaron Story* (New York: Harper Paperbacks, 1991), p. 152.
20. Paxton, "The Redlegs' Miraculous Twins," August 3, 1957.
21. "Confusion Reigns as Braves Down Reds," *Cincinnati Enquirer*, September 23, 1954, p. 30.
22. Tom Swope, "Giles Weighs Unique Red Protest," *Cincinnati Post*, September 23, 1954, p. 19.
23. Lou Smith, "Reds, Braves to Play Off Protested Tilt," *Cincinnati Enquirer*, September 24, 1954, p. 34.
24. United Press International, "Decision Right: Grimm Agrees on Giles Ruling," *Cincinnati Enquirer*, September 24, 1954, p. 34.
25. Earl Lawson, "Thinks It Over All Night, Then—Johnny Bangs Out Crucial Hit," *Cincinnati Times-Star*, April 24, 1957.

Chapter Four

1. Danny Peary, *We Played the Game: 65 Players Remember Baseball's Greatest Era, 1947–1964* (New York: Hyperion, 1994), p. 296.
2. Birdie Tebbetts with James Morrison, *Birdie: Confessions of a Baseball Nomad* (Chicago: Triumph, 2002), p. 125.
3. Peary, *We Played the Game*, p. 296.
4. Ibid.
5. Gregory Korte, "Complex Was Troubled from Beginning," *Cincinnati Enquirer*, September 1, 2002.
6. Pat Harmon, "Temple's No. 1 Asset—Patience," *Cincinnati Post*, April 20, 1956, p. 34.
7. Milton Richman, "Reds Earned Honors," *Cincinnati Post*, July 10, 1956, p. 14.
8. Daniel, "The People's Choice," *Cincinnati Post*, July 10, 1956, p. 14.
9. Harry T. Paxton, "The Redlegs' Miraculous Twins," *Saturday Evening Post*, August 3, 1957, p. 58.
10. Hank Aaron with Lonnie Wheeler, *I Had a Hammer: The Hank Aaron Story* (New York: Harper Paperbacks, 1991), p. 157.
11. Harold Harrison, "It's Just Singles for Temple," Associated Press, August 3, 1955.

Chapter Five

1. Earl Lawson, "Johnny Temple Tired of Taking," *Cincinnati Times-Star*, March 7, 1957.
2. "Sport, a Game of Inches," *Time*, July 8, 1957, p. 42.
3. David Maraniss, *Clemente: The Passion and Grace of Baseball's Last Hero* (New York: Simon & Schuster, 2006).
4. Bruce Markusen, *Roberto Clemente: The Great One* (Champaign, IL: Sports Publishing, 1998), p. 280.
5. Earl Lawson, "Prelude to Punch," *Cincinnati Times Star*, June 22, 1957, p. 1.
6. Associated Press, "One-Punch Pinson a Weak Hitter," June 21, 1962.
7. "Sport, a Game of Inches," p. 47.
8. John Thorn, ed., *The National Pastime: The Best Baseball Stories, Articles, and Statistical Records* (New York: Bell, 1987), p. 33.
9. Bob Pille, "Six Weeks Enough for Temple," *Cincinnati Post*, November 19, 1957.
10. Ibid.

Chapter Six

1. Bob Husted, "Temple Jewel of Consistency," *Cincinnati Enquirer*, August 9, 1958.
2. Earl Lawson, "Home Run Surprise to Temple, He Admits," *Cincinnati Times-Star*, April 30, 1958, p. 29.
3. Bob Husted, "The Johnny Temple Story," *Cincinnati Enquirer*, May 16, 1959.
4. William Collins, "Reds Lose Birdie; Dykes to Fill In," *Cincinnati Enquirer*, August 14, 1958.

5. Lee Allen, "New Pilot Must Be Executive," *Cincinnati Enquirer*, August 20, 1958.

Chapter Seven

1. Peary, *We Played the Game*, p. 437.
2. *Ibid.*
3. Earl Lawson, *Cincinnati Seasons: My 34 Years with the Reds* (South Bend, IN: Diamond Communications, 1987), p. 62.
4. United Press International, "Cincy's Temple Beefs to Giles Over $75 Fine," May 26, 1959.
5. Earl Lawson, "Giles Explains Umpire's Ruling," *Cincinnati Post*, May 26, 1959.
6. Johnny Temple, "Johnny on the Spot," *Cincinnati Post*, June 10, 1959.
7. Peary, *We Played the Game*, p. 437.
8. Roy Terrell, "Don't Let Hutch Get Mad," *Sports Illustrated*, September 21, 1959, p. 9.
9. Associated Press, "Reds Fire Mayo, Hire Hutchinson from Last-Place Seattle Team," *Pittsburgh Post-Gazette*, July 9, 1959, p. 20.
10. *Ibid.*
11. Furman Bisher, "Roughneck at Second Base," *Sport*, January 1960, p. 37.
12. Lester J. Biederman, "Temple Calls Himself Better 2nd Baseman than Bill Mazeroski," *Pittsburgh Press*, May 30, 1959.
13. *Ibid.*
14. Johnny Temple, "Johnny on the Spot," *Cincinnati Post*, July 8, 1959.
15. Dick Forbes, "Al Players Thrill for La Crowd," *Cincinnati Enquirer*, August 3, 1959.
16. Earl Lawson, "Not Like All-Star Game, Says Musial," *Cincinnati Post & Times Star*, August 4, 1959.
17. "Players Voted Against Star Game: Temple," *Chicago Daily Tribune*, August 3, 1959.
18. "Temple Getting Adjusted in His New Surroundings," *Cincinnati Enquirer*, March 20, 1960.
19. From a personal letter written by Waite Hoyt to Lee Allen, December 9, 1959, National Baseball Hall of Fame Library, Cooperstown, New York.
20. Dick Forbes, "Johnny in Tears," *Cincinnati Enquirer*, December 17, 1959.
21. Bob Vanderberg, *Frantic Frank Land: Baseball's Ultimate Wheeler and Dealer* (Jefferson, NC: McFarland, 2013), p. 106.
22. Clay Coppedge, *Texas Baseball: A Lone Star Diamond History from Town Teams to the Big Leagues* (Charleston, SC: History Press, 2012), p. 70.
23. Associated Press, *Victoria (TX) Advocate*, December 17, 1959, p. 15.
24. Harry Grayson, "Temple Anchors Indian Infield," unknown source, 1960.
25. John Wilson, "Johnny Temple Never Gives Less than His Best," *Houston Chronicle*, June 2, 1963, p. 4.
26. Associated Press, "Temple Tightens Tribe's Infield," December 16, 1959.
27. *Ibid.*
28. Pat Harmon, "Indians Swap Mclish, Two Infielders," *Cincinnati Post & Times Star*, December 1959.

Chapter Eight

1. Roger Kahn, "Shakeup at Yankee Stadium," *Sport*, January 1960, p. 75.
2. Hal Lebovitz, "Surprise-Package Francona," *Sport*, January 1960, p. 51.
3. Bruce Weber, "Jim Brosnan, Who Threw Literature a Curve, Dies at 84," NYTimes.com, July 4, 2014.
4. Dan Daniels, Daniel's Dope (column), "Lane Bars Indians from Any Writing," *New York World Telegram*, March 7, 1960.
5. Milton Gross, *New York Post*, March 29, 1960.
6. *Ibid.*
7. Regis McAuley, "Temple Is Ousted Defending Rookie," *Cincinnati Post & Times Star*, April 4, 1960.
8. UPI, "Indians Swap Colavito for Kuenn of Detroit," *Cincinnati Enquirer*, April 18, 1960, p. 1.
9. Terry Pluto, "50 Years Later, the Cleveland Indians' Trade of Rocky Colavito Still Stinks," http://blog.cleveland.com/plutoblog, April 16, 2010.
10. Stan Isaacs, "Temple Steps Back and Looks—At Temple," *Newsday*, May 1960.
11. *Ibid.*
12. *Ibid.*
13. Harry Grayson, "Temple Finds Al Pitchers Tough," *Cincinnati Post & Times Star*, May 25, 1960.
14. *Ibid.*
15. Earl Lawson, "Temple Wants to Live Here," *Cincinnati Post & Times Star*, June 14, 1960.
16. "Temple Tantrum," from a July 29, 1960, article in the Johnny Temple clippings file at the National Baseball Hall of Fame

Museum Library, Cooperstown, New York, July 29, 1960.
17. Lou Smith, Lou Smith's Notes (column), *Cincinnati Enquirer*, August 3, 1960, p. D3.
18. Associated Press, "Tigers, Tribe Swap Managers," *Cincinnati Enquirer*, August 4, 1960, p. D2.
19. Edward Linn, "Ballplayers Vs. Fans," *The Saturday Evening Post*, August 12, 1961, p. 53.
20. *Ibid*.
21. Associated Press, "Tigers, Tribe Swap Managers."
22. *Ibid*.
23. Peary, *We Played the Game*, p. 468.
24. "Billy Martin," FBI Reading Room: The Vault, File: 9–37793, https:/vault.fbi.gov/reading-room-index, p. 44.

Chapter Nine

1. George McLeod, "'Too Many Trades Cooked Tribe,' Says Temple," source unknown, Johnny Temple clippings file, National Baseball Hall of Fame Library, Cooperstown, NY.
2. *Ibid*.
3. *Ibid*.
4. "Temple Shudders Over Last Season," February 4, 1961, source unknown, Johnny Temple clippings file, National Baseball Hall of Fame Library, Cooperstown, NY.
5. *Ibid*.
6. *Ibid*.
7. *Ibid*.
8. "Cleveland Indians," *Sports Illustrated*, April 10, 1961, www.si.com/vault/1961/04/10/624828/clevelandindians.
9. *Ibid*.
10. *Ibid*.
11. *Ibid*.
12. Harry Grayson, "Temple Says Schmidt 'A Minor Leaguer,'" *Cincinnati Post & Times Star*, May 4, 1961.
13. *Ibid*.
14. Lou Smith, Lou Smith's Notes (column), *Cincinnati Enquirer*, July 12, 1961.
15. "I'll Swing at Any Fan Who Runs Onto Field—Piersall," *The Sporting News*, September 20, 1961, p. 11.
16. "Temple on Coats: Fires at the Head," September 11, 1961, source unknown, Johnny Temple clippings file, National Baseball Hall of Fame Library, Cooperstown, NY.
17. "I'll Swing at Any Fan Who Runs Onto Field—Piersall," *The Sporting News*.
18. "Johnny Doffs Hat to Piersall as a Top-Drawer Competitor," *The Sporting News*, November 15, 1961, p. 5.
19. *Ibid*.
20. *Ibid*.
21. Bob Dolgan, "After the Cheers Die," November 1977, source unknown, Johnny Temple clippings file, National Baseball Hall of Fame Library, Cooperstown, NY.
22. Tebbetts with Morrison, *Birdie*, p. 22.
23. "Temple Says This Season His Finale," *Houston Chronicle*, August 15, 1962, Sec. 7, p. 3.
24. *Ibid*.
25. "One-Punch Pinson a Weak Hitter," June 21, 1962, source unknown, Johnny Temple clippings file, National Baseball Hall of Fame Library, Cooperstown, NY.
26. Mickey Herskowitz, "Johnny Temple Instills Pride in Colt Rejects," *Houston Post*, September 2, 1962, Sec. 4, p. 2.
27. Clark Nealon, "Fiery Johnny Temple Predicts Colts to Be on the Move in '63," *Houston Post*, March 10, 1963.
28. Mickey Herskowitz, "Suitable for Framing," *Houston Post*, May 26, 1963.
29. "Temple Fined Third Time," source unknown, Johnny Temple clippings file, National Baseball Hall of Fame Library, Cooperstown, NY.
30. Clark Nealon, "Fiery Temple Backs Away from Ump Conspiracy Rap," *Houston Post*, July 13, 1963.
31. *Ibid*.

Chapter Ten

1. "Temple Is Reds Coach," December 15, 1963, source unknown, Johnny Temple clippings file, National Baseball Hall of Fame Library, Cooperstown, NY.
2. *Ibid*.
3. Earl Lawson, "Hutch to Use His New Coach as Base Runner," *Cincinnati Post & Times Star*, March 2, 1964.
4. *Ibid*.
5. Pete Rose and Roger Kahn, *Pete Rose: My Story* (New York: Macmillan, 1989), p. 108.
6. Peary, *We Played the Game*, p. 575.
7. *Ibid*.
8. Pete Rose with Rick Hill, *My Prison Without Bars* (Emmaus, PA: Rodale, 2004), p. 50.

9. Peary, *We Played the Game*, p. 575.
10. *Ibid.*
11. Rose with Hill, p. 51.
12. Author's interview with Dave Bristol, September 24, 2002.
13. "Hutch to Use His New Coach as Base Runner."
14. *Ibid.*
15. Lester Biederman, "Toupee Topper for Temple—Even Barber Doesn't Know," *Pittsburgh Press*, August 15, 1964.
16. Michael Y. Sokolove, *Hustle: The Myth, Life, and Lies of Pete Rose* (New York: Fireside, 1992), p. 59.
17. Lawson, *Cincinnati Seasons*, p. 65.
18. Peary, *We Played the Game*, p. 575.
19. Sokolove, *Hustle*, p. 61.
20. Biederman, "Toupee Topper for Temple—Even Barber Doesn't Know."
21. Earl Lawson, "Temple, Otero Fight in Reds Clubhouse," *Cincinnati Post and Times Star*, August 29, 1964, p. 1.
22. Lou Smith, "Jokes Aftermath of 'Non-Title' Bout," *Cincinnati Enquirer*, August 30, 1964.
23. Lou Smith's Notes, "Jokes Aftermath of 'Non-Title' Bout," *Cincinnati Enquirer*, August 30, 1964.
24. Lawson, "Temple, Otero Fight in Reds Clubhouse," p. 1.
25. *Ibid.*
26. Rose and Kahn, *Pete Rose*, p. 117.

Chapter Eleven

1. Richard West, "Houston TV Ratings War," *Texas Monthly*, May 1974, www.texasmonthly.com/content/houston-tv-ratings-war.
2. Jack Gallagher, "Oilers Can't Be Faulted for Releasing Bobby Maples," *Houston Post*, August 26, 1966.
3. *Ibid.*
4. *Ibid.*
5. Bob Dolgan, "After the Cheers Die," November 1977, source unknown, Johnny Temple clippings file, National Baseball Hall of Fame Library, Cooperstown, NY.
6. Jack Murray, "Temple and His Temper," *Cincinnati Enquirer*, September 19, 1976, p. C11.
7. Richard Morris, "A Love Affair—Johnny Temple Returns to Lake Lure," *Asheville Citizen-Times*, August 24, 1975, p. 2B.
8. Dolgan, "After the Cheers Die."
9. Earl Lawson, "The Fall of Johnny Temple," *Cincinnati Post*, November 18, 1977, p. 3.
10. Mike Bass, "Temple Remembered," *Cincinnati Post*, Johnny Temple clippings file, National Baseball Hall of Fame Library, Cooperstown, NY.

Bibliography

Books

The Baseball Encyclopedia. 8th ed. New York: Macmillan, 1990.
Bryant, Howard. *The Last Hero: A Life of Henry Aaron.* New York: Pantheon Books, 2010.
Cook, William A. *Big Klu: The Baseball Life of Ted Kluszewski.* Jefferson, NC: McFarland, 2012.
____. *Diamond Madness: Classic Episodes of Rowdyism, Racism and Violence in Major League Baseball.* Mechanicsburg, PA: Sunbury Press, 2013.
____. *Pete Rose: Baseball's All-Time Hit King.* Jefferson, NC: McFarland, 2004.
____. *The Summer of '64: A Pennant Lost.* Jefferson, NC: McFarland, 2002.
Coppedge, Clay. *Texas Baseball: A Lone Star Diamond History from Town Teams to the Big Leagues.* Charleston, SC: History Press, 2012.
Lawson, Earl. *Cincinnati Seasons: My 34 Years with the Reds.* South Bend, IN: Diamond Communications, 1987.
Peary, Danny, ed. *We Played the Game: 65 Players Remember Baseball's Greatest Era, 1947–1964.* New York: Hyperion, 1994.
Riechler, Joseph L., ed. *The Baseball Encyclopedia,* 7th ed. New York: Macmillan, 1988.
Rose, Pete, with Rick Hill. *My Prison Without Bars.* Emmaus, PA: Rodale, 2004.
Sokolove, Michael Y. *Hustle: The Myth, Life, and Lies of Pete Rose.* New York: Fireside, 1992.
The Sporting News editors. *Baseball: A Doubleheader Collection of Facts, Feats & Firsts.* New York: Galahad, 1992.
Tebbetts, Birdie, with James Morrison. *Birdie: Confessions of a Baseball Nomad.* Chicago: Triumph, 2002.
Thorn, John, ed. *The National Pastime: The Best Baseball Stories, Articles, and Statistical Records.* Society for American Baseball Research. New York: Bell, 1987.

Archives and Libraries

The Cincinnati Museum Center at Union Terminal, Cincinnati Historical Society, Cincinnati, OH.
Library of Cincinnati and Hamilton County, Cincinnati, OH.
Monmouth County Library, Manalapan, NJ.
The National Baseball Hall of Fame Library, Cooperstown, NY.

Articles

Bisher, Furman. "Roughneck at Second Base." *Sport* 29, no. 1 (January 1960).
Edmonds, Ed. "The Enduring Legacy of Curtis Charles Flood: His Courageous Legal Struggle for Personal Dignity." 2006, http://www3.nd.edu/~ndlaw/faculty/edmonds/, accessed June 8, 2016.
Paxton, Harry T. "The Redlegs' Miraculous Twins." *The Saturday Evening Post*, August 3, 1957.

Websites

www.baseball-reference.com
http://bleacherreport..com
www.nytimes.com
www.salisburypost.com.

Index

Aaron, Hank 32, 48–49, 66, 93–94–95, 134–135
Abrams, Cal 24
Acker, Tom 53, 58
Adair, Jerry 142–143
Adams, Bobby 15
Adams, K.S. Bud 127
Adcock, Joe 15, 21, 24, 32, 58
All-Star Games 50–53, 65, 66–68, 91, 93–96, 116–117, 134–135, 168; ballot box stuffing 49–50–51, 66–67; inaugural game, 1933 50; player selection: 50, 67, 78–79
Allen, Dick 134
Allen, Lee 63, 99
Allor, Bernarde 145
Alston, Walter 50, 52, 67
Amalfitano, Joey 144
American Association (Major League) 3
American Association (Minor League) 20
American Cancer Society 172
American Football League (AFL) 165
American League 2–3, 35, 52, 60, 64–65, 67–68, 93–95, 97–99, 103, 105–107, 110, 112, 115, 117, 120–123, 130, 132, 134–135, 143, 146
Anderson, Sparky 56
Antonelli, Johnny 11, 123, 130
Apache Junction, Arizona 145
Aparicio, Luis 57, 117
Appalachian State 6
Arroyo, Louis 142–143
Ashburn, Richie 69
Asheville Citizen-Times 168
Aspromonte, Ken 116, 118, 131, 137
Atlanta Braves 112; *see also* Boston Braves; Milwaukee Braves

Baczewski, Fred 30
Bailey, Ed 27, 43–44, 48, 50–51, 53–54, 56, 66–68, 78, 86, 90, 133
Baker, Del 26
Baker, Gene 59

Ballanfant, Lee 34
Ballantine, South Carolina 167
Baltimore Orioles 116, 131, 139–140, 142–143
Banks, Ernie 40, 78, 93
Barker, Ray 139
Barlick, Al 34
Baseball Encyclopedia 5
Baseballreference.com 5
Baseball Writers Association of America (BBWAA) 64
Bauer, Hank 106
Baumer, Jim 133
Bavasi, Buzzie 38
Beaumont, Texas 12
Beckett, Josh 172
Bell, Buddy 24, 45
Bell, Gary 130
Bell, Gus 23–24, 30–34, 36–37, 39, 43, 45–48, 50, 53–54, 56, 58, 60, 66, 68, 78, 84, 86, 91, 94, 101
Bench, Johnny 141, 155
Benson, Vern 7
Berra, Yogi 3, 95, 118, 141
Berry, Charlie 138
Biltmore Hotel
Bisher, Furman 6, 100
Black, Joe 44, 46, 49
Blackwell, Ewell, "The Whip" 20
Blair, Gwenda 47; *The Trumps: Three Generations That Built an Empire* 47
Blanchard, John 137
Blasingame, Don 76, 79, 97, 133–134, 150–151, 154, 160
Bloebaum, Buddy 158
Blue, Vida 134
Bolling, Frank 135
Bond, Walt 111–112, 114, 137
Boone, Bob 134
Boone, Bret 134
Borkowski, Bob 31, 34–35, 37
Boston Braves 3, 18, 20–22, 24, 103; *see also* Milwaukee Braves

Index

Boston Red Sox 16, 26, 106, 111–112, 120, 122, 147, 172
Boswell, Ken 62
Boudreau, Lou 103
Bouton, Jim 108; *Ball Four* 108
Bowen, Carroll 7
Boyer, Clete 138, 153
Boyer, Ken 52, 95
"Bradley's Bullpen" 164
Bragan, Bobby 26, 81, 101
Brecheen, Harry, "The Cat" 70
Breeding, Marv 143
Brewer, Jim 125
Bridges, Rocky 24–26, 28, 30, 45, 76, 118
Briggs Stadium (Detroit) 121
Briles, Nelson 62
Bristol, Dave 153
Brooklyn Dodgers 3, 8, 11, 18, 22–23, 25–26, 30–31, 35, 38–39, 43, 49, 54–55, 75–76, 83, 102–103, 114, 119; *see also* Los Angeles Dodgers
Brosnan, Jim 11, 87, 94, 108–109, 153; *The Long Season* 108; *Pennant Race* 108
Brown, Bobby 11
Brown, Dick 108
Brown, Joe 98
Bruckner, Earle 20
Bruton, Bill 37, 48
Bryant, Howard 45; *The Last Hero—A Life of Henry Aaron* 45
Bryson, George 65
Buhl, Bob 29
Buncombe County Clerk (Supreme Court, Asheville, NC) 5
Bunning, Jim 67–68, 132, 134, 136
Burdette, Lew 31–32, 85
Burgess, Smokey 15, 39–40, 43–44, 46–49, 54–56, 86–87, 97–98
Burtschy, Edward, "Moe" 17
Bush, August, "Gus" 101

Cabrera, Miguel 134
Callahan, Ben 8
Candlestick Park (San Francisco) 96
Cardenas, Leo, "Chico" 1, 134, 155
Carolina League 44
Carrasquel, Chico 103
Carter, Gary 141
Cash, Norm 108, 112, 114, 123, 132
Catawba College 6–8
CBS 165
Cepeda, Orlando 95
Chacon, Elio 134
Chapman, Ben 16
Chicago Cubs 3, 14–15, 17, 20, 30, 35, 37, 43, 45, 54–55, 59, 61, 71, 77, 96–99, 102, 125, 129, 145
Chicago White Sox 3, 57, 98–99, 101–102, 104–108, 113, 120–121, 123–124, 133–134, 169
Chipman, Bob 22

Chiti, Harry 139–140
Christ Hospital (Cincinnati) 155
Cincinnati, Ohio 2
Cincinnati Baseball Writers Association 56, 65, 84
Cincinnati Enquirer 64, 76, 81, 100, 168–139
Cincinnati Post (*Cincinnati Post & Times Star*) 87, 101, 109, 133, 144, 170
Cincinnati Red Stockings 45
Cincinnati Reds/Redlegs 2–4, 8, 10, 12–45, 47–49, 52–61, 63, 65–68, 71–72, 74–75, 77–79, 81–88, 90–91, 94, 96–102–104, 108, 110, 115, 118, 123–127, 132–134, 138–139, 141–142, 144–145, 147–148–149–163, 168
Cincinnati Times Star 16, 63, 87
Clemente, Roberto 53, 62–63, 98, 134–135
Clemmens, Roger 134
Cleveland Indians 2, 45, 90, 98–100, 108–109, 111–123–124, 126–127, 129–132, 134, 136, 138–140, 144, 149, 151, 153, 172
Clevenger, Tex 102, 125
Coates, Jim 136–137
Cobb, Ty 20, 30, 162
Colavito, Rocky 95, 99, 107, 112–114, 117, 123, 130, 132, 135
Coleman, Gordy 66, 99, 103, 108, 124, 151
Coleman, Jerry 11
Collum, Jackie 42
Columbia, South Carolina 46, 169, 171
Columbia Reds 10–12
Comiskey Park (Chicago) 99, 106, 120–121
Conley, Gene 125
Continental League 127
Cooper, Walker 151
Corinthian Broadcasting Company 166
Cotton, Lamar 145
County Stadium (Milwaukee) 34, 36, 48, 55, 60
Courtney, Clint 77
Craft, Harry 143, 145
Crandall, Del 28–29, 32, 34, 36, 90, 93, 133
Critz, Hughie 3
Crockett, Jimmy 169
Crone, Ray 48–49
Cronin, Joe 122
Crosley, Powell, Jr. 20, 26, 28, 42, 75–76, 81, 84, 86, 99, 149; Stadium Advisory Committee 76
Crosley Field (Cincinnati) 2, 12, 15, 17, 20, 25, 29–32, 46, 55, 63, 68, 71, 76–77, 79, 84, 87, 90, 94, 96–97, 124, 144, 150–151, 158, 160–161
Crowe, George 44, 46, 54, 56, 66, 68, 77–78, 83
Cucinello, Tony 3–4, 37
Cueto, Johnny 70
Culliman, Craig, Jr. 127
Cunningham, Joe 96

Index

Daley, Richard J. (mayor) 107
Daniel, Dan 64
Dark, Alvin 17
Dascoli, Frank 88–89
Day, Laraine 81
Dean, Dizzy 23
Demeter, Steve 112
Derringer, Paul 14
Detroit Tigers 14, 107, 112–114, 119, 122–123, 127, 136, 149, 172
Devine, Bing 108
DeWitt, William O., "Bill," Sr. 113, 119, 122, 127, 132–133, 149–150, 154–157, 159–160
DiMaggio, Joe 141
Dittmer, Jack 2, 32, 49
Dixon, Hal 34
Doby, Larry 107
Donovan, Dick 98–99, 104, 139
Douglas, Whammy 86
Drabowsky, Moe 71
Drummond, Cal 120
Drysdale, Don 93, 95, 137
Dunn & Bradstreet 166
Duran, Ryne 114
Durocher, Leo 81
Dyck, Jim 49
Dykes, Jimmy 48, 82, 119, 122, 127, 131, 138–139

Eastern Kentucky College 6
Ebbets Field (Brooklyn) 18, 22, 55, 76, 88
Edwards, Johnny 159
82nd Airborne (NC) 6
Ellis, Sammy 158
Elmira, New York 11
Elston, Don 68, 94
Enis, Bill 165
Erskine, Carl 88
Escalera, Nino 37
ESPN 70, 166
Essegian, Chuck 138
Evans, Chesty 150

Face, Elroy 93–94, 96, 98, 117
Fazio, Ernie 147
Feeney, Chub 50
Fenway Park (Boston) 120, 122
Ferrarese, Don 108
Ferrick, Tom 42
Finley, Charles O. 126
Fiscalini, John 10
Fisk, Carlton 141
Flood, Curt 44, 58, 71–73
Foiles, Hank 63
Forbes, Dick 100
Forbes Field 53, 94, 144
Ford, Whitey 11, 52, 70, 105–106, 136, 142, 150–151
Foster, George 100
Fowler, Art 33, 39, 42–47, 88

Fox, Nellie 52, 57, 94, 117
Francona, Terry 112, 172
Francona, Tito 103, 107, 112, 130
Franklin, Ron 166
Frazier, Joe 56
Freeman, Hershell 43–44, 46, 49, 53, 69
Freese, Gene 133–134, 151, 153–154
Frey, Lonnie 3
Frick, Ford 66, 94
Friend, Bob 96, 98, 117

Gabriel, Charlie, "The Slinging Kid" 7
Galbreath, John W. 98
Gallagher, Jack 165
Gargiola, Joe 93, 109; *Baseball: It's a Funny Game* 109
Gatewood, Charles 145
Gentile, Jim 135, 143
Gibson, Bob 70
Gibson, Sam 7
Giles, Warren 14, 18, 35–36, 50, 60, 64–65, 71, 77, 88–89, 103–104, 147
Gilliam, Jim 38, 76, 95
Gleason, Jackie 156
Golenbock, Peter 124; *Wild High and Tight—The Life and Death of Billy Martin* 124
Gooden, Dwight 95
Gorbus, Glen 40
Gordon, Joe 101–103, 113, 119–120, 122, 131
Gossage, Rich, "Goose" 134–135
Grammas, Alex 44, 83
Grant, Jim, "Mudcat" 115, 123
Grayson, Harry 133
Green, Gene 139
Greenberg, Hank 27
Greene, Bill 7
Greengrass, Jim 20–22, 29, 31–32, 40, 73
Griffey, Ken, Jr. 51, 134
Griffey, Ken, Sr. 100
Griffith, Calvin 99
Griffith Stadium 51
Grimm, Charlie, "Jolly Cholly" 36–37, 54
Groat, Dick 40, 63, 98
Gross, Don 82
Grove, Lefty 3
Guglielmo, Augie 73
Gwynn, Tony 172

Haddix, Harvey 11, 33, 49, 82, 86–87, 97–98
Hale, Bob 136
Haney, Fred 54, 78–79, 93
Hansen, Ron 143
Hanshin Tigers 154
The Hardball Times 92
Harmon, Chuck 25, 43–44, 56
Harnett, Gabby 141
Harper, Tommy 150
Harrell, Billy 103

Harridge, William 50, 60, 64–65
Harris, Bucky 120
Hatton, Grady 15–18, 21–22, 25, 28, 30
Hazel, Bob 11
Hearn, Jim 22
Hebner, Richie 62
Held, Woodie 103, 105, 109, 130
Hemus, Solly 108
Henly, Gail 24
Henry, Bill 98–99, 117
Hiller, Frank 18
Hiroshima Carp 154
Hitchcock, Billy 143
Hoak, Don 60, 66–67, 69, 85–87, 97–98, 146
Hodges, Gil 68, 115
Hoeft, Billy 142
Hofheinz, Roy (judge) 127
Hope, Bob 101
Hornsby, Rogers 19–26, 29, 43, 76
Houk, Ralph 138
Houston, Texas 126–127
Houston Astros 56
Houston Colt .45s 112, 126, 139, 143–147, 149, 155, 158, 160–161
Houston Oilers 127, 165
Houston Post 165
Houston Sports Association 127
Howard, Elston 138, 142
Hoyt, Waite 14, 60, 98–99, 104
Hubbard, Cal 118
Husted, Bob 76–77
Hutchinson, Fred 90, 94, 97, 99, 118, 133, 149–150, 154–161, 163

International League 45
Isaacs, Stan 114–115

Jablonski, Ray 45, 48, 56
Jackowski, Bill 34
Jackson, Larry 117
Jackson, Lou 1, 98
Jay, Joey 133
Jeffcoat, Hal 43–44, 53, 87
Jessell, George 93
Jeter, Derek 2
John, Dick 165
Johnson, Lou 1
Johnson, Randy 134
Johnson, Walter 115
Jolly, Dave 37
Jones, Willie, "Puddin' Head" 90–91, 94, 96

Kaat, Jim 70
Kahn, Roger 152, 158; *Pete Rose: My Story* 152, 158
Kaline, Al 132
Kansas City Athletics 98, 101, 105, 107, 172, 123, 126, 131, 154; *see also* Oakland Athletics; Philadelphia Athletics
Kansas City Chiefs 165

Kansas City Royals 50
Kasko, Eddie 90, 94, 110, 134
Katy Freeway (U.S. Interstate 10) 166
Kay, Art 139
Kell, George 107
Keller, Charlie 141
KHOU-TV (Houston) 164–166
Killebrew, Harmon 99
Kiner, Ralph 23, 91
Kirkland, Willie 123, 130, 137
Kirsey, George 127
Klaus, Bobby 156
Klippstein, Johnny 43–45, 48–49, 58, 88
Kluszewski, Ted 10, 15, 20–21, 24, 26, 29–31, 33–34, 37–40, 42–43, 46–49, 50–52, 54–56, 59–61, 63, 66, 68–69, 81, 87–88, 99–100, 115, 157
Klutz, Clyde 7
Korean War 11
Koufax, Sandy 1
KPRC (Houston) 165
Kramer, Jerry 108; *Instant Replay* 108
Kraus, Pete 10
KTRH AM (Houston) 164
Kubek, Tony 118
Kuenn, Harvey 112–114, 116, 120, 122–123, 130
Kuhn, Bowie 168

Labine, Clem 54
Ladd, Ernie, "The Big Cat" 165
Lake Lure, North Carolina 168–170
Landrith, Hobbie 43
Lane, Frank 101–105, 107–108–109, 112–114, 118–119, 123–124, 126, 130–131
Larkin, Barry 100
Lasker, Sid 165
Latman, Barry 112, 118
Law, Vern 96, 98, 117
Lawrence, Brooks 30, 42–44, 50, 53–54, 82, 91
Lawson, Earl 16, 28, 62–66, 87–89, 108, 115, 143–144, 157, 159, 161, 168, 170
Lazzeri, Tony 103
Lee, Pinky 46
Leiber, Hank 129
Leonard, Wilbur G. (U.S. Attorney) 126
Leppert, Don 62
Lewis, J. Norman 91
Lexington, North Carolina 5
Lincecum, Tim 70
Lipon, Johnny 30
Loes, Billy 68
Logan, Johnny 30–33, 37, 40, 60, 78
Lombardi, Ernie 1, 3, 14, 100, 140–141
London, Mike 6–7
Long, Dale 51–52
Lopez, Al 26
Lopez, Hector 118, 153
Los Angeles Angels 131
Los Angeles Coliseum 1, 88, 95

Index

Los Angeles Dodgers 1, 38, 82–83, 88, 96–97, 144, 147, 172; *see also* Brooklyn Dodgers
Louis, Joe 9
Lumpe, Jerry 131
Lynch, Jerry 56, 71, 83, 110–111

Macon Telegraph 157
Madison, New Jersey 83
Maglie, Sal 30, 54
Mahoney, Jim 139
Mains, Thomas 169
Major League Players Association 72
Malden, Karl 137
Maloney, Jim 160–161
Malzone, Frank 95
Manley, Abe 23
Manley, Effa 23
Mantle, Mickey 52, 105–106, 132, 135–138, 142, 150, 156, 171
Maris, Roger 98, 105, 123–124, 132, 135–136–138, 142
Marquis, Bob 21
Marshall College 6
Marshall Willard 28
Martin, Billy 2, 11, 62, 99, 102, 104, 108, 123–126, 133, 151, 156
Maryville College 6
Mathews, Eddie 32, 34–36, 67, 95, 135
Mattick, Bobby 44
Mattingly, Don 51
Mauch, Gene 125
Mays, Willie 11, 51–52, 66, 68, 76, 94, 117, 135
Mazeroski, Bill 4, 78, 92, 93, 98, 127–128
McCarthy, Joe, (Senator) 27
McClymonds High School 44, 72
McCool, Billy 158
McCovey, Willie 158, 171
McCullough, Reverend Paul 11
McDaniel, Lindy 117
McDermott, Mickey 16
McDevitt, Denny 88
McDougal, Gil 95, 106, 114
McDowell, "Sudden Sam" 131–132
McGwire, Mark 124
McInerty, James, Jr. 137
McKecnie, Bill 56
McKeesport Daily News 62
McLain, Denny 1, 169
McLish, Cal 99, 101–102, 104, 108, 123–124–126, 151
McMillan, Roy 12, 15, 17, 21, 37–38, 40–42, 44–47, 49–52, 54, 56–57, 60, 66, 69–70–71, 76, 78, 100, 109, 133, 146, 150, 154, 157, 161
McNally, Dave 72
McPhee, Bid 3, 100
Meggyesy, Dave 108; *Out of Their League* 108
Mendez, Robert 137

Merriman, Lloyd 11, 34
Messersmith, Andy 72
Metkovich, George 37
Metro, Charlie 10
Meyer, Russ 24
Miller, Marvin 72
Miller, Stu 82
Miller, Tex 9
Mills, Buster 26
Milwaukee Braves 11, 24–25, 28–37, 39–41, 43–44, 48–49, 54–55, 58, 60, 79, 82, 84–85, 91, 96, 98, 126, 133, 135; *see also* Boston Braves
Milwaukee Brewers 101, 112
Minnesota Twins 112, 172
Minoso, Minnie 68, 108, 121, 123
Mize, Johnny 2, 134
Mizel, Vinegar Bend 77
MLB Network 70
Montreal Expos
Mooresville, North Carolina 8, 71
Moran, Billy 157
Morgan, Joe 4, 168
Municipal Stadium (Cleveland) 107, 113–115, 120, 123, 136, 138
Municipal Stadium (Kansas City) 116
Murdough, John 89, 100
Murray, Eddie 2
Murray, Jack 168
Musial, Stan 33, 52, 66, 89, 93–94, 96, 101, 117
Myers, Alton 9

Nankai Hawks 154
Napp, Larry 120
National League 2–4, 14–15, 18, 26, 35, 39–40, 43, 49–50, 52, 54–57, 60, 64–69, 78, 88–89, 93–95, 97, 102, 110, 117, 126–128, 132, 134–135, 143, 145, 147, 162
Nettles, Craig 134
Nevel, Ernie 21
New York Daily News 62
New York Giants 3, 17, 22, 30–31, 33, 75, 79, 129, 142; *see also* San Francisco Giants
New York Mets 62, 140, 145, 162
New York Post 106
New York State Employees Retirement System 47
New York Times 54
New York Yankees 2–3, 20, 55, 70, 81, 83, 98, 102–103, 105–106, 114–116, 118, 122–124, 130, 132, 134–138, 142–143, 150
Newark Eagles 23
Newcombe, Don 11, 54, 82–83, 88, 91, 96, 118
Newsweek 114
Newton, North Carolina 6
Niekro, Phil 134
Nixon, Richard 93

Nuxhall, Joe 13, 33, 45–47, 50, 53, 56, 100, 161–162

Oakland Athletics 112; *see also* Kansas City Athletics; Philadelphia Athletics
O'Brien, John 63
Occidental Winter League (Venezuela) 71
O'Connell, Danny 37, 41
O'Doul, Lefty 26
Oliver, Al 62
O'Malley, Peter 83
O'Malley, Walter 1, 168
Ortiz, David 172
Otero, Reggie 118, 155, 160–161, 167
O'Toole, Jim 84–85, 87, 96, 134, 152

Pacific Coast League 45, 90, 102, 159
Palys, Stan 40, 56
Pastora Milkers 71, 73
Paterson, New Jersey 58
Paul, Gabe 19–20, 23–27, 38, 40, 42–43, 46, 58, 71–72, 74, 79, 81–82, 86–87, 89–92, 97–100–101, 104, 126–127, 139–141, 149
Pavletich, Don 158–159
Pedoria, Justin 172
Pellagrini, Eddie 15–16, 21–22
Pena, Orlando 94
Pendleton, Jim 37, 86, 90
Pennsylvania National Guard 11
Perez, Tony 2, 100
Perkowski, Harry 22
Perry, Jim 114, 130, 138
Philadelphia Athletics 3, 8, 17; *see also* Kansas City Athletics; Oakland Athletics
Philadelphia Phillies 11, 15–16, 28, 33, 35–37, 40, 58, 72, 77, 82, 86, 112, 118, 125, 127, 159, 162
Phillips, Bubba 103, 108, 130
Phillips, Buz 7
Piersall, Jim 114, 119–122, 130, 136–137, 139; *Fear Strikes Out* 120, 137
Pillette, Duane 73
Pinson, Vada 66, 71–72, 84, 91–92, 94, 96, 134, 144, 150–153, 157, 160
Pioneer League 10
Pittsburgh Pirates 4, 23, 33, 36, 41, 49, 53, 62–63, 65, 82, 84, 86–87, 90, 96–98, 102, 128, 134, 144, 154
Pizzaro, Juan 133
Podbielan, Bud 33
Podres, Johnny 117, 147
Pollet, Howie 155
Polo Grounds (New York) 22, 75
Post, Wally 31, 34, 36–39, 42–43, 46–49, 54, 58–60, 66, 82
Power, Vic 103, 105, 112, 115, 130, 136–137, 153
Powers, Johnny 86
Purkey, Bob 78, 82, 90–91, 134, 161

Quay, Luke 62–63

Raffensberger, Ken 15, 20
Rather, Dan 165
Reeds, North Carolina 5, 8, 27
Reeds High School (West Davidson) 6
Reese, Pee Wee 40, 81
Repulski, Rip 10
Reynolds, Allie 91, 103
Rice Hotel 127
Richardson, Bobby 143
Rickey, Branch 23–24, 71, 127
Ridzik, Steve 40
River Downs Race Track 152
Roberts, Robin 101, 118, 144
Robinson, Brooks 142
Robinson, Frank 10, 43–44, 46–48, 50–51, 54, 56–60, 66–68, 72, 78, 84–85, 88, 91–92, 94–96, 99, 134, 150–153, 155, 157, 161
Robinson, Jackie 16, 23, 38
Roger Bacon High School 17
Rogovin, Saul 28
Romano, John 108, 130, 136, 139
Rose, Harry 152
Rose, Pete 2, 4, 150–160, 162–163, 169, 171; *My Prison Without Bars* 153
Rossi, Joe 24
Ruiz, Chico 159
Runge, Ed 111–112
Runnels, Pete 117, 146–147
Ruth, Babe 124, 132, 136, 142
Rutherford, Johnny 18
Ryan, Connie 15, 28
Ryan, Nolan 134

Saguaro National Monument 129
St. Louis Browns 19
St. Louis Cardinals 15, 30, 33, 35–36, 41–42, 49, 54, 56, 59, 66, 68, 72, 77, 87, 90, 97, 101, 108, 112, 124, 127, 133, 151, 155–156, 162
Salisbury Post 6–7
Salt Lake City Bees 132
San Diego Chargers 165
San Diego Padres 135, 172
San Diego Padres (AAA) 154, 159
San Francisco Giants 78, 82–83–84, 94, 96–97, 123, 130, 133, 144, 151, 158, 162; *see also* New York Giants
Sanchez, Raul 125
Sands, Jerry 8
The Saturday Evening Post 69
Savannah Indians 11, 71
Sawatski, Carl 11, 32
Schaeffer, Harry 12–13
Schecter, Leonard 106
Scheffing, Bob 77
Schilling, Curt 134
Schmidt, Bob 133
Schmidt, Willard 72

Index

Schmitz, Johnny 21
Schoendienst, Red 4, 59, 68, 79, 101, 106, 144, 151
Score, Herb 113–114, 123
Seals Stadium (San Francisco) 82, 96
Seattle Mariners 56
Seaver, Tom 62, 70
Seghi, Phil 158, 160–162
Seminick, Andy 15, 18, 27, 37
Sewell, Luke 15, 17–19, 21, 24
Sheffing, Bob
Short, Bill 114
Simmons, Curt 11, 67
Simpson, Harry, "Suitcase" 153
Sisler, Dick 15, 155, 159, 161, 163
Skowron, Bill, "Moose" 106, 138, 142
Slaughter, Enos 23
Smalley, Roy 31
Smart, Curley 150
Smith, Al (MLB player) 105
Smith, Al (MLB umpire) 118
Smith, Frank 32–33, 37
Smith, Hal 10
Smith, Lou 64–65
Smith, Mayo 86–87, 90–91, 97
Snider, Duke 1
Snyder, George 8–9
Sosa, Sammy 124
South Atlantic League (Sally League) 10, 58
Southern Association 103
Southern League 169
Spahn, Warren 22, 32–34, 36
Speacht, Bill 7
Spencer, Darrell 83, 97
Sport Magazine 6, 100
The Sporting News 56, 138–140, 170
Sports Illustrated 108, 130
Sportsman Park (St. Louis) 67
Stallard, Tracy 138
Stallcup, Virgil 15
Stankey, Eddie 2, 81
Staub, Rusty 62
Stengel, Casey 67, 106, 112, 156
Stone, Ron 165
Surkont, Max 22, 25
Swifton Village (Apartments) 46–47

Tampa, Florida 16, 28, 44, 58–59, 100, 142, 154
Tangerine Bowl 6
Taylor, Ben 13
Tebbetts, Birdie 3, 27–29, 32–37, 39, 42, 48–50, 54, 56–60, 68, 70 74–77, 79, 81, 117, 140–141, *Birdie: Confessions of a Baseball Nomad* 140
Tebbetts, Mary 79
Temple, Alma 5
Temple, Aubrey J. 5
Temple, Chub 8–9
Temple, Coy E. 5
Temple, Johnny Ellis 1–18, 21–22, 24–33, 36–42, 44–54, 56–71, 73–74, 76–79, 82–84, 87–97, 99–101, 103–105, 108–112, 114–118, 123–124, 127, 129–150, 154–172; All-Star Games 2, 37, 50–52, 66, 68, 92–93, 95–96, 134–135, 143; arrest record in Buncombe County 169–171; Baltimore Orioles 139–140, 142–143, 145, 161; Catawba College 6–8; Cincinnati Reds 13–18, 21–22, 24–26, 32–33, 36–42, 44, 47–49, 53–54, 56–67, 69–71, 76–78, 82–84, 87–91, 94, 96–97, 100, 110–111, 124, 134, 139, 147–148–150, 154–163; Cleveland Indians, 99–100, 103–105, 108–112, 115–118, 123–124, 129–132, 134, 136–140, 144, 161; Earl Lawson incident 62–64, 143–144; first major league hit 18; first home run at Crosley Field 77; first major league home run 22; Houston Colt .45s 143–149, 161; Johnny-on-the-Spot newspaper columns 88–90, 93, 101, 108–109; KHOU-TV (Houston) 164–166; KTRH AM (Houston) 164; Manager Pastora Milkers 71, 73–74; marriage to Becky Sheely 10–11; minor leagues 8–13; suit filed in Arizona Superior Court 145; The Rancho Del Jefe 129–130, 138–139, 141–142; toupée 156–157, 159; U.S. Navy 7
Temple, Leslie 5
Temple, Mike 46, 73, 117, 129, 157, 166, 171
Temple, Rebekah (Becky) Sheely 10, 45–46, 73, 100, 129, 145, 155, 167–171
Temple, Shelbourne L. 5
Tennessee Titans 127
Terry, Ralph 142
Texas A&M 166
Texas League 11, 13, 28
Texas Monthly 164
Thomas, Frank 53, 86–87, 90–91, 94, 97–99, 104
Thome, Jim 134
Thomson, Bobby 48, 77
Three Rivers Stadium 62
Thurman, Bob 43–44, 54, 56
Thurman, Senator Strom 167
Time Magazine 66, 68
Tomanek, Dick 105
Toots Shor's 156
Torre, Frank 48–49
Triandos, Gus 10, 94–95
Trice, Bob 153
Trump, Donald 47; *The Art of the Deal* 47
Trump, Fred 47
Tucson, Arizona 109, 111, 129, 131
Tulsa Oilers 11, 13, 16, 18, 20–21, 25
Turley, "Bullet" Bob 106
Turner, Jim 155
Tuttle, Bill 172
Tyler, Texas 71

Umont, Frank 138
U.S. Naval Academy 7

U.S. Navy 7, 11
U.S. Supreme Court 72
USS *Randolph* 7

Valentine, Corky 31, 33, 37
Valenzuela, Fernando 70
Valo, Elmer 17
Vander Meer, Johnny 14
Veeck, Bill, Jr. 19, 108, 121; *Veeck as in Wreck* 108
Venezuelan Winter League 26, 28
Vincent, Al 12
Virginia Military Institute (VMI) 6

Wagner, Leon 97
Walcott, Jersey Joe 9
Walker, Harry, "The Hat" 26
Walker, Jerry 95
Walls, Lee 98
Walters, Bucky 14
Ward, Arch 50
Ward, Preston 105
Washington Nationals (AL expansion team) 139, 144, 154
Washington Nationals/Senators (AL) 30, 77, 102
Wehmeier, Herman 17, 46
Weiss, George 105
Welch, Bob 83
Wertz, Vic 103
West, Governor John 167
West, Richard 164
Westbrook State Hospital 120

Western Carolina College 6
Western Carolina League 9
Western Hills High School 150
White, Bill 135
White, Charlie 33
White, Ernie 26
White Rock, North Carolina 171
Wilkins, Bobby 8
William & Mary College 6
Williams, Dee 129
Williams, Stan 117
Williams, Ted 11, 50, 52, 95, 120, 122
Wilson, Bert 14
Winchell, Walter 156
Winfield, Dave 134
WLW-TV (Cincinnati) 57
Woodeshick, Hal 158
World Series: 1919 169; 1939 141; 1940 14, 27; 1941 103; 1948 103; 1956 83; 1957 11, 106; 1958 24, 105; 1959 99, 114; 1960 128; 1961 138; 2004 112; 2009 112
Wrigley Field (Chicago) 54, 77, 125
Wrona, Walt 13
Wyers, Colin 92
Wynn, Early 93, 96, 105, 107, 109, 120

Yankee Stadium (New York) 2, 106, 114, 136–137, 142
Yellowstone National Park 10
Young, Dick 62

Zimmer, Don 11

www.ingramcontent.com/pod-product-compliance
Ingram Content Group UK Ltd.
Pitfield, Milton Keynes, MK11 3LW, UK
UKHW042010140426
5217IPUK00015B/1094